D0713025

THE INSANITY DEFENSE, THE WORLD OVER

THE INSANITY DEFENSE, THE WORLD OVER

Rita J. Simon
and
Heather Ahn-Redding

A division of
ROWMAN & LITTLEFIELD PUBLISHERS, INC.
Lanham • Boulder • New York • Toronto • Oxford

LEXINGTON BOOKS

A division of Rowman & Littlefield Publishers, Inc.
A wholly owned subsidary of The Rowman & Littlefield Publishing Group, Inc.
4501 Forbes Boulevard, Suite 200
Lanham, MD 20706

PO Box 317
Oxford
OX2 9RU, UK

British Library Cataloguing in Publication Information Available

Library of Congress Cataloging-in-Publication Data

Simon, Rita James.
  The insanity defense, the world over / Rita J. Simon and Heather Ahn-Redding.
    p. cm. — (Global perspectives on social issues)
  Includes index.
  ISBN-13: 978-0-7391-1591-6 (cloth : alk. paper)
  ISBN-10: 0-7391-1591-X (cloth : alk. paper)
  1. Insanity—Jurisprudence. 2. Competency to stand trial. I. Ahn-Redding, Heather. II.
Title. III. Series.
K5077.S56 2006
345'.04—dc22   2006003107

Printed in the United States of America

⊗™ The paper used in this publication meets the minimum requirements of American
National Standard for Information Sciences—Permanence of Paper for Printed Library
Materials, ANSI/NISO Z39.48-1992.

Contents

Tables

Part I

1

Introduction: A Comparative Analysis of the Defense of Insanity

CONTINUING IN THE TRADITION OF the "The World Over" volumes that focused on juvenile justice systems, abortion, euthanasia, pornography, marriage and divorce, education, death penalty, the use and distribution of illicit drugs and women's roles and statuses, this book examines and compares the criteria and procedures surrounding the defense of insanity across twenty-two countries. In addition to the criteria for each of the countries, we report the burden of proof, is it on the side of the defense or the prosecution, and the degree, beyond a reasonable doubt or by a preponderance of the evidence, the form the verdict takes, typically who decides, a judge or a jury, what role do experts play in the proceedings, what happens to the defendant if he or she is found not guilty by reason of insanity, and, when available, the frequency with which the defense of insanity is introduced and for what types of offenses, that is, violent acts, property, etc.

Before reporting these data on a country-by-country basis, a brief history of the defense of insanity is provided.

Development of the Insanity Defense Standards

The notion of a plea that refutes criminal responsibility dates back to the ancient days of Greek philosophy. Plato (427–347 B.C.) pondered the dilemma of dealing with mentally disturbed individuals who committed crimes. He proposed that such persons were not responsible for their acts in the same way that most others were and should not be punished by the same means. Focusing on restitution rather than punishment, Plato noted:

Someone may commit an act when mad or afflicted with disease . . . [and if so,] let him pay simply for the damage; and let him be exempt from other punishment. Except that if he has killed someone and his hands are polluted by murder, he must depart to a place in another country and live there in exile for a year.[1]

Plato also went a step further and proposed a humane method for early civil commitment procedures:

If anyone is insane, let them not be seen openly in the city, but let the relatives of such a person watch over him in the best manner they know of; and if they are negligent, let them pay a fine.[2]

Legal codes that separated madmen from the criminally responsible can be traced back to the second-century writing of Jewish law embodied in the Talmud, which stated:

Idiots, lunatics and children below a certain age ought not be held criminally responsible because they could not distinguish good from evil, right from wrong and were thus blameless in the eyes of God and man. It is an ill thing to knock against a deaf mute, an imbecile, or a minor. He that wounds them is culpable, but if they wound others they are not culpable . . . for with them only the act is a consequence while the intention is of no consequence.[3]

Separation of those who cannot be held criminally culpable may also be traced to the legal code of sixth century Rome, the Justinian Code.[4] The Code states:

There are those who are not to be held accountable, such as a madman and a child, who are not capable of wrongful intention . . . Since a wrong is only able to exist by the intention of those who committed it, it follows that these persons . . . are not considered to have committed a wrong.[5]

The Insanity Defense under Islamic Criminal Law

In no civilized penal code is a person held criminally responsible for conduct he committed while he was insane, even if he recovers his sanity after the commission of the criminal act or omission.[6]

Under Islam, it is believed that man has free will—he can rationally choose what to do and what not to do. Hence, he is responsible for the consequences of his actions—good or bad.

Criminal responsibility under Islamic law requires both the commission of a legally recognized crime and the criminal capacity to commit such a crime. In the absence of one of these elements, a person cannot be held criminally responsible for his actions.

Insanity is one of the defenses to, or one of the reasons for withholding, criminal responsibility under Islamic law. An insane person (whether permanently or temporarily insane) is deprived of the consciousness and/or willingness to commit a crime:

> He (1) cannot know the difference between right and wrong, (2) cannot understand the nature or consequences of his actions, (3) cannot understand what kinds of conduct are prohibited by criminal laws, or (4) can understand all of the above but did not commit the prohibited act willingly.[7]

In this respect, it covers both cognitive and volitional incapacity.

There are two types of legally recognized insanity defenses under Islamic law: (1) prolonged or total insanity; and (2) interrupted or sporadic insanity. A totally insane person is absolutely deprived of the mental capacity to rationally perceive the nature of and circumstances surrounding his action.

A sporadically insane person is excused from criminal responsibility only if he committed the crime while he was insane, regardless of whether he subsequently regains sanity. However, the reverse does not hold true. A sporadically insane person who commits a crime while sane shall be held criminally responsible, regardless of whether he subsequently becomes insane.

In the latter case of subsequent insanity, two issues may arise, both of which are viewed differently by each of the four Sunni[8] schools of jurisprudence. Firstly, if the accused subsequently becomes insane after the crime and after the commencement of the trial, but before a verdict is rendered, the issue of his fitness to stand trial or legal/criminal capacity may arise.

An accused who is unfit to stand trial or lacks legal capacity cannot be punished according to the *Malikis*[9] and the *Hanafis*.[10] Hence, "insanity prior to a verdict is grounds for suspending the trial until the person recovers from his insanity."[11] The *Hanbalis*[12] and the *Shafi'is*[13] believe otherwise. However, all four schools recognize an accused as unfit for trial if insanity ensues after the crime but before the trial begins.

Secondly, in the case of insanity after a verdict, if the crime was proved by confession rather than by evidence, the verdict is suspended as the convicted, in the absence of his rational faculties, is deprived of the right to withdraw his confession at the time of execution of the verdict.[14]

Even if the convicted is unable to withdraw his confession after the verdict due to insanity, his confession may still be disqualified on the grounds that it does not satisfy the conditions for the admissibility of a confession. It casts doubt on the convicted's ability to freely render, understand the substance, foresee the consequences, and assert the certainty of a confession. This is the *Hanbalis* and *Shafi'is* belief.

The *Malikis* believe likewise with the variation that if the punishment is not retribution, then the verdict is suspended and indemnity is paid.[15] However, the punishment of retribution may still be executed at the request of the executor of a blood feud.[16]

By contrast, the *Hanafis* believe that withdrawal of a confession by the convicted or testimony by a witness which casts doubt on the case and punishment should not be executed, and indemnity, instead of retribution, should be paid. This is so because under Islamic law in order for evidence to be definite and conclusive, there must be corroboration between the testimonies or confessions, and other facts and circumstances of the case. In the absence of such corroboration or consistency, there is no strength in the complainant's case.

In addition, more preference and importance is given to direct evidence (testimony or confession) than to circumstantial evidence. Circumstantial evidence is treated as indicative of the crime. However, in the absence of direct evidence, circumstantial evidence is sufficient to prove commission of the crime.

However, in the case of *ta'azir*[17] crimes, withdrawing a confession has no effect on the proceedings of the trial or the execution of the verdict.

Modern Legal Codes

England provides a solid foundation for modern legal codes on the insanity defense. In 1265, British jurist and scholar Lord Bracton introduced the original "wild beast test" which likened the defendant to a wild beast due to his complete lack of understanding.[18] Bracton asserted that some simply are not aware of what they are doing and act in a manner "as to be not far removed from the brute."[19] In 1582, William Lambarde wrote a leading text known as *Eirenarcha: Or of the Office of the Justices of the Peace*, which was a comprehensive account of the structure of the local government in relation to the justices of the peace at the end of the sixteenth century.[20] In this work, Lambarde suggested that fools and lunatics were not appropriate recipients of that era's severe criminal sanctions.[21]

English case law followed the lead of writings such as those by Bracton and Lambarde. In a 1723 case, *Rex v. Arnold*,[22] Justice Tracy enhanced Bracton's wild beast test and held that to be insane, a defendant "must be totally deprived of his understanding and memory so as not to know what he is doing, no more than an infant, brute or a wild beast."[23] This early description of insanity not only sets the stage for further developments of the insanity defense, but it also foreshadows the current concept of psychosis as generally described in the American Psychiatric Association, Diagnostic and Statistical Manual of Mental Disorders (DSM-IV, 1994).[24]

In 1800, the case of *Rex v. Hadfield*[25] involved acquittal of a defendant whose brain was permanently exposed due to a head injury.[26] Hadfield believed God required his sacrifice in order to save the world, therefore he chose to fire a shot at

King George III in order to assure his execution.[27] Hadfield's lawyer, Thomas Erskine, proposed a new test for insanity that addressed persons like Hadfield, who had bouts of normal and abnormal spells. The test focused on the defendant's behavior at the time of the offense rather than requiring a constant "frenzy or raving madness" because "delusion . . . is the true character of insanity."[28]

Perhaps the most well-known English case pertaining to the insanity defense is *M'Naghten*,[29] which created a common law standard in many countries. The defendant, Daniel M'Naghten, was acquitted by virtue of insanity for killing Prime Minister Robert Peel's private secretary, Edward Drummond, mistaking him for the prime minister.[30] At trial, nine medical witnesses described Mr. M'Naghten's condition and countless delusions of persecution.[31] The *M'Naghten* standard held that the accused is not responsible for his criminal act if "labouring under such a defect of reason, from disease of mind as not to know the nature and quality of the act he was doing; of if he did 'know' it, that he did not know he was doing what was wrong."[32] Within a decade, England and most of the United States state courts adopted the *M'Naghten* test. The test, however, was widely criticized for its narrow focus on cognitive impairment, thus neglecting the defendant's ability to *control* his behavior.

The *M'Naghten* criticisms prompted an upgrade to the test in the United States, and most jurisdictions adopted a new "irresistible impulse" test.[33] The language of this test focused on the complete causal element of the mental disease as leading to certain conduct, thus destroying free will in commission of a crime.[34] Also meeting resistance, this test was criticized for potentially leading to invalid insanity defenses because an irresistible "attack" could be easily feigned. Accordingly, yet another test, the "product test," was introduced in *Durham v. United States*,[35] which held that "an accused is not criminally responsible if his unlawful act was the product of a mental disease or defect."[36] But given the fact that "mental defect" and "product" were vague terms, the test created jury confusion due to "a confusing mass of . . . fruitless disputation between lawyer and witness about legal and psychiatric labels and jargon."[37]

Finally, in the 1962 case of *McDonald v. United States*,[38] the Washington D.C. Court of Appeals adopted a test established by the American Law Institute (ALI). The ALI standard basically combined the *M'Naghten* and irresistible impulse tests, and many states adopted its standard in the Model Penal Code. The standard held that criminal responsibility could be excused if the defendant "lacks *substantial* capacity to *appreciate* the criminality [wrongfulness] of his conduct or to conform [it] to the law."[39] The test makes it clear that a defendant's cognitive or volitional impairment need only be substantial at the time of the offense in order to "earn" a defense of insanity.

After two decades, and in response to the Hinckley verdict in the United States, critics began to attack the ALI test's volitional prong. Both the American Bar Association (ABA) and the American Psychological Association

(APA) recommended eliminating the volitional requirement (to "conform the conduct to the law"). Both associations adhered to the "appreciation" factor in the test in order to avoid a return to *M'Naghten*'s "knowledge" feature.[40] Consequently, the ABA recommended a new test for insanity: "[A] person is not responsible for criminal conduct if, at the time of such conduct, and as a result of the mental disease or defect, that person was unable to appreciate the wrongfulness of such conduct."[41]

Influenced by the criticisms and debates over the defense, Congress adopted the Federal Insanity Defense Reform Act (IDRA)[42] in 1984. The Act virtually tracked the APA proposal; however, it placed the burden of proof on the defendant by clear and convincing evidence.[43] The goal of the shift in burden was not only to deter a defendant from a "convenient" plea of insanity, but it would also lessen the repercussions from battling experts as in the Hinckley case.[44] The shift would render a defendant "unsuccessful" under the insanity defense if the jury could not determine, with certainty, the defendant's insanity due to conflicting expert testimony.

So much for background. We turn now to a country-by-country analysis.

Notes

1. Plato, *The Laws*, vol. 5, trans. George Burges (London: Dell and Daldy, 1868).

2. Plato, *The Laws*, vol. 5.

3. Rita J. Simon and David E. Aaronson, *The Insanity Defense* (Westport, CT: Praeger, 1988), 10 (citing Barbara A. Weiner, "Not Guilty by Reason of Insanity: A Sane Approach," *Chicago-Kent Law Review* 1057-85 [1980]).

4. A collection of early Roman laws and legal principles. The code was drawn up by a committee of leading lawyers who were appointed by Emperor Justinian I in A.D. 528. (From World Book Online, © 2000 World Book, Inc. <www.worldbook.bigchalk.com/293360.htm>).

5. Simon and Aaronson, *The Insanity Defense*, 10, note 47 (citing David W. Carrither, "The Defense of Insanity and Presidential Peril," *Society* 23–27, no. 6 [July/Aug. 1985]).

6. Ahmad Fathi Bahnassi, *The Islamic Criminal Justice System*, ed. M. Cherif Bassiouni (Dobbs Ferry, NY: Oceana Publications, 1982), xiii, xix.

7. Nagaty Sanad, *The Theory of Crime and Criminal Responsibility in Islamic Law: Shari'a* (Office of International Criminal Justice, University of Illinois, Chicago, 1982), 89–91.

8. Bahnassi, *The Islamic Criminal Justice System*, 186.

9. "One of the four Sunni schools of jurisprudence named after its founder," Malek. Bahnassi, *The Islamic Criminal Justice System, supra* note 6 at 251.

10. "One of the four Sunni schools of jurisprudence named after its founder," Abuhanifa. Bahnassi, *The Islamic Criminal Justice System, supra* note 6 at 251.

11. Bahnassi, *The Islamic Criminal Justice System*, 186.

12. Bahnassi, *The Islamic Criminal Justice System*, 187.

13. Bahnassi, *The Islamic Criminal Justice System*, 187.

14. Mohammad Salam Madkour, *Defining Crime Responsibility According to Islamic Legislation*, trans. United Nations Social Defence Research Institute (Ministry of Interior, Kingdom of Saudi Arabia, 1976, 1980), 124.

15. Saleh Ibn Mohammad Al-Laheidan, *Means of Evidence in Islamic Law*, trans. United Nations Social Defence Research Institute (Ministry of Interior, Kingdom of Saudi Arabia, 1976, 1980), 181.

16. Al-Laheidan, *Means of Evidence in Islamic Law*, 157.

17. Al-Laheidan, *Means of Evidence in Islamic Law*, 159.

18. See John Biggs, *The Guilty Mind: Psychiatry and the Law of Homicide*, 1st ed. (New York: Harcourt Brace, 1955), 82.

19. See Karl Menniger, *The Crime of Punishment* (New York: Viking Press, 1968), 112.

20. See Gilbert Geis and Joseph F. Dimento, "Empirical Evidence and the Legal Doctrine of Corporate Criminal Liability," *Am. J. Crim. L.* 29 (2002): 341, 342.

21. Geis and Dimento, "Empirical Evidence," 341.

22. How. St. Tr. 16 (1723), 695.

23. How. St. Tr. 16 (1723), 764.

24. DSM-IV, page 273 (stating that "psychotic" is "conceptually defined as a loss of ego boundaries or a gross impairment in reality testing." Features vary with each type of psychotic disorder, such as schizophrenia, and are much more specific).

25. How. St. Tr. 27, 1281.

26. Hadfield was nearly decapitated as a soldier at the Battle of Flanders. See How. St. Tr. 27, 1320. See also Daniel N. Robinson, *Wild Beasts and Idle Humours: The Insanity Defense from Antiquity to the Present* (Cambridge, MA: Harvard University Press, 1996).

27. See Robinson, *Wild Beasts*.

28. *Rex v. Hadfield*, How. St. Tr. 27, page 1314.

29. *Daniel M'Naghten's Case* (or *Regina v. M'Naghten*), Eng. Rep. 2 (1843), 718.

30. *Daniel M'Naghten's Case*, 719.

31. See Thomas Szasz, *Psychiatric Justice* (Syracuse, NY: Syracuse University Press, 1988), 289 (citing *Daniel M'Naghten: His Trial and the Aftermath* [London: Gaskell, 1977], 22–29).

32. *M'Naghten*, Eng. Rep. 2, page 722.

33. See *Parsons v. State*, 2 So. 854 866 (Ala. 1886) (one of the first courts to apply the test).

34. See *Parsons v. State*.

35. 214 F.2d 862 (DC Cir. 1954).

36. 214 F.2d 862 (DC Cir. 1954), 874–75.

37. *Washington v. United States*, 390 F.2d (DC Cir. 1967), 444, 447.

38. 312 F.2d 847 (DC Cir. 1962).

39. Model Penal Code 401(1) (proposed official draft 1962) (emphasis added). Note: the Code excluded "psychopathic personalities," such as chronic antisocial criminal behavior, from the class of mental diseases or defects.

40. Barbara Ann Stoltz, "Congress and Criminal Justice Policy-Making: The Federal Insanity Defense" (unpublished, 1986).

41. Stoltz, "Congress and Criminal Justice," 8. See also American Bar Association, Criminal Justice Mental Health Standards, standard 7-6.1 (1984).

42. The IDRA is part of the Comprehensive Crime Control Act of 1984, Pub. L. 98-473, tit.2, ch.4, 98 Stat. 1837, 2057-68 (1984), 401–6.

43. 18 U.S.C. 20(b).

44. See S. Rep. No. 225, 98th Cong., 1st Sess. 379 (1984), 230–31.

References

Al-Laheidan, Saleh Ibn Mohammad. *Means of Evidence in Islamic Law.* Trans. United Nations Social Defence Research Institute, Ministry of Interior, Kingdom of Saudi Arabia, 1976, 1980.

Bahnassi, Ahmad Fathi. *The Islamic Criminal Justice System.* Ed. M. Cherif Bassiouni. Dobbs Ferry, NY: Oceana Publications, 1982.

Biggs, John. *The Guilty Mind: Psychiatry and the Law of Homicide,* 1st ed. New York: Harcourt Brace, 1955.

Comprehensive Crime Control Act of 1984. Pub. L. 98-473, tit. 2, ch. 4, 98 Stat. 1837, 2057–68 (1984).

Daniel M'Naghten's Case (or *Regina v. M'Naghten*). Eng. Rep. 2 (1843).

Geis, Gilbert, and Joseph F. Dimento. "Empirical Evidence and the Legal Doctrine of Corporate Criminal Liability." *Am. J. Crim. L.* 29 (2002).

Madkour, Mohammad Salam. *Defining Crime Responsibility According to Islamic Legislation.* Trans. United Nations Social Defence Research Institute. Ministry of Interior, Kingdom of Saudi Arabia, 1976, 1980.

Menniger, Karl. *The Crime of Punishment.* New York: Viking Press, 1968.

Parsons v. State. 2 So. 854 866 (Ala. 1886).

Plato. *The Laws,* vol. 5. Trans. George Burges. London: Dell and Daldy, 1868.

Rex v. Hadfield. How. St. Tr. 27.

Robinson, Daniel N. *Wild Beasts and Idle Humours: The Insanity Defense from Antiquity to the Present.* Cambridge, MA: Harvard University Press, 1996.

Sanad, Nagaty. *The Theory of Crime and Criminal Responsibility in Islamic Law: Shari'a.* Office of International Criminal Justice, University of Illinois, Chicago, 1982.

Simon, Rita J., and David E. Aaronson. *The Insanity Defense.* Westport, CT: Praeger, 1988.

Stoltz, Barbara Ann. "Congress and Criminal Justice Policy-Making: The Federal Insanity Defense." Unpublished, 1986.

Szasz, Thomas. *Psychiatric Justice.* Syracuse, NY: Syracuse University Press, 1988.

Washington v. United States. 390 F.2d (DC Cir. 1967).

World Book Online. © 2000 World Book, Inc. <www.worldbook.bigchalk.com/293360.htm.>

Part II
NORTH AMERICA

2

Canada

CANADA BORDERS THE NORTH ATLANTIC OCEAN in the east, the North Pacific Ocean in the west, the Arctic Ocean in the north, and the United States in the South. It is a nation of 31.4 million inhabitants in ten provinces and three territories (Eaves, Lamb and Tien 2000: 616). The official languages are English and French. Within Canada, 28 percent are Anglophones, 23 percent Francophones, 15 percent Europeans, 6 percent Asian/Arab/African, 2 percent indigenous Amerindian, and 26 percent have mixed backgrounds (U.S. Department of State 2003). Roman Catholicism is practiced by 46 percent of the population, followed by Protestantism (36 percent), Judaism (4.2 percent), Islam (2 percent), and other (11.8 percent).

The Canadian government is a confederation, founded on July 1, 1867, with a parliamentary democracy. Its constitution is "the amended British North America Act of 1867 patriated to Canada on April 17, 1982, Charter of Rights and Freedoms, and unwritten customs" (U.S. Department of State 2003). Queen Elizabeth II is the recognized head of state though there is also a prime minister and cabinet. The legislative branch is a bicameral parliament with a 301-member House of Commons and a 105-member Senate. The judicial branch consists of the Supreme Court.

Background

The origins of the Canadian legal system can be traced back to seventeenth- and eighteenth-century English and French law. The system was primarily

British after 1759, except in Quebec, where the Napoleonic Code was the basis of civil law (Eaves, Lamb and Tien 2000: 615). Throughout the nineteenth century, various laws were passed that would affect mentally ill offenders, such as the County Asylum Act of 1808 (England), amendments to the Criminal Lunatics Act of 1816, and the Insane Prisoners Act 1840 (Menzies 2002: 382). It wasn't until after *M'Naghten* (1843) that people could raise the insanity defense (Eaves et al. 2000: 616).

The first institution for the mentally ill was established in British Columbia. The Victoria Lunatic Asylum was open from 1872 to 1878 (Menzies 2002: 380). In 1878, the New Westminster Asylum was opened. It was later called the Public Hospital for the Insane. Another facility, Provincial Mental Home in Essondale, opened in 1913. From 1874 to 1950 in British Columbia, there were 387 people who were criminally insane (found not guilty by reason of insanity [NGRI], not fit for trial) or who were insane inmates (Menzies 2002: 381). These forensic patients were considered Warrant of the Lieutenant Governor cases and sent to asylums under the Criminal Code of Canada or the Penitentiary Act. As set forth in the Canadian Code of 1892, these individuals could be confined indefinitely (Menzies 2002: 382).

Since 1964, British Columbia's Mental Hospitals Act (now known as Health Act) has undergone many amendments (Menzies 2002: 400). The Forensic Psychiatry Act, established in 1974 in British Columbia, created the independent Forensic Psychiatric Services Commission that could address mental health issues objectively (Eaves et al. 2000: 622). The commission was charged with providing forensic psychiatric services to courts and to "persons remanded for psychiatric examination or held under the Criminal Code of Canada or Mental Health Act; and to plan, organize, and conduct research and education with respect to forensic psychiatric cases" (Eaves et al. 200: 622).

The Criminal Code underwent changes in 1992 when Parliament abolished "mandatory indeterminate confinement of NGRI and unfit criminal defendants under warrants of the lieutenant governor" (Menzies 2002: 440). These changes were made to conform to the Canadian Charter of Rights and Freedoms (Grant 1997: 419).

Criminal laws are found in the Criminal Code of Canada (Eaves et al. 2000: 616). The rights of Canadians are found in the Charter of Rights and Freedoms. In the Charter, section 15 sets forth equal rights to all people, including the mentally ill (Eaves et al. 2000: 615). Prior to 1992, the term "not guilty by reason of insanity" (NGRI) was used (Grant 1997: 420). It was mandatory that NGRI offenders were sent to psychiatric hospitals for indefinite periods—judges couldn't impose other sentences (Grant 1997: 420). The impetus for the change was the 1991 case *R. v. Swain*.[1] The Supreme Court found that it was unconstitutional to mandate that all NGRI defendants be confined in "strict-custody" hospitals and that it was not in alignment with section 7 of the Canadian Charter of Rights and Freedoms, which "requires that the accused be detained no longer than is necessary to determine whether he or she currently presents a danger and that this decision must be made pursuant to clear criteria" (Grant 1997: 421).

Bill C-30, which changed the Criminal Code, came into law following *Swain* in 1992 and renamed the insanity defense to the mental disorder defense, while also changing NGRI to "not criminally responsible on account of mental disorder" (NCRMD) (Grant 1997: 422). Under this new verdict, judges were given more discretion to decide on the case. If they render a disposition that does not release the offender totally, the review board is required to review the decision within ninety days. Judges could also ask the review board to determine the disposition within forty-five days (see Eaves et al. 2000: 618). This new legislation also changed the maximum evaluation period to determine fitness to stand trial from thirty to five days (Holley, Arboleda-Flórez, and Crisanti 1998: 43–45).

In 2003, there were nearly 36,400 inmates (including remand and pretrial prisoners) in Canada's 168 prisons, 5 percent of whom were female (ICPS 2005). The prison population rate was 116 per 100,000 national residents. Between 1989 and 1999, the prison population increased by 19 percent, while between 1998 and 1999 it decreased by 1 percent (Barclay and Tavares 2002: 7). Prisoners with sentences less than two years serve time in the provincial prison system and those with sentences over two years are incarcerated in the federal system (Eaves et al. 2000: 623).

Legal Criteria

No person is criminally responsible for an act committed or an omission made while suffering from mental disorder that rendered the person incapable of appreciating the nature and the quality of an act or omission or of knowing that it was wrong. (Criminal Code of Canada)[2]

Offenders who are "unfit to stand trial" cannot participate in their defense due to a mental disorder and are thus unable to understand the nature of the proceedings, the potential outcomes of the proceedings, and communicate with their defense counsel (Department of Justice Canada [DJC] 2003a). If the court believes a person's fitness to stand trial could be restored within sixty days, they can order treatment (Eaves et al. 2000: 618).

The Criminal Code, which was altered in 1992, describes when and how assessments can be made by the court in order to determine the following: fitness of the accused to stand trial; whether the accused had a mental disorder at the time of the crime that might affect criminal responsibility; mental state of a women who is accused of infanticide (Eaves et al. 2000: 618).

An offender may be found not criminally responsible (NCR) if, at the time of the offense, the individual was unable to appreciate the nature or quality of the act or know that it was wrong due to a mental disorder (Luettgen, Chrapko, and Reddon 1998).[3] To "appreciate" indicates a broader state of awareness than to "know." This is a departure from *M'Naghten*. There must be an appreciation of the factors involved in the act and a mental capacity to measure and foresee the consequences of the violent conduct (Hucker 2004). The "nature and quality" refers to the physical consequences of the act (Hucker 2004). "Knowing that the act or omission was wrong" indicates knowledge of the legal and moral wrongfulness of the action. "Moral" refers to societal, not individual, moral codes. A defendant must be able to apply that knowledge in a rational manner (Hucker 2004).

The term "mental disorder" refers to a "disease of the mind" in Canada's Criminal Code (DJC 2003a; see Hucker 2004). This does not include voluntary intoxication nor transcient mental states, yet those with personality disorders may be eligible to use the defense (Hucker 2004). Other mental illnesses that may render a defendant "not criminally responsible" are major mental disorders, paraphilias, post-traumatic stress disorder, and dissociative identity disorder (also known as multiple personality disorder) (Hucker 2004).

Defendants have used automatism as a defense in which "the state of a person who, though capable of action, is not conscious of what he is doing. It means an unconscious, involuntary act, where the mind does not go with what is being done" (Hucker 2004; see *R. v. Rabey* 1981). Porter et al. (2001) describe automatism as "the performance of unconscious, automatic acts conducted during a dissociative state and often followed by amnesia" (26). When this defense is used, a psychiatric evaluation is necessary to determine whether the defendant has a mental disorder or whether he or she experienced a nonmental disorder automatism at the time of the crime (Hucker 2004; see *R. v. Stone* 1999). For a successful use of automatism as a defense, the defense must show that the defendant acted involuntarily at the time of the offense. If a mental condition is determined to be present, and if the condition is a danger to society, then the person is considered to have a "disease of the mind" (Hucker 2004). A trial judge may determine whether the defendant experienced a nonmental disorder automatism. If so, the defendant is acquitted. Nonmental disorder automatism may be caused by a cerebral concussion, hypoglycemia, medically administered drugs, idiosyncratic or pathological intoxication, dissociative states, sleepwalking, parasomnias, and other sleep disorders (e.g., sudden waking, night terrors) (Hucker 2004).

Burden of Proof

If the court believes that an offender is unfit to stand trial, it may raise the issue of fitness at any time prior to the delivery of a verdict (DJC 2003b). This also applies to the defendant and prosecutor, but the party that raises the issue of fitness bears the burden of proof. As stated by the DJC (2003b): "The burden of proof that the accused has subsequently become fit to stand trial is on the party who asserts it, and is discharged by proof on the balance of probabilities."

If an individual is rendered unfit to stand trial, an inquiry must be held in two years, and every two years after until the defendant is acquitted or found guilty (DJC 2003b). A defendant may order an inquiry. At such an inquiry, "the burden of proof that sufficient evidence can be adduced to put the accused on trial is on the prosecutor" (DJC 2003b).

Under the Criminal Code, the court and defendant may order a mental evaluation (DJC 2003b). In cases where a summary judgment may be made against the defendant, a prosecutor may apply for a mental evaluation order if the issue is raised by the defense or if the prosecutor provides evidence that the accused may be unfit to stand trial. If the prosecutor suspects that the defendant may be rendered not criminally responsible due to his or her mental state at the time of the defense, the court can only order an assessment if the defendant also raises the issue regarding criminal intent or if the prosecutor provides evidence to support the notion that the individual should not be held criminally responsible because of a mental disorder. If the individual is not fit to be tried, "any plea that has been made shall be set aside and any jury shall be discharged" (DJC 2003b).

Form of Verdict

A defendant may be found "not criminally responsible" (Hucker 2004; Luettgen, Chrapko, and Reddon 1998). In 1992, new legislation changed the verdict of "not guilty by reason of insanity" to "not criminally responsible on account of mental disorder" (Eaves, Lamb and Tien 2000: 618).

Who Decides?

If the issue of fitness is raised before a trial, the judge can order a jury to render a decision (DJC 2003b).[4] If the issue is raised during a trial, the jury will also "be sworn to try that issue in addition to the issues in respect of which it is already sworn" (DJC 2003b). If a defendant is brought before a court with no jury, or "before a court at a preliminary inquiry or at any other stage of the proceedings", the court makes a decision regarding fitness (DJC 2003b).

A court has the power to order a mental evaluation of the accused for any of the following reasons:

1) to determine whether the individual is competent to stand trial,
2) to determine whether the individual was suffering from a mental condition during the time of the defense that may render him not criminally responsible,
3) to determine the mental state of certain females who have contributed toward the death of a newborn baby,
4) to make an appropriate disposition, and
5) to determine whether the defendant should be committed to an institution for treatment if the individual is convicted (DJC 2003b).

Regarding responsibility, a judge or jury may "render a verdict that the accused committed the act or made the omission but is not criminally responsible on account of mental disorder" (DJC 2003b). The Criminal Code allows murder charges to be changed to manslaughter if the homicide occurs "in the heat of passion caused by sudden provocation" (McSherry 2004: 454).[5] In NCRMD cases, judges or the review board determine whether to absolutely discharge the offender, discharge the offender conditionally, or order "indeterminate custody in a psychiatric facility" (Grant 1997: 422). Essentially, the Board is responsible for taking into account public safety, the defendant's mental state and needs, and the defendant's integration back into the community (Grant 1997: 422).

Role of Experts

In determining criminal responsibility, psychiatrists examine police reports, witness/victim statements, prior mental health history, prior criminal behavior, clinical interviews and mental status examinations, and results of psychological and neurological testing (Hucker 2004). Furthermore, whether there was a motive and whether the defendant planned the offense in advance are taken into consideration. Psychiatrists may also look at whether the defendant displayed any abnormal functioning prior to the crime. They may inquire as to the defendant's behavior prior to the offense and, if the accused did not know that the offense was wrong, attempt to determine if the defendant's understanding of the act was due to a mental disorder.

In determining whether the defendant had any knowledge of the wrongfulness of the offense, his or her behavior after the offense may be assessed (Hucker 2004). For example, did the defendant try to avoid apprehension and/or destroy evidence? Did the defendant notify the police? Did the defendant state that he or she knew the offense was wrong at the time of the offense, and did the defendant display signs of remorse or guilt?

What Happens to the Defendant?

The Mentally Disordered Offender (MDO) Protocols, first established in 1992, "describe the different stages that MDOs move through when they enter the criminal justice system—point of arrest, arrival at the detention point, first appearance in court, referral for fitness evaluation, competency evaluation, trial, presentence report, imprisonment, and discharge to the community" (Eaves et al. 2000: 627). Under the Criminal Code that was altered in 1992, for persons to be unfit to stand trial, they must have a mental disorder that renders them unable to defend themselves or instruct an attorney throughout the court proceedings prior to a verdict, as well as not be able to understand the "nature and object of the proceedings" and its consequences, nor to communicate with their defense attorney (Eaves et al. 2000: 628). If a defendant is found not fit to be tried, a trial may proceed when the individual is deemed fit to stand trial (DJC 2003b).

After *Swain* (1991), Bill C-30 changed the Criminal Code because mandating that NGRI offenders be sent to secure facilities indeterminately was considered unconstitutional. It thus provided for alternative dispositions for offenders who were now called NCRMD, stating that these dispositions must be that which is the "least onerous and least restrictive to the accused" (Grant 1997: 422). If a defendant is found NCRMD, he or she is deemed not guilty due to the mental disorder (DJC 2003b). Furthermore,

(a) the accused may plead *autrefois acquit* in respect of any subsequent charge relating to that offence;
(b) any court may take the verdict into account in considering an application for judicial interim release or in considering what dispositions to make or sentence to impose for any other offence; and
(c) the National Parole Board or any provincial parole board may take the verdict into account in considering an application by the accused for parole or pardon in respect of any other offence. (2003b)

Under *Orlowski* (1992), the accused must be absolutely discharged if the review board or court can "make an affirmative finding that the accused is not a significant threat to the safety of the public" (Grant 1997: 423).[6] Thus, to order an absolute discharge, the review board or court must believe that the offender poses no significant threat to the public. This case also established that "an accused could be a threat to the public without being a significant threat" (Grant 1997: 423), and if this is the case, the offender can be given a conditional discharge or can be sent to a psychiatric facility. The *Orlowski* decision also stated that "if the board is concerned that an accused with an appropriate history is not a present significant threat and will not become one if he continues with prescribed medications, but the board also has the opinion that he may be a significant threat if he does not take his medication, the board cannot be said to have an opinion that the accused is not a significant threat" (Grant 1997: 424). If the board or court is uncertain, they do not have to issue an absolute discharge, as stated by Justice McEachern: "If the board does not have that opinion, then it need not order an absolute discharge" (Eaves et al. 2000: 620). In 1999, three cases argued that placing the burden on the accused to show that he or she is not a significant threat to the public is a violation of the Canadian Charter of Rights and Freedoms (Eaves et al. 2000: 621).[7] As a result, unless they can determine "with certainty" that the accused is not a significant public threat, the court or the review board must order an absolute discharge.

Compulsory Commitment Treatment (CCT) in Canada can take the form of conditional leave or community treatment (Gray and O'Reilly 2005: 15). A person on conditional leave can leave the hospital but must continue to adhere to certain guidelines. Renewable leave is possible in British Columbia, Alberta, Manitoba, New Brunswick, and Yukon. Leave is for three months in Ontario and ten days in Prince Edward Island (Gray and O'Reilly 2005: 17). Community treatment orders—enacted in Saskatchewan in 1994 and in Ontario in 2000—do not require individuals to be in hospitals. In both jurisdictions the person must have been hospitalized in the past. In Ontario, a person given a community treatment order is one who is "in need of treatment or care and supervision in the community; if not treated, serious bodily harm to self or others or substantial mental or physical deterioration or impairment is likely" (Gray and O'Reilly 2004: 16).

Stuart et al. (2001) examined all pretrial mentally disordered offenders in Alberta from 1989 to 1991 who were admitted to the Alberta Hospital Edmonton and Calgary General Hospital Forensic Services for pretrial fitness evaluations. The study examined differences in assessment lengths in years pre- and post-Bill C-30 (which was passed in 1992). During the six years, 3,405 offenders were admitted. Stuart et al. had data on 3,344 (98.2 percent) of the 3,405. They looked at the data regarding 2,091 fitness assessments, of which there were 256 pretrial assessments in 1989, 388 in 1990, 420 in 1991, 310 in 1992, 387 in 1993, and 330 in 1994 (Stuart et al. 2000: 532, figure 2).

On average, the assessments lasted twenty-four days in 1989, twenty-two days in 1990, nineteen days in 1991, twenty-two days in 1992, twenty-one days in 1993, and twenty-two days in 1994 (Stuart et al. 2001: 532, figure 3).

In British Columbia, there is an inpatient Forensic Psychiatric Institute (FPI) (built 1997) with the capacity to house over two hundred patients and six community clinics (Eaves et al. 2000: 623). The FPI evaluates the mental statuses of the accused, determines whether defendants are fit to stand trial, treats people found NCRMD or unfit to stand trial, treats mentally ill inmates who are transferred to the facility, and assesses offenders who could possibly be indeterminately hospitalized under the Criminal Code's *Dangerous Offender* provisions (Eaves et al. 2000: 624).

According to Eaves et al. (2000):

> The Forensic Psychiatric Community Services (Clinics) provide a wider array of services than the FPI: (1) Court ordered NCRMD and fitness assessments. (2) Presentence assessments of persons suspected of mental disorder, sex offenders, and persons charged with spousal assault. (3) Community management of persons found NCRMD and unfit. (4) Community management of mentally disordered persons on bail, parole, and probation. (5) Community treatment for sex offenders. (624)

Changes to the Criminal Code in 1997 "prescribe[d] indefinite incarceration for designated dangerous offenders and long-term supervision (up to ten years) for long-term offenders, following a definite period of incarceration" (Eaves et al. 2000: 629).

Frequency of Use

In 1992, fifteen offenders were acquitted due to insanity in Saskatchewan, a province with 1 million people (Stuart, Arboleda-Flórez, and Crisanti 2001: 528). In British Columbia, the insanity defense was used in 0.2 percent of cases. Throughout Canada, "there may have been only 1,000 people falling under the insanity provisions and held on Lieutenant Governor's Warrants at the time Bill C-30 was enacted" (Stuart et al. 2001: 528).

Eaves et al. (2000) observed that after the 1992 legislation that changed the Criminal Code, "there have been significant increases in the numbers of persons found NCRMD and also an increase in discharges of such persons to the community" (623).

Between March 1, 1990, and February 28, 1991, according to a study by Christopher Webster[8] (cited by Grant 1997: 426), there were twenty-three new admissions on warrants in British Columbia, of whom seven had been found

NGRI. Another study by Ogloff (1991) reported that within the Forensic Psychiatric Institute, the number of admissions resulting from NGRI verdicts was eleven in 1988, fourteen in 1989, and seven in 1990. There were thirty-eight new NCRMD's in the forensic system in 1993, and forty in 1994 (Grant 1997: 426).

Grant (1997) examined 112 new NCRMD patients in British Columbia from May 1992 to year-end 1994 (425). There were 28 women (25 percent) and 84 men (75 percent) (428). Among the 112 cases, 7 (6.25) were charged with murder and 6 (5 percent) charged with attempted murder (427). Only 4 (57.1 percent) were actually found by the review board to be a significant public threat (Grant 1997: 435). Among the 112 cases, the offenders were charged with offenses against the person (71.43 percent); property crimes (19.64 percent); and public-order offenses (8.93 percent) (Grant 1997: 425). Of those charged with offenses against the person, 18.75 percent (15) were found by the review board to be a significant threat (Grant 1997: 435).

Of the 28 women, 64.3 percent (18) were charged with offenses against the person, as opposed to 73.8 percent (62) of the 84 men. Approximately 29 percent (8) of the women were charged with property offenses, in comparison to 16.7 percent (14) of the men, and 7.1 percent (2) of the women were charged with public-order offenses, as opposed to 9.5 percent (8) of the men (Grant 1997: 429). The most frequent diagnosis was schizophrenia (33.3 percent) followed by bipolar disorder (26.7 percent), other psychoses (13.3 percent), organic brain disorders (9.3 percent), personality disorders (4.0 percent), and other disorders (2.7 percent) (Grant 1997: 430, table 3).

One among the 112 was given an absolute discharge and 67 percent (112) were conditionally discharged (Grant 1997: 429). Of the 28 women, 42.9 percent were given conditional discharges, 28.6 percent received conditional discharge (with custody), and 28.6 percent were given custody orders. Of the 84 men, 35.7 percent were given conditional discharges, 33.3 percent were given custody orders, 29.8 percent were given conditional discharges (with conditions), and 1.2 percent were absolutely discharged (Grant 1997: 433, table 6). Grant also reports that of the 112 cases, 20 were seen as threats by the review board, 1 was not considered a threat, in 80 of the cases the board was unable to determine whether the person was a threat, and in 11 cases there was no reference.

Holley, Arboleda-Flórez, and Crisanti (1998) studied the records of 455 forensic and nonforensic defendants. Of the sample, 250 had been sent to a forensic unit in Calgary to undergo a forensic evaluation in 1998, and 205 were in pretrial custody but did not receive forensic evaluations (Holley et al. 1998: 44–45). Of the forensic offenders, 58 percent had been charged with one or more violent offenses, compared to 22 percent of the nonforensic offenders (Holley et al. 1998: 48). Other charges included property, traffic, and "other." The forensic patients were 0.4 times less likely to be convicted in comparison to the control group of offenders who did not undergo psychiatric evaluations (51). Holley et al. (1998) stated: "forensic offenders were found to be significantly *less likely* to be convicted and, if convicted, significantly *less likely* to be given a sentence involving prison time" (55).

Luettgen et al. (1998) conducted a study within the Alberta Hospital Edmonton. They examined 109 individuals who were at the hospital for at least thirty days between September 1982 and September 1993. Of the patients, 37 had been found NCR before the start of the study (Sept. 1982) and were already receiving treatment during the study period. On average, the patients were 34.1 years old (91). The most common diagnosis was schizophrenia (77.1 percent), followed by bipolar disorder (6.4 percent), major depression (5.5 percent), psychoactive substance-induced organic mental disorder (3.7), dementia (1.8), organic syndromes (1.8), paranoid delusional disorder (1.8), brief psychotic episode (0.9), and personality disorder (0.9) (Luettgen et al. 1998: 92, table 1). Of the 109 patients, 88 percent (96) had been charged with violent crimes, 8.3 percent (9) with nonviolent crimes, and 3.7 percent (4) with sexual crimes (Luettgen et al. 1998: 93, table 2). Of those who were discharged, the average duration of hospitalization was 3.8 years.

Menzies (2002) analyzed a sample of one hundred forensic patients in British Columbia who were sent to the Victoria Lunatic Asylum, the Public Hospital for the Insane, and the Provincial Mental Home in Essondale by courts or prisons from 1874 to 1950—a period of seventy-seven years (380). Of the one hundred patients, eighty-nine were men. The most common charges were property (25 percent), murder/manslaughter (23 percent), and violence/others (17 percent). Other charges were vagrancy, public order/drunkenness, damage/arson, robbery, violent sex, nonviolent sex, drugs, attempted suicide, and no charges laid (Menzies 2002: 386, table 3). Sentences of less than a month were given to 1 percent of the group, 11 percent were given two to three months, 14 percent were given four to six months, 4 percent were given seven to twelve months, 5 percent were given one to two years, 16 percent were given two to five years, 2 percent were given six to ten years, and 2 percent were given eleven to fifteen years (Menzies 2000: 386). In addition, 3 percent received life sentences, 2 percent had death sentences commuted, 38 percent received no conviction, and 1 percent received indeterminate sentences. The total time that the patients spent in the hospital ranged from forty to forty-nine years (3 percent) to less than one year (15 percent)

TABLE 2.1
Cases of Criminal Insanity in British Columbia by Year and Sex

Year of Admission	Total General Admissions	Total Criminal Insanity Admissions	Criminally Insane as Percentage of Total
1872–1879	144	4	2.7
1880–1889	205	12	5.9
1890–1899	659	29	4.4
1900–1909	1,559	22	1.4
1910–1919	3,774	21	0.8
1920–1929	4,963	41	1.5
1930–1939	6,264	94	1.6
1940–1949	9,117	143	1.5
1950	1,415	21	1.4
Total	**28,100**	**387**	**1.4**

Source: Menzies 2002: 382, table 1.

(Menzies 2000: 386). The rest spent thirty to thirty-nine years (4 percent), twenty to twenty-nine years (21 percent), ten to nineteen years (16 percent), five to nine years (6 percent), four years (6 percent), three years (6 percent), two years (10 percent), and one year (13 percent) (Menzies 2000: 386). These mentally ill offenders were categorized by Menzies into five groups: murderous lunatics, criminals for life, recalcitrants and resisters, the ordinarily afflicted, and manipulators and malingerers (391).

Notes

1. *R. v. Swain* (1991) 1 S.C.R. 933.
2. RS 1985 c. C-46, s 16(1) (cited by Scottish Law Commission 2003).
3. See Martin's Annual Criminal Code 1997.
4. "If the judge directs that the issue of fitness of the accused be tried before the accused is given in charge to a jury for trial on the indictment, a jury composed of the number of jurors required in respect of the indictment in the province where the trial is to be held shall be sworn to try that issue and, with the consent of the accused, the issues to be tried on the indictment" (DJC 2003b).
5. Section 232(1).
6. *Orlowski v. British Columbia (Attorney General)* (1992), 16 B.C.A.C. 204, 28 W.A.C. 204, 75 C.C.C. (3d) 138.
7. *Orlowski v. British Columbia* 1999; *Bese v. British Columbia* 1999; *Winko v. British Columbia* 1999.
8. See Hodgins, Webster, and Paquet 1991.

References

Barclay, Gordon and Cynthia Tavares. 2002. "International comparisons of criminal justice statistics 2000." Issue 05/02. Retrieved June 15, 2004, <www.homeoffice.gov/uk/rds/pdfs2/hosb502.pdf>.

Bese v. British Columbia (Forensic Psychiatric Institute), [1999] 2 S.C.R. 722.

Department of Justice Canada. 2004. "Part XX.1: Mental Disorder" from *Criminal Code*. Retrieved May 16, 2005 (http://laws.justice.gc.ca/en/C-46/index.html).

Department of Justice Canada. 2003a. "Consolidated Statutes and Regulations: Criminal Code Chapter C-46" on *Criminal Code* website. Retrieved July 5, 2004, <http://laws.justice.gc.ca/en/C-46/41228.html>.

Department of Justice Canada. 2003b. "Mental Disorder Part XX.1: Interpretation" on Criminal Code website. Retrieved July 5, 2004, <http://laws.justice.gc.ca/en/C-46/44143.html>.

Eaves, Derek, Diane Lamb, and George Tien. 2000. "Forensic Psychiatry Services in British Columbia." *International Journal of Law and Psychiatry* 23, nos. 5–6: 615–31. Retrieved online June 6, 2005, <www.sciencedirect.com>, Elsevier Sciences, Ltd.

Grant, Isabel. 1997. "Canada's New Mental Disorder Disposition Provisions: A Case Study of the British Columbia Criminal Code Review Board." *International Journal of Law and Psychiatry* 20, no. 4: 419–43. Retrieved online June 6, 2005, <www.sciencedirect.com>, Elsevier Sciences, Ltd.

Gray, John E. and Richard L. O'Reilly. 2005. "Canadian Compulsory Community Treatment Laws: Recent Reforms." *International Journal of Law and Psychiatry* 28: 13–22. Retrieved online June 6, 2005, www.sciencedirect.com, Elsevier Sciences, Ltd.

Hodgins, Sheilagh, Christopher Webster, and Jean Paquet. 1991. *Annual Report Year Three Canadian Database: Patients Held on Lieutenant Governors' Warrants*.

Holley, G., J. Arboleda-Flórez, and A. Crisanti. 1998. "Do Forensic Offenders Receive Harsher Sentences? An Examination of Legal Outcomes." *International Journal of Law and Psychiatry* 21, no. 1: 43–57. Retrieved online June 6, 2005, www.sciencedirect.com, Elsevier Sciences, Ltd.

Hucker, Stephen. 2004. "Criminal Responsibility" from ViolenceRisk.com website, <www.violence-risk.com>. Division of Forensic Psychology, McMaster University, Hamilton, Ontario, Canada.

International Centre for Prison Studies [ICPS]. 2005. "World Prison Brief: Entire World—Prison Population Totals, Prison Brief for Canada." International Centre for Prison Studies, Kings College London. Retrieved May 9, 2005, <www.kcl.ac.uk/depsta/rel/icps/worldbrief/world_brief.html>.

Luettgen, James, Wendy E. Chrapko, and John R. Reddon. 1998. "Preventing Violent Re-Offending in Not Criminally Responsible Patients: An Evaluation of a Continuity of Treatment Program." *International Journal of Law and Psychiatry* 21, no. 1: 89–98. Retrieved online June 6, 2005, <www.sciencedirect.com>, Elsevier Sciences, Ltd.

Martin's Annual Criminal Code. 1997. Aurora, Ontario: Canada Law Books.

McSherry, Bernadette. 2004. "Criminal Responsibility, "Fleeting" States of Mental Impairment, and the Power of Self-Control." *International Journal of Law and Psychiatry*

27: 445–57. Retrieved online June 6, 2005, <www.sciencedirect.com>, Elsevier Sciences, Ltd.

Menzies, Robert. 2002. "Historical Profiles of Criminal Insanity." *International Journal of Law and Psychiatry* 25: 379–404. Retrieved online June 6, 2005, <www.sciencedirect.com>, Elsevier Sciences, Ltd. Table reprinted with permission from Elsevier.

Ogloff, J. R. P. 1991. *The Use of the Insanity Defence in British Columbia: A Qualitative and Quantitative Analysis*. Technical report prepared for the Department of Justice, Canada.

Orlowski v. British Columbia (Forensic Psychiatric Institute), [1999] 2 S.C.R. 625.

Orlowski v. British Columbia (Attorney General) [1992], 75 C.C.C. (3d) 138.

Penitentiary Act, Canada. RSC 1906, c. 147, s. 53.

Porter, Stephen, Angela R. Birt, John C. Yuille, and Hugues F. Hervé. 2001. "Memory for Murder: A Psychological Perspective on Dissociative Amnesia in Legal Contexts." *International Journal of Law and Psychiatry* 24: 23–42. Retrieved online June 6, 2005, <www.sciencedirect.com>, Elsevier Sciences, Ltd.

R. v. Stone (1999) 2 S.C.R. 290.

R. v. Swain (1991) 1 S.C.R. 933.

R. v. Rubey (1981).

Stuart, Heather, Julio Arboleda-Flórez, and Annette S. Crisanti. 2001. "Impact of Legal Reforms on Length of Forensic Assessments in Alberta, Canada." *International Journal of Law and Psychiatry* 24: 527–38. Retrieved online June 6, 2005, <www.sciencedirect.com>, Elsevier Sciences, Ltd.

United States Department of State. 2003. "Background Note: Canada." Washington, D.C.: U.S. Department of State. Retrieved online June 14, 2004, <www.state.gov/r/pa/ei/bgn/2089.htm>.

Winko v. British Columbia (Forensic Psychiatric Institute), [1999], 2 S.C.R. 625.

3

United States

THE UNITED STATES OCCUPIES A LARGE portion of North America, stretching across the continent between Mexico and Canada, and includes Hawaii in the Pacific Ocean and Alaska on the northwestern border of Canada. With 263.4 million people, the United States is the third-largest nation in the world in population, behind only China and India. In area, it is the fourth-largest country after Russia, Canada, and China.

Three-fourths of the United States population live in urban areas, and more than forty metropolitan areas have populations over 1 million. Approximately 83 percent of Americans are Caucasian, 12.5 percent are African American, 4 percent are Asian or Pacific Islander, and 0.8 percent are American, Indian, Eskimo, or Aleut. Hispanic Americans make up 14 percent of the population.

The United States is a democratic nation headed by a president who holds executive power. The Congress, consisting of the House of Representatives and the Senate, exercises legislative power. The judicial power rests in the hands of the Supreme Court, which interprets the highest law of the land, the Constitution.

For administrative purposes the country is divided into fifty territories known as states, and the District of Columbia, the nation's capital. Each state has its own executive, legislative, and judicial powers. Each state is also subject to the laws made by the federal government, which surpasses any state law.

English is the official language and is the language of instruction for educational purposes and on official documents.

There is no established religion in the United States. Under the Constitution, individuals have the freedom to practice whichever religion they choose. Fifty-six percent of Americans are Protestant, 26 percent are Roman Catholic, and 2 percent are Jewish. There are many other religions represented in smaller minorities, such as Muslims, Hindus, and Buddhists.

Background

In 1851, what have become known as the *M'Naghten* rules were adopted in the federal and most of the state courts of the United States. Under the prevailing *M'Naghten* standard—sometimes referred to as the "right-wrong test"—a person cannot be convicted if, at the time the criminal act was committed, that person was laboring under such a defect of reason (from a disease of the mind) as not to know the nature and quality of the act he or she was doing—or, if that person did know it, as not to know that the action was wrong. The easy reception of the *M'Naghten* rules into the law of the United States suggests that there was no well-developed test of insanity. Before 1800, there were probably not enough reported cases to require—or permit—the law to develop. By 1858, Circuit Justice Nathan Clifford was able to observe: "All of the well-considered cases since 1843, in both countries, are founded upon the doctrine laid down by the fourteen judges, in the opinion delivered in the House of Lords at that time."[1]

The word "know" has been the source of much of the controversy and criticism of the *M'Naghten* standard. Critics often assume that "know" refers only to cognitive or intellectual awareness, and they argue that there are few—if any—persons who have absolutely no intellectual awareness of what they are doing. In fact, in most of the *M'Naghten* jurisdictions, the word "know" is not defined at all, leaving the jury free to determine the meaning based on the expert testimony received at trial. Of those jurisdictions that have addressed the question, the majority have favored a broader construction of the word. In these states, the word "know" encompasses "affective" or "emotional" knowledge.[2] As Gregory Zilboorg argued in an article written in 1939, "know" means knowledge "so fused with affect that it becomes a human reality"[3]; in the words of Abraham Goldstein, "know" refers to knowledge that "can exist only when the accused is able to evaluate his conduct in terms of its actual impact upon himself and others and when he is able to appreciate the total setting in which he is acting."[4] In some of the jurisdictions adopting the restrictive view of the word "know," the limitation may be of little significance because of the availability of the "irresistible impulse" control test, in addition to *M'Naghten*.

The irresistible impulse test recognizes insanity as a defense when mental disease prevents the defendant from controlling his or her conduct. The irresistible impulse test predates the *M'Naghten* case. In 1840—just a few years before *M'Naghten*—an English judge instructed the jury in a case where a man named Oxford was charged with treason for firing a pistol at Queen Victoria: "If some controlling disease was, in truth, the acting power within him which he could not resist, then he will not be responsible."[5] The *M'Naghten* rules did not mention this test, probably because the answers to the House of Lords were confined to questions put to the judges in a particular case, which concerned a defendant who had acted because of a delusion. After *M'Naghten*, English trial judges instructed juries only in terms of the right-wrong test, and irresistible impulse was expressly rejected in 1863 as "a most dangerous doctrine."[6]

In the United States, the leading case on the irresistible impulse test came in the 1887 trial of *Parsons v. State*. After instructing the jury on the *M'Naghten* test, the judge stated that, even if this test were not met, the defendant could not be legally responsible:

1) [i]f by reason of the duress of such mental disease, he had so far lost the power to choose between the right and wrong, and to avoid doing the act in question, as that his free agency was at the time destroyed;
2) and if, at the same time, the alleged crime was so connected with such mental disease, in the relation of cause and effect, as to have been the product of it solely.[7]

Jurisdictions using this standard seldom mentioned the phrase "irresistible impulse" in instructions to the jury. The rule is usually stated in terms of a capacity for self-control or free choice. Also, the jury is not ordinarily told that the defendant must have been acting on a sudden impulse or that his or her acts must have been totally irresistible. For this reason, the "irresistible impulse" test is unfortunately named.[8]

In 1946 , the United States Supreme Court upheld the appellate court's application of the *M'Naghten* standard in *United States v. Fisher*.[9] The Court rejected the doctrine of partial insanity or diminished capacity in the District of Columbia, in the absence of legislation authorizing this doctrine. The question raised was whether it may be possible for a mental disorder to be shown to support a conviction of murder in the second degree, but not of murder in the first degree, on the ground that the defendant's mind at the time was incapable of a deliberate and premeditated design to kill another person.

The *Fisher* case involved the death of the librarian at the Cathedral of St. Peter and St. Paul in Washington, D.C., at the hands of a janitor, Julius Fisher. Psychiatrists testifying for the defense said that Fisher had a mental age of eleven years, a "psychopathic personality of a predominantly aggressive type, and that evidence of a deranged mental condition indicated that he was unable to resist the impulse to kill."[10] Counsel for Fisher requested that the jury also be instructed on the question of Fisher's capacity for the premeditation and deliberation necessary to convict for first degree murder, and to take into account the entire personality of the defendant as it was developed by expert evidence in the case. The request was refused.

The jury was charged as follows:

> Insanity, according to the criminal law, is a disease or defect of the mind which renders one incapable to understand the nature and quality of his act, to know that it is wrong, to refrain from doing the wrong act.[11]

Fisher was found guilty of first degree murder, and he was sentenced to die. The United States Court of Appeals for the District of Columbia Circuit Court and the United States Supreme Court in a 5–4 vote upheld the verdict.[12] In a dissenting opinion, Justice Frank Murphy wrote:

> [T]here are persons who, while not totally insane, possess such low mental powers as to be incapable of the deliberation and premeditation requisite to statutory first degree murder. Yet under the rule adopted by the court below, the jury must either condemn such persons to death on the false premise that they possess the mental requirements for a first degree murderer or free them completely from criminal responsibility and turn them loose among society. The jury is forbidden to find them guilty of a lesser degree of murder by reason of their generally weakened or disordered intellect. Common sense and logic recoil at such a rule.[13]

Other state courts have reached the opposite conclusion and recognized the possibility of such unsoundness of mind as to constitute partial diminished capacity, without establishing a total lack of criminal responsibility. It is argued that, just as intoxication—while not an excuse for crime—may disprove the presence of some particular state of mind, a mental disorder could be of such a nature as to produce the same result. If the state of mind required for the guilt of the particular grade or degree of the offense charged be missing—whether because of mental disease or defect or for any other reason—that crime has not been committed.

In the years following *M'Naghten*, only one state—New Hampshire—adopted a rule that was not in line with this standard. The New Hampshire rule was later adopted and modified as the *Durham* rule. In 1868, a New Hampshire jury was trying to decide whether a defendant who had killed his victim with an ax in the course of a robbery was insane. Chief Justice Ira Perley instructed the jury along the following lines:

> If [the jury] found that the defendant killed Brown in a manner that would be criminal and unlawful if the defendant were sane, the verdict should be "not guilty by reason of insanity" if the killing was the offspring or product of men-

tal disease in the defendant; that neither delusion, nor knowledge of right and wrong, nor design, nor cunning in planning and executing the killing, and escaping or avoiding detection, nor ability to recognize acquaintances, or to labor or transact business or manage affairs, is, *as a matter of law,* a test of mental disease; but that *all* symptoms and *all* tests of mental disease are *purely matters of fact* to be determined by the jury.[14]

Under such instructions the issue of the accused's mental condition—whether he had the capacity for criminal intent—became a question of fact and, therefore, a matter for the jury to determine, not for the court to define.

A few years later, the New Hampshire court made this point even more explicit, when it used the following analogy in its instructions to the jury:

Whether the defendant had a mental disease seems as much a question of fact as whether he had a bodily disease; and whether the killing of his wife was the product of that disease was also as clearly a matter of fact as whether thirst and a quickened pulse are the product of a fever.[15]

The decisions in *State v. Pike* (1870)[16] and *State v. Jones* (1871)[17] are today the law in New Hampshire. But the New Hampshire rule has had little impact outside the borders of that state, and failed to gain adoption in any other jurisdiction for almost a century. Other jurisdictions continued to adhere to the *M'Naghten* "right from wrong" formula.

In 1954, the United States Court of Appeals for the District of Columbia handed down its decision, discarding the *M'Naghten* rule and introducing a different legal basis for determining criminal responsibility, in *Durham v. United States.*[18]

Unlike many trials involving a defense of insanity, Monte Durham's crime was housebreaking, rather than murder. The defendant, a twenty-six-year-old resident of the District of Columbia, had a long history of mental disorder and petty thievery. He had been committed on several occasions to mental hospitals and had served time in prison for passing bad checks. He received a medical discharge from the navy. On at least two occasions, he had attempted suicide. The judge in the district court instructed the jury along the lines of the *M'Naghten* rule, and the defendant was found guilty.

On appeal, after deciding to grant the defendant a new trial on other grounds, the court went on to announce its new rule for insanity. Speaking for the court, Judge David L. Bazelon stated the new formula:

The rule we now hold must be applied on the retrial of this case and in future cases is not unlike that followed by the New Hampshire court since 1870. It is simply that an accused is not criminally responsible if his unlawful act was *the product of mental disease or mental defect.* We use "disease" in the sense of a condition which is considered capable of either improving or deteriorating. We use "defect" in the sense of a condition which is not considered capable of either improving or deteriorating and which may be either congenital, or the result of injury, or the residual effect of a physical or mental disease.

Thus your task would not be completed upon finding, if you did find, that the accused suffered from a mental disease or defect. He would still be responsible for his unlawful act if there was not a causal connection between such mental abnormality and the act. These questions must be determined by you from the facts which you find to be fairly deducible from the testimony and the evidence in this case.[19]

The adoption of the *Durham* rule in the District of Columbia was widely hailed in most psychiatric and some legal circles as the beginning of a new era. As Seymour Halleck stated in 1960: "It is doubtful whether any single case in the criminal law has stirred more comment than *Durham.*"[20] The *Durham* decision was regarded as a sign that the law would recognize the growing prestige and knowledge of psychiatry, and would work with it in the disposition of criminal cases, especially those in which the issue of insanity was introduced.

The *Durham* rule, however, did not gain wide acceptance. In the decade following its adoption in the District of Columbia, thirty state and five federal courts reviewed and rejected the rule. Two states—Vermont and Maine—adopted it for civil actions but retained *M'Naghten* for criminal cases.

Twenty-eight years later in the district court in Washington, D.C., a jury found John Hinckley not guilty by reason of insanity under still another set of legal rules. The *Hinckley* jury was instructed along these lines:

A person is not responsible for criminal conduct if at the time of such conduct, as a result of mental disease or defect, he lacks substantial capacity either to appreciate the criminality (wrongfulness) of his conduct or to conform his conduct to the requirements of law.[21]

With slight alterations, this formulation—which was written by the American Law Institute in 1962—became the law in a majority of the states and, until October 1984, in the federal circuits. In the words of Judge Irving Kaufman of the appellate bench:

This test focuses not only on the defendant's understanding of his conduct, which remains a key element in any inquiry into mental capacity, but also on the defendant's ability to control his actions. It would absolve from criminal punishment an individual who knows what he is doing yet is driven to crime by delusions, fears or compulsions. This result conforms to the modern view of the mind as a unified entity whose functioning may be impaired in numerous ways.[22]

The first reported jury trial involving a defense of insanity after an attempt had been made on the life of a president occurred in 1835. Richard Lawrence fired at President Jackson from a range of about thirteen feet as he was walking through the rotunda of the capitol.

> The cap went off with a loud report, but the powder did not ignite and the pistol did not fire. Lawrence dropped the first pistol and transferred the other to his right hand. Meanwhile, Jackson rushed at Lawrence with his cane upraised. Lawrence fired the second pistol into Jackson's chest at pointblank range. It also misfired. Subsequent examination of the pistols showed that they were properly loaded. Their misfiring was attributed to humidity and near-miraculous good fortune.[23]

Lawrence pleaded not guilty by reason of insanity. The prosecutor—Francis Scott Key—cooperated with the defense in establishing a liberal test for insanity.

> Lawrence was to be found not guilty by reason of insanity for the deed was the "immediate, unqualified offspring of the disease"—even if at the time of the attack he comprehended the nature of the act and knew the difference between right and wrong.[24]

The jury found Lawrence not guilty by reason of insanity, and he spent the rest of his life in mental institutions.

Forty-six years later, in July 1881, Charles Guiteau shot and killed President James Garfield four months after Garfield had assumed office. Prior to his successful assassination of the president of the United States, Guiteau had engaged in many bizarre activities, and his life demonstrated instability and lack of control over his behavior. There was a history of mental illness in the family. One of Guiteau's uncles died insane; the sanity of two of his sisters was questioned; and Guiteau's two first cousins were committed to asylums. Shortly before the assassination, Guiteau received a message that God wanted him to save the country from ruin by eliminating Garfield.

> Guiteau bought a forty-four caliber pistol with borrowed money. He paid an extra dollar in order to get a fancier handle, because he thought it would look better in a museum. The owner of the gunshop showed Guiteau how to load the revolver and suggested a spot where Guiteau could practice.[25]

During the trial Guiteau claimed that he had acted as an agent of God and was thus guiltless. It took the jury one hour and five minutes to find him guilty and sane, and he was hanged in front of a large crowd. Reports indicate that the spectators in the court applauded when the jurors announced their verdict, and the newspapers and public officials commended their act. An autopsy done after Guiteau's death found syphilitic lesions on his brain.

Forty years later, in October 1921, John Schrank shot and wounded in the chest the then–presidential aspirant, Theodore Roosevelt.

> Standing about six feet from Roosevelt, Schrank would most likely have killed Roosevelt, had the bullet not spent much of its force passing through Roosevelt's metal glass case and the fifty-page manuscript of a speech he was to give, which was folded double in the breast pocket.

As early as 1901, McKinley's ghost had appeared to Schrank in a dream and accused Roosevelt of the (McKinley) assassination.

> On the eleventh anniversary of President McKinley's death, while Roosevelt was campaigning on the Bull Moose platform, the ghost of McKinley again appeared to Schrank, touched him on the shoulder, and told him not to let a murderer become president.[26]

This apparently confirmed Schrank's conviction that he must be the agent of God to see that Roosevelt did not live to win what Schrank construed to be a third term—although, of course, it would not be a *full* third term, since Roosevelt had only been elected once in his own right.

Having determined to kill Roosevelt, Schrank set out to stalk him on his campaign tours. In more than 2,000 miles and twenty-four days of travel in eight states, Schrank managed to be in the same city at the same time as Roosevelt in only three instances: Chattanooga, Chicago, and Milwaukee. Schrank said his nerve momentarily failed him in Chattanooga. He refrained from shooting Roosevelt in Chicago for fear of damaging the reputation of that city. He finally acted in Milwaukee. After Schrank's arrest, the court appointed five psychiatrists to examine him. They unanimously reported that he was not competent to stand trial. Schrank spent the rest of his life in Wisconsin mental institutions.[27]

On February 15, 1933, Giuseppe Zangara attempted to assassinate president-elect Franklin Roosevelt. Following World War I, Zangara had served for five years in the Italian army. Sometime during this period he had bought a pistol in order to assassinate the king of Italy, but was discouraged by the guards and crowds surrounding the king. At the age of twenty-three—shortly after his discharge from the Italian army—he emigrated to the United States.[28]

In the winter of 1932–1933, Zangara was apparently determined to kill President Hoover, but the cold weather in Washington deterred him. When he learned that president-elect Roosevelt planned to be in Miami, Zangara went to Miami. The shot that he presumably fired at Roosevelt hit and killed Mayor

Anton Cermak of Chicago, who was sitting next to Roosevelt. Zangara was found to be sane, and he was electrocuted.

In November 1963, Jack Ruby pleaded insanity after he fatally shot Lee Harvey Oswald—the presumed assassin of President John F. Kennedy—before millions of television witnesses. A jury found Ruby guilty, and he was sentenced to life imprisonment.[29]

In 1968, attorneys for Sirhan Sirhan—the assassin of presidential aspirant Robert Kennedy—pleaded "diminished responsibility" for their client, claiming that he was "not capable of mature consideration when the act was committed."[30] After seventeen hours of deliberation, the jury found Sirhan guilty of first degree murder. The same jury also deliberated on Sirhan's sentence. It took the jurors nearly twelve hours to decide that Sirhan should be condemned to death in the gas chamber.

In 1972, when Arthur Bremer introduced a plea of insanity after he shot and paralyzed George C. Wallace—the governor of Alabama and a presidential candidate—it took a jury ninety minutes to determine that Bremer was sane and guilty.[31] He was sentenced to sixty-three years in prison.

In the staff report to the National Commission on the Causes and Prevention of Violence (1968), the authors quoted psychiatrist Donald Hastings as concluding that all of the presidential assassins (those who were successful, and those who failed)—with the exception of the Puerto Rican nationalists who attempted to kill Truman—were "mentally disturbed persons who did not kill to advance any national political plan."[32] Dr. Hastings—the report claimed—"goes so far as to diagnose their mental illness as schizophrenia, in most instances a paranoid type."

But in every trial with the exception of Lawrence's, the juries found the defendants guilty as charged. There were no public outcries in response to any of these verdicts; no media denouncement of the failure of the jury system; no official demands for changes in the rule of law. The public, the press, and the officials supported the juries' verdicts. Their silence indicated that justice had been done in the eyes in the public, the media, and the government.

Was the jury in the *Hinckley* case less competent, less wise, and more ignorant of the law than the juries who found Guiteau, Zangara, Bremer, Ruby, and Sirhan guilty of their heinous acts? We do not know firsthand what happened in the deliberating rooms of any of these trials. We know what the final verdict was; and, in recent trials, we also know how individual jurors reacted to their experiences, after the fact. But questions remain about juries' competence to decide the complex issues involved after a defense of insanity has been raised. We know that the jury did not fare well in the court of public opinion after its verdict was announced in the *Hinckley* trial.

Following the controversy over the *Hinckley* verdict, various professional associations convened special committees to study and recommend adoption of a policy vis-à-vis the retention or abolition of the defense of insanity. The National Mental Health Association, the American Psychiatric Association, and the American Bar Association all came out in favor of retaining the defense. The National Mental Health Association noted:

> The Commission strongly believes that this virtual elimination of the insanity defense is unnecessary for the protection of the public, unwise as a matter of public policy and a radical departure from one of the basic precepts of our jurisprudence . . . [T]he insanity defense, in some form, has been a part of our Anglo-American justice system for centuries.
>
> Certainly proposals which seek to abolish this defense should bear a significant burden of proof in order to demonstrate the urgent need to simply eliminate this concept from our jurisprudence. The Commission does not believe that the proponents of abolition have demonstrated in any fashion that they have met that burden.[33]

The American Psychiatric Association statement contained the following:

> The insanity defense rests upon one of the fundamental premises of the criminal law, that punishment for wrongful deeds should be predicated upon moral culpability. However, within the framework of English and American law, defendants who lack the ability (the capacity) to rationally control their behavior do not possess free will. They cannot be said to have "chosen to do wrong." Therefore, they should not be punished or handled similarly to all other criminal defendants. Retention of the insanity defense is essential to the moral integrity of the criminal law.[34]

The American Bar Association supported retention, and approved the following new test for insanity:

> RESOLVED, that the American Bar Association approves, in principle, a defense of nonresponsibility for a crime which focuses solely on whether the defendant, as a result of mental disease or defect, was unable to appreciate the wrongfulness of his or her conduct at the time of the offense charged.[35]

After reviewing the American Bar Association policy positions and the position statement of the American Psychiatric Association, the Committee on Legal Issues of the American Psychological Association endorsed in principle the position of the American Bar Association that the insanity defense be retained. Swimming against the tide of this professional opinion, the American Medical Association adopted a policy favoring abolition of the insanity defense. The report on which the AMA's policy was based concluded:

[The insanity defense] has outlived its principal utility, it invites continuing expansion and corresponding abuse, it requires juries to decide cases on the basis of criteria that defy intelligent resolution in the adversary forum of the courtroom, and it impedes efforts to provide needed treatment to mentally ill offenders. As a result, it inspires public cynicism and contributes to erosion of confidence in the law's rationality, fairness, and efficiency.[36]

Within the Reagan administration there were strong sentiments in favor of abolishing the defense of insanity. Precedent for this position dates back to the Nixon administration. In congressional deliberations over revising the federal criminal code, the Nixon administration included a provision in a proposed comprehensive criminal code reform bill that would have abolished the insanity defense as follows:

Section 501. Insanity.

It is a defense to a prosecution under any federal statute that the defendant, as a result of mental disease or defect, lacked the state of mind required as an element of the offense charged. Mental disease or defect does not otherwise constitute a defense.[37]

Legal Criteria

The Insanity Defense Reform Act of 1984 represents the first federal codification of the insanity defense. The new standard provides for the affirmative defense that "the defendant, as a result of a severe mental disease or defect, was unable to appreciate the nature and quality or the wrongfulness of his acts." This formulation does not allow an insanity defense based on a defendant's inability to conform his conduct to the requirements of the law, as provided by the American Law Institute standard.

A description of the legal criteria adopted by each of the fifty states is listed in table 3.1.

Burden of Proof

The Insanity Defense Reform Act (1984) shifts the burden of proof from the prosecution to the defendant, who must prove insanity by a standard of clear and convincing evidence. Following the passage of the 1984 act, two-thirds of the states have placed the burden of proof on the defendant, most by the standard of by a preponderance of the evidence.

Form of Verdict

The verdict form of the federal law is not guilty only by reason of insanity. For the fifty states, the verdict forms are shown in table 3.1.

Who Decides?

Usually a jury trial is held.

Role of Experts

The 1984 act limits the role of experts such that:

No expert witness testifying with respect to the mental state or condition of a defendant in a criminal case may state an opinion or inference as to whether the defendant did or did not have the mental state or condition constituting an element of the crime charged or of a defence thereto. Such ultimate issues are matters for the trier of fact alone.

Given the above statement regarding limitations on expert testimony, the expert will not be allowed to express opinions on the following questions:

1) Was the defendant insane?
2) Could the defendant tell right from wrong?
3) Could the defendant appreciate the wrongfulness of his conduct?

It is much less clear whether the expert will be allowed to answer a question as to whether the defendant possessed a "severe mental disease or defect" at the time of the crime. The congressional report mentioned above suggests that an expert witness might be permitted to address this question.

When the Federal Rules of Evidence was adopted in 1975, the power of the trial judge to appoint expert witnesses was affirmed, and procedures were devised to facilitate the use of this authority. Many state evidence codes—modeled on the Federal Rules of Evidence—have adopted similar procedures. Rule 706 provides:

Rule 706. Court Appointed Experts

a) Appointment. The court may on its own motion or on the motion of any party enter an order to show cause why expert witnesses should not be appointed, and may request the parties to submit nominations. The court may appoint any expert witnesses agreed upon by the parties, and may appoint expert witnesses of its own selection. An expert witness shall not be appointed by the court unless he consents to act. A witness so appointed shall be informed of his duties by the court in writing, a copy of which shall be filed with the clerk, or at a conference in which the parties shall have opportunity to participate. A witness so appointed shall advise the parties of his findings, if any; his deposition may be taken by any part; and he may be called to testify by the court or any party. He shall be subject to cross-examination by each party, including a party calling him as a witness.

b) Compensation. Expert witnesses so appointed are entitled to reasonable compensation in whatever sum the court may allow. The compensation thus fixed is payable from funds which may be provided by law in criminal cases and civil actions and proceedings involving just compensation under the fifth amendment. In other civil actions and proceedings the compensation shall be paid by the parties in such proportion and at such time as the court directs, and thereafter charged in like manner as other costs.

c) Disclosure of appointment. In the exercise of its discretion, the court may authorize disclosure to the jury of the fact that the court appointed the expert witness.

d) Parties' experts of own selection. Nothing in this rule limits the parties in calling expert witnesses of their own selection.

What Happens to the Defendant?

Under federal rules and in most states a defendant who is found not guilty by reason of insanity is committed to a mental institution until such time as medical authorities recommend his release. It is the court, however, that has the final authority concerning the defendant's release.

Frequency of Use

The defense of insanity is introduced in about 2 percent of capital cases. When it is introduced it is successful about 20 percent of the time.

TABLE 3.1

Insanity Defense Standards in the United States by State[38]

State	Insanity Test	Bifurcated Trial	Verdict(s)	Treatment: (M)andatory (D)iscretionary	Release Authority
Alabama	M'N	N	NGBD	D	Court
Alaska	M'N (nature and quality prong only)[39]	N	NGBI/GBMI	D for NGBI; M for GBMI	Court
Arizona	M'N (nature and quality)[40]	N	NGBI/GBI	D	Court
Arkansas	A.L.I. (minus "substantial")	N	NGBD	D	Court
California	M'N	Y	NGBI	D	Court
Colorado	M'N and irresistible impulse	N	NGBI	M	Court
Connecticut	A.L.I.[41]	N	NGBD	D	Court
Delaware	A.L.I. (criminal prong only)	N	NGBI	M	Court
District of Columbia	A.L.I.	Y	NGBI	M	Court
Florida	M'N	Y[42]	NGBI	D	Court
Georgia	M'N and delusional comparison	N	NGBI/GBMI/GBMR	M for NGBI; D for GBMI/GBMR	Court
Hawaii	A.L.I.[43]	N	Acquitted for physical or mental disorder	D	Court
Idaho[44]			GBI	D	Court
Illinois	A.L.I.[45]	N	NGBI	D	Court
Indiana	A.L.I. (no control prong)[46]	N	Not responsible by insanity	D	Court
Iowa	M'N	N	NGBI	M	Court
Kansas	M'N	N	NGBD	M	Court
Kentucky	A.L.I.	N	NGBI	D	Court
Louisiana	M'N	N	NGBI	M	Court

	A.L.I. (no control prong)[47]				
Maine	A.L.I. (no control prong)[47]	Y	Not responsible for mental defect reasons	M	Court
Maryland	A.L.I.	Y	Not responsible by reason of insanity	D	Court
Massachusetts	A.L.I.	N	NGBI	D	State Hospital[48]
Michigan	A.L.I.	N	NGBI	M	N/S
Minnesota	M'N	Y	NGBI	M	Court
Mississippi	M'N	Y	ABI	D	N/S
Missouri	M'N[49]	N	NGBD	M	Court
Montana[50]	N/A		GBI	D	Court
Nebraska	M'N	N	NGBI	D	Court
New Hampshire[51]		Y	NGBI	M	Court
New Jersey	M'N	Y	NGBI	D	Court
New Mexico	M'N or irresistible impulse	N	NGBI	D	Court
New York	A.L.I.	N	Not responsible by reason of mental defect	D	Court
North Carolina	M'N	N	NGBI	M	Court
North Dakota[52]	A.L.I.	Y	NG, lack of criminal responsibility	D	Court Annual Review
Ohio	M'N	N	NGBI	D	Court
Oklahoma	M'N	Y	AGI	D	Court
Oregon	A.L.I.	N	Guilty except for insanity	D	Psych. Security Review Board
Pennsylvania	M'N	Y	NGBI	D[53]	Court
Puerto Rico	A.L.I.	B	NGBI	D	Court
Rhode Island	A.L.I.	B	NGBI	D	Court

(continued)

TABLE 3.1
(continued)

State	Insanity Test	Bifurcated Trial	Verdict(s)	Treatment: (M)andatory (D)iscretionary	Release Authority
South Carolina	M'N	N	NGBI	M (120 days)	Chief Admin. Judge
South Dakota	M'N	N	NGBI	D	Court
Tennessee	A.L.I.	N	NGBI	M	Court
Texas	M'N and Irresistible Impulse	N	NGBI	D for nonviolent, M for violent	Court
Utah[54]			GBI	D	Court
Vermont	A.L.I.	N	NGBI	D	Dev./Mental Health Services[55]
Virginia	M'N and Irresistible Impulse	N	NGBI	D	Court
Washington	M'N	N	NGBI	D	Court
West Virginia	A.L.I.	N	NGBD	M	Court
Wisconsin	A.L.I.	N	NGMI/D	D	Court
Wyoming	A.L.I.	N	NGMI/D	D	Court
Federal	M'N	N	NGBI	M[56]	Court[57]

M'N = M'Naghten
A.L.I. = American Law Institute
GBMI = Guilty But Mentally Ill
NGBD = Not Guilty by Reason of Mental Disease or Defect

NGBI = Not Guilty by Reason of Insanity
ABI = Acquitted by Reason of Insanity
N/S = Not Stated

Mental health state laws available at <www.megalaw.com/top/mentalhealth.php>.

Notes

1. *United States v. Holmes*, 26 F. Cas. 349, 358 (No. 15,382) (Cir.Ct.D.Me.).

2. Wayne R. LaFave and Austin W. Scott Jr., *Handbook on Criminal Law* (St. Paul, MN.: West Publishing Co., 1972), 276–77.

3. Gregory Zilboorg, M.D., "Misconceptions of Legal Insanity," 9 *Am .J. Orthopsychiatry* 540 (1939): 522–53.

4. Abraham S. Goldstein, *The Insanity Defense* (New Haven, CT: Yale University Press, 1967), 49.

5. *Regina v. Oxford*, 175 Eng. Rep. 941, 950 (1840).

6. *Regina v. Burton*, 176 Eng. Rep. 354, 357 (1863).

7. *Parsons v. State*, 81 Ala. 577, 2 So. 854 (1887).

8. LaFave and Scott, *Criminal Law*, 284.

9. *United States v. Fisher*, 328 U.S. 463, 66 S. Ct. 1318 (1946).

10. John Biggs, *The Guilty Mind* (New York: Harcourt, Brace, 1955), 138–39.

11. Biggs, *The Guilty Mind*, 142–43.

12. Biggs, *The Guilty Mind*, 143.

13. Biggs, *The Guilty Mind*, 143–44.

14. Rita J. Simon, *The Jury and the Defense of Insanity* (Boston: Little, Brown, 1967), 25 (emphasis in original).

15. Simon, *The Jury and the Defense of Insanity*, 31.

16. *State v. Pike*, 49 N.H. 399 (1870).

17. *State v. Jones*, 50 N.H. 369 (1871).

18. *Durham v. United States*, 94 U.S. App. D.C. 228, 214 F.2d 862 (1954).

19. Simon, *Jury and Insanity*, 32.

20. Seymour Halleck, "Insanity Defense in the District of Columbia—A Legal Lorelie," 49 *Geo. L.J.* 294 (1950).

21. American Law Institute, *Model Penal Code*, sec. 4.01 (Philadelphia: ALI, 1962).

22. Irving Kaufman, "The Insanity Plea on Trial," *New York Times Magazine*, August 8, 1982: 18.

23. Rita J. Simon, "Assassination Attempts Directed at the Office of the President of the United States," in James F. Kirkham, Sheldon Levy, and William Crotty, eds., *Assassination and Political Violence*, vol. 8: *Report of the National Commission on the Causes and Prevention of Violence* (Washington, D.C.: U.S. Government Printing Office, 1969), 49–50.

24. Simon, "Assassination Attempts," 50.

25. Simon, "Assassination Attempts," 53.

26. Simon, "Assassination Attempts," 56.

27. Simon, "Assassination Attempts," 57.

28. Simon, "Assassination Attempts."

29. Simon, "Assassination Attempts," 61.

30. Simon, "Assassination Attempts," 62.

31. Valerie P. Hans and Neil Vidmar, *Judging the Jury* (New York: Plenum Press, 1986), 190.

32. Simon, "Assassination Attempts," 62.

33. Ingo Keilitz and Junius P. Fulton, *The Insanity Defense and Its Alternatives: A Guide for Policy Makers* (Williamsburg, VA.: Institute on Mental Disability and the Law, National Center for State Courts, 1984).

34. APA, *Statement on the Insanity Defense.*

35. American Bar Association, *American Bar Association Policy on the Insanity Defense* (approved by the ABA House of Delegates on February 9, 1983).

36. Committee on Medicolegal Problems, American Medical Association, "Insanity Defense in Criminal Trials and Limitations of Psychiatric Testimony: Report of Board of Trustees," 251 *J.A.M.A.* 2967 (1984).

37. Criminal Code Reform Act of 1973, S. 1400, 93d Cong., lst sess. (March 17, 1973). See also Heathcote W. Wales, "An Analysis of the Proposal to 'Abolish' the Insanity Defense in S.1: Squeezing a Lemon," 124 *U. Pa. L. Rev.* 687 (1976).

38. Adapted from Bureau of Justice Statistics (2000): table 38.

39. Wrongfulness prong is basis for GBMI verdict.

40. Wrongfulness prong is basis for GBMI verdict.

41. Requires lack of capacity to conform behavior.

42. At discretion of trial court.

43. Expands disability defense so conduct can be as a result of "physical or mental disease, disorder, or defect."

44. Insanity defense abolished; evidence of mental defect may negate an offense element.

45. Requires lack of substantial capacity to conform.

46. Mental disease/defect must be severely abnormal mental condition that grossly and demonstrably impairs perception.

47. Mental disease/defect must be severely abnormal mental condition that grossly and demonstrably impairs perception.

48. District attorney must be informed of release and given opportunity to file civil commitment.

49. *M'Naghten* and incapacity to conform conduct to requirements of law.

50. Insanity defense abolished; evidence of mental defect may negate an offense element.

51. Legislature has not adopted a test: courts have held that the insanity must negate criminal intent for NGBI verdict.

52. Availability of insanity defense tied to the elements of offense. Effectively abolishes insanity defense for crimes not requiring intention, knowledge, or recklessness.

53. If court has reasonable grounds to believe imposition is necessary due to his or her dangerous character.

54. Insanity defense abolished, evidence of mental defect may negate an offense element.

55. Court may retain the release authority.

56. Unless defense can prove by clear and convincing evidence that his release would not create a substantial risk of bodily injury or serious damage to property due to a present mental disease or defect.

57. Upon certification by director of mental facility that defendant's release or conditional release would no longer create a substantial risk.

References

American Law Institute. 1962. Model Penal Code, Proposed Official Draft, §4.01.

Biggs, John. *The Guilty Mind.* New York: Harcourt, Brace, 1955.

Bureau of Justice Statistics. 2000. *State Court Organization, 1998.* Washington, D.C.: U.S. Department of Justice, Bureau of Justice Statistics.

Committee on Medicolegal Problems, American Medical Association. "Insanity Defense in Criminal Trials and Limitations of Psychiatric Testimony: Report of Board of Trustees." 251 *J.A.M.A.* 2967 (1984).

Davis v. United States (165 U.S. 373, 378 (1897)

Durham v. United States 214 F. 2d 862, 869 et seq. (D.C. Cir. 1957).

Durham v. United States 214 F. 2d at 874–875.

Goldstein, Abraham S. 1967. *The Insanity Defense.* New Haven, CT: Yale University Press.

Halleck, Seymour. "Insanity Defense in the District of Columbia—A Legal Lorelie." 49 *Geo. L.J.* 294 (1950).

Hans, Valerie P., and Neil Vidmar. *Judging the Jury.* New York: Plenum Press, 1986.

Internal Revenue Service. "The Internal Revenue Manual," Part 31, chapter 3, section 5 (31.3.5.1). Retrieved July 2, 2004, <www.irs.gov/irm/part31/ch03s05.html#d0e38718>.

Kaufman, Irving. "The Insanity Plea on Trial." *New York Times Magazine,* August 8, 1982.

Keilitz, Ingo, and Junius P. Fulton. *The Insanity Defense and Its Alternatives: A Guide for Policy Makers.* Williamsburg, VA.: Institute on Mental Disability and the Law, National Center for State Courts, 1984.

LaFave, Wayne R., and Austin W. Scott Jr. *Handbook on Criminal Law.* St. Paul, MN.: West Publishing Co., 1972.

McDonald v. United States, 312 F. 2d 847, 851 (D.C. Cir. 1962).

Monson, Candice M, Deborah D. Gunnin, Michael H. Fogel and Lori L. Kyle. 2001. "Stopping (or Slowing) the Revolving Door: Factors Related to NGRI Acquittees' Maintenance of a Conditional Release." *Law and Human Behavior* 25, no. 3: 257–67.

Overholser v. Russell, 283 F. 2d 195, 198 (D.C. Cir. 1960).

Report of the Canadian Royal Commission on Insanity as a Defense in Criminal Cases. 1955: 12–13.

Report of the Royal Commission on Capital Punishment 80 (1953).

Simon, Rita J. "Assassination Attempts Directed at the Office of the President of the United States." In James F. Kirkham, Sheldon Levy, and William Crotty, eds., *Assassination and Political Violence,* vol. 8: *Report of the National Commission on the Causes and Prevention of Violence.* Washington, D.C.: U.S. Government Printing Office, 1969.

———. *The Jury and the Defense of Insanity.* Boston: Little, Brown, 1967.

State v. Reidell 14 Atl. 550, 551 (Del. 1888).

TheFreeDictionary.com. 2004. "Insanity defense." Farlax, Inc. The article was derived from Wikipedia.org. Retrieved June 28, 2004, <http://encyclopedia .thefreedictionary.com/Insanity percent20defense>.

Wales, Heathcote M. "An Analysis of the Proposal to 'Abolish' the Insanity Defense in S.1: Squeezing a Lemon." 124 *U. Pa. L. Rev.* 687 (1976).

Zilboorg, Gregory, M.D. "Misconceptions of Legal Insanity." 9 *Am .J. Orthopsychiatry* 540 (1939).

Part III

SOUTH AMERICA

4

Argentina

THE FEDERAL REPUBLIC OF ARGENTINA is the second largest country in South America and occupies much of the southern portion of the continent. The Republic, which is located between Uruguay and Chile, has a population of 39.5 million. The majority of the population is white with Italian or Spanish ancestry (97 percent), while other ethnic groups include Amerindians and mestizos, who are white-Amerindians (CIA 2005). Roman Catholics make up 90 percent of the population, and the church plays a major role in shaping the country's laws and policies, especially those concerning women's issues. Other practiced religions are Protestantism (2 percent) and Judaism (2 percent). While the official language in Argentina is Spanish, English, Italian, German, French, and many Native American languages are also spoken.

Argentina is a major agricultural producer, but is also highly industrialized, with the vast majority of its citizens (86 percent) living in urban centers. Major industries include food processing, motor vehicles, chemicals, steel, printing, and textiles (CIA 2005). Argentine exports include edible oils, fuel, cereal, and motor vehicles, while its imports include machinery, chemicals, and plastics.

Argentina is a federal republic headed by a president, who is assisted by a Council of Ministers. Legislative powers are vested in a national congress consisting of a senate and a Chamber of Deputies. All constitutional provisions have been repeatedly suspended and then reinstated. As of 1994, several parts of Argentina's Constitution were revised, although the basic system of government remained unchanged.

Background

At the federal level, there are seventeen appellate courts, district and territorial courts, and a Supreme Court (Fischer 2002). There are different court systems in each Argentine province, each of which consists of "supreme, appellate, and lower courts" that try civil, criminal, and labor cases (Fischer 2002).

Criminal trials in Argentina are largely oral and take place in a two-phase Criminal Forum (Fischer 2002; Kozameh et al. 2001). During the first phase, a judge determines whether there is enough evidence to try the defendant. If so, the second phase involves three judges who ultimately determine guilt. In some provinces judges take part in criminal investigations, whereas in other regions judges and prosecutors may work together.

Argentina has 30 federal and 136 provincial institutions, as well as other police facilities (ICPS 2005). As of 2003, there were 38,604 prisoners in Argentina, of whom 9.5 percent were women (ICPS 2005). The same year, the prison population rate was 107 per 100,000 national population.[1]

Legal Criteria

Anyone who at the time of the commission of the crime could not appreciate the unlawfulness of the deed or control his actions by reason of insufficiency or diseased disturbance of his mind or by unconsciousness or by error of fact or ignorance is not responsible.

Burden of Proof

The Argentine Supreme Court has ruled "that it is the defendant's burden to prove the existence of any justification or excuse invoked by him, once his participation in a crime has been objectively determined." It is not clear, however, whether the burden is beyond a reasonable doubt or by preponderance of the evidence.

Form of Verdict

A defendant may be found not guilty by reason of insanity.

Who Decides?

A judge renders the decision.

Role of Experts

Experts conduct insanity evaluations that focus on determining whether the accused was suffering from a mental disturbance at the moment of the crime so that he or she could not fulfill the cognitive and volitional component mentioned in the legal criteria. The experts are subject to cross-examination.

What Happens to the Defendant?

The defendant is automatically committed to an insane asylum if found not guilty by reason of insanity. Release is dependent on a judicial hearing in the presence of a public prosecutor and on the presentation of a medical experts' report that in their view the patient no longer constitutes a danger to himself or others. The average stay is two years.

Note

1. See <www.nationmaster.com/country/ar/Crime>.

References

Central Intelligence Agency (CIA). 2005. "France." The World Factbook. <www.odci.gov/cia/publications/factbook/geos/fr.html>.

Fischer, Susanna. 2002. "Argentine Legal System and Structure." Susanna Fischer's website, Columbus School of Law, The Catholic University of America. Retrieved August 11, 2005, <http://faculty.cua.edu/fischer/ComparativeLaw2002/comphome2002.htm>.

International Centre for Prison Studies (ICPS). 2005. "World Prison Brief: Entire World—Prison Population Totals, Prison Brief for Argentina." International Centre for Prison Studies, Kings College London. Retrieved May 10, 2005, <www.kcl.ac.uk/depsta/rel/icps/worldbrief/world_brief.html>.

Nationmaster.com. "South America, Argentina, Crime." Retrieved August 11, 2005, <www.nationmaster.com/country/ar/Crime>.

Kozameh, Ernesto Nicolás, Julio O. Trajtenberg, Nicolás Kozameh Jr., and Ezequiel Trajtenberg. 2001. "Guide to the Argentine Executive, Legislative, and Judicial System." Published July 15, 2001. Retrieved August 11, 2005, <www.llrx.com/features/argentina.htm>.

5

Brazil

THE FEDERATIVE REPUBLIC OF BRAZIL is a democratic nation located in South America and is bordered by the Atlantic Ocean and all other South American nations with the exception of Chile and Ecuador. Brazil's 177 million people live in twenty-seven states and a federal district throughout regions of the north, northeast, centre-west, southeast, and south (U.S. Department of State 2003; ICL 1993; Taborda et al. 2001: 579; Scuro 2003). Each state has its own constitution. The official language is Portuguese, but Spanish, English, and French are also spoken.

Approximately 55 percent of the population is white and of Portuguese, Spanish, Polish, Italian and German ancestry, while other ethnic groups include blacks (6 percent), mixed white and black (38 percent), and persons of Japanese, Arab, or Amerindian descent (1 percent). Approximately 80 percent of Brazilians are Roman Catholic.

Brazil's Constitution was promulgated on October 5, 1988, and has undergone over forty amendments (GSLR 2003). The Brazilian government consists of three independent branches: executive, legislative, and judicial (ICL 1993). National laws supercede state laws (Taborda et al. 2000). The executive branch consists of a popularly elected president, while the legislative branch is composed of an 81-member Senate and a 513-member Chamber of Deputies (U.S. Department of State 2003). The justice system consists of federal and common courts (Prisoners Abroad 2002: 4) and the judicial branch contains an 11-member Supreme Federal Tribunal.

Because Brazil is a civil law country, legislative statutes define crimes and dictate various sanctions. Under the Federal Supreme Court of Justice, whose function it is to administer the law, are three types of superior courts that handle criminal cases (Prisoners Abroad 2002: 4). These courts are the Superior Court of Justice (STJ), the Superior Electoral Court (TSE), and the Superior Military Court (STM) (4).

Background

Until 1822, Brazil remained under Portuguese rule. Early penal codes were the Criminal Code of the Empire of Brazil (1830), the Penal Code of the United States of Brazil (1890), and the Consolidation of the Penal Laws (1932) (Taborda 2001: 383). These older codes referred to the mentally ill through phrases such as "mad people of all kinds," "native imbecility," "senile deterioration," "deaf-mute when born," and "complete deprivation of their senses and intelligence" (Taborda 2001: 384).

Early Portuguese law permitted a husband who caught his wife with another man to kill her (Human Rights Watch). This law was repealed in 1830 when Brazil developed a new penal code. The new 1890 Penal Code, however, provided that offenders "under a state of total perturbation of the senses and intelligence" (Human Rights Watch website) at the time of the crime were not criminally responsible, so men who murdered unfaithful wives and who were believed to have undergone periods of "momentary insanity" (Human Rights Watch website) were often acquitted by using a "crimes of passion" defense or "honour defense" (Human Rights Internet [HRI] 1998).

It was not until the 1940 Penal Code that "violent emotion cannot be used to exculpate the defendant but only as a mitigating factor reducing the sentence of up to a third" (Benninger-Budel and O'Hanlon 2003: 79). Still, men who kill their spouses attempt to circuitously use insanity to reduce their sentences by using pleas of "'violent emotion,' 'temporary insanity' and 'unjust provocation'" (HRI 1998). When "temporary insanity" is used successfully, as happens more in rural areas of Brazil, the offense is called "privileged homicide" and may result in one to six years in prison rather than the normal twelve- to thirty-year sentence for homicide (HRI 1998). Men who successfully use the "honour defense," in which they argue that their actions were in self-defense, may be alleviated of criminal responsibility (Benninger-Budel and O'Hanlon 2003: 79).

Imputability became an issue in the Penal Codes of 1940 and 1984 (Taborda 2001: 383). The Penal Code of 1940, which was the first to include "semi-imputable" as a category of mental status, required an offender to be totally or partially impaired "of the *cognitive* or *volitive* elements, during the committing of the crime, on account of mental disturbance," a requirement that is still currently used under the Penal Code of 1984 (Taborda 2001: 384).

Within the criminal justice system, crimes are set forth through five codes: civil, criminal, commercial, civil procedure, and criminal procedure (Scuro 2003; GSLR 2003). Today, other relevant laws are the Penal Execution Law,[1] the Health Organic Law,[2] the Penal Code,[3] and the Procedural Code[4] (Taborda et al. 2000: 581).

When individuals are arrested, the manner with which they are dealt depends on the nature of the offense as well as the individual's social status (FloridaBrasil.com 1997). If an arrestee has a degree from a university, he or she has the right to special treatment and cannot be placed in the same cell as arrestees with lower education. Arrestees with limited financial resources are guaranteed free legal assistance by the constitution (Prisoners Abroad 2002: 3). Due to a lack of resources, however, students in their last year of legal studies often assist defense lawyers with administrative and judicial duties.

When a crime has been committed, the Brazilian police undergo an "inquest" to collect evidence and gather information about the incident (Taborda 2001: 372). The next step involves the judiciary during which an individual is tried. The Public Ministry, or Ministerio Publico, prosecutes criminal offenses whereas judges are charged with protecting the rights of the accused (Prisoners Abroad 2002: 2). For the more serious crimes, a person may be tried by a judge and a jury, while less severe crimes are tried by a single judge. If the defense, prosecutor, or judge requests, the offender may be given the Penal Imputability Exam or the Drug Addiction Exam (Taborda 2001).

Through pretrial diversion, many offenders are placed, for example, in detoxification facilities, community service centers, treatment centers, and may be ordered to participate in counseling or job assistance (Scuro 2003). Thus, many mentally ill offenders are diverted from prison to treatment facilities (Scuro 2003).

Criminal cases are inquisitorial and their outcomes are products of secret votes among jurors (Scuro 2003). Counsel is required in order for a defendant to be tried and sentenced. Aggravating and mitigating circumstances may be taken into consideration during sentencing and the maximum term of incarceration is thirty years. A sentence of incarceration may be given to an offender convicted of homicide, major assault, rape, kidnapping, theft, violent robbery, embezzlement, and corruption (Scuro 2003). The death penalty may be used only during wartime and in cases of foreign aggression (Scuro 2003). Under the constitution, convicted offenders cannot receive life sentences (ICL 1993).

Under the Federal Prison Department's auspices are correctional institutions, penitentiaries, houses of custody and treatment, penal and agricultural colonies, houses of correction, military prisons, houses of detention, and correctional institutions for minors (Winslow 2005). There are over 1,500 prisons, approximately 2,800 jails, and 5 facilities for juveniles (Winslow 2005).

There is a prison hospital in Porto Alegre that provides outpatient and inpatient care to inmates from the Porto Alegre Central Prison, located in the state Rio Grande do Sul (Taborda et al. 1999). There are approximately 1,800 maximum-security male inmates in Porto Alegre Central Prison (as of 1999). As of 1999, there were 11,000 inmates in the state's prisons. Forensic psychiatric hospitals are different from prison hospitals. Through inpatient treatment, prisons treat mentally ill inmates and inmates who develop psychological disorders while incarcerated. Offenders who were court-ordered to be evaluated before any civil or criminal proceedings take place are sent to the forensic psychiatric hospital.

There are more people incarcerated in Brazil than any other South American country; Brazil's incarceration rate ranks fifth in the world (ICPS 2005). Rates of violent crime are high in Brazil. In the 1990s, there were more homicides in Brazil than in the United States, Canada, Japan, Australia, Portugal, Britain, Austria, and Germany combined (Scuro 2003). Much of this violence can be attributed to drug trafficking. As of June 2004, there were 330,642 persons (including pretrial and remand prisoners) incarcerated in Brazil, an incarceration rate of approximately 183 per 100,000 national population (ICPS 2005). An estimated 3.3 percent of the prisoners were female. In 2004, there were 868 penal institutions. Lemgruber (2004) reports that from 1995 to 2003, 112,132 new prison spaces were added and the prison population doubled from 147,760 to over 300,000. Each prison has a psychologist and social worker (Scuro 2003).

Legal Criteria

The legal criteria for insanity is based on the *M'Naghten* rule, which states that a person is not held responsible if the defendant suffers from a mental illness and is unable to understand the illicit nature of his act on account of disease.

Form of Verdict

Offenders in the Brazilian criminal justice system can be convicted due to semi-imputability, which is similar to a "guilty but mentally ill" (GBMI) verdict in the United States, and thus criminally committed; acquitted due to the offender's lack of imputability, which indicates that the offender is not guilty by reason of insanity (NGRI); or acquitted because of an innocent verdict (Taborda 2001: 372–73). An individual who is found to be not imputable becomes an "intern," rather than a "prisoner," a term that is reserved for general offenders in the penal system (Taborda 2001; Taborda et al. 2000).

Who Decides?

A judge may decide the "minimum duration and the setting" of compulsory treatment of semi-imputable and not imputable offenders (Taborda 2001: 374).

Role of Experts

The Penal Execution Law sets forth provisions for prisons for general and mentally ill offenders. This law also dictates what happens to offenders who are found NGRI, as well as the roles of psychiatric experts in cases where mentally ill offenders are committed to a hospital (Taborda et al. 2000: 581).

Forensic psychiatrists are key to determining the outcome of a criminal case in which the offender is suspected of being *lato sensu* (mentally ill) (Taborda 2001: 373). Taborda (2001) describes the role of a forensic psychiatrist as " a clinician and as an expert" (375). The forensic psychiatrist administers treatment— outpatient or inpatient—as determined by the judge (Taborda 2001: 375). He or she is also responsible for administering several psychiatric examinations, such as the Penal Imputability Exam (PIE), an evaluation that involves interviews and psychological tests (Taborda 2001; Taborda et al. 2000). The PIE is used

> to detect whether the defendant suffers from a *lato sensu* mental illness and whether, on account of this disease, he would be unable to understand the illicit nature of the act or to make decisions based on this understanding, since, according to Brazilian law, the legal concept of inimputability comprehends not only the cognitive element (as in the M'Naghten rule) but the volitional element as well (similar to the concept of "irresistible impulse" formulated in Ohio, in 1834). (Taborda et al. 2000: 585)

After the administration of the PIE, the expert provides the judge with the following information:

> "Identification of the examinee; History of the Crime According to the Accusation; History of the Crime According to the Examinee; Synthesis of the Process (a report on the main points of the process); Personal History (medical and psychiatric histories inclusive); Family History; Mental Status Examination; Physical Exam (neurological exam inclusive); Complementary Exams (psychological tests inclusive); Diagnosis; Medical-Legal Comments; Conclusion; [and] Answer to the Queries Formulated by the Judge and by the Parties." (Taborda et al. 2000: 585).

What Happens to the Defendant?

Rio Grande do Sul is the only state with "an organized penitentiary system spread all over its territory" (Taborda et al. 2000: 580). In other states, mentally ill offenders are often placed in facilities for general prison populations, and even if they are sent to a psychiatric hospital, they may not receive adequate forensic psychiatric care (Taborda et al. 2000: 580).

Punishment in Brazil is perceived as a "condition for the devolution of freedom" and based on the "presumed social adaptability" of the defendant (Scuro 2003). Under the Penal Code, offenders found to be NGRI (not imputable), and some who are found to be semi-imputable, cannot be punished (Taborda et al. 2000: 581). Other mentally ill offenders may be given probation rather than prison (Scuro 2003).

If an offender is acquitted because of NGRI (inimputability), he or she will undergo compulsory treatment in a forensic psychiatric hospital (Taborda 2001: 373). Criminally committed offenders in the Rio Grande do Sul are sent to the Forensic Psychiatric Hospital Maurício Cardoso (FPH), which is responsible for all inpatient treatment and all outpatient treatment within the state's capital (Taborda et al. 2000). If an offender is found semiimputable (similar to GBMI), psychiatric treatment may be ordered and the offender committed (Taborda 2001: 373). The disposition of the case depends largely on the condition of that specific individual. In the Rio Grande do Sul, some semi-imputable offenders are sent to the FPH (Taborda et al. 2000). Some offenders who are semi-imputable and all offenders who are not imputable undergo treatment for a minimum time as determined by a judge and with no maximum (Taborda 2001: 374–75).

To be discharged, a criminally committed intern is legally required to take the Verifying of Dangerousness Stoppage Exam (VDSE), an evaluation in which a psychiatrist determines whether he or she is still mentally ill (Taborda 2001: 380; Taborda et al. 2000). If so, then the examination will be administered on an annual basis. If a penal order for criminal commitment is withdrawn due to the VDSE results, the offender is free (Taborda et al. 2000). In São Paulo, if a patient's level of dangerousness is no higher than the average mentally ill individual, the psychiatrist will recommend discharge to the court (Taborda et al. 2000: 585). In Rio Grande do Sul, however, patients undergo Progressive Discharge in which they are ordered by the court to be reintegrated into society in phases to ensure that the individual is ready for release.

The Hospital of Safekeeping and Tratamento Psiquiátrico (HCTP), located on the Island of Itamaracá, is a facility where mentally ill criminal offenders serve a "penalty-treatment" (Inverse 2005). Their length of stay is determined by a judge.

Frequency of Use

According to Taborda (2001), the defense of insanity in Brazil "is rather ordinary and presents chances of being successful" (386). Taborda et al. report in 2000 that there were 595 FPH patients, of whom 74 percent had committed violent crimes and 9 percent had committed sexual offenses (584). Of the 595 patients, 91 percent were male and 75 percent were white (Taborda et al. 2000: 584). Nearly one-third (31 percent) had been in the hospital for over a decade.

Notes

1. Law 7210/84.
2. Law 8080/90.
3. Law 7209/84.
4. Decree-law 3689/41.

References

Associação Internacional de Direito Penal (AIDP). 2002. "Criminal Responsibility of Minors in National and International Legal Order." Congressos Anteriores. Vienna, Austria, 26 a 28 de Setembro de 2002. Retrieved June 2, 2005, <www.aidpbrasil.org .br/cong2002b_2.asp>/.

Benninger-Budel, Carina and Lucinda O'Hanlon. 2003. "Violence against Women: For the Protection and Promotion of the Human Rights of Women." Ten reports. OMCT (The World Organisation against Torture). Switzerland. Retrieved May 11, 2005, <www.omct.org/pdf/vaw/publications/2003/vaw_reports2003_eng.pdf>.

FloridaBrasil.com. 1997. "Penal Code in Brazil." Retrieved May 9, 2005, <www .floridabrasil.com/brazil/about-Brazil-National-Security-Penal-Code.htm>.

Global Studies Law Review (GSLR). 2003. "Brazil, Background and Legal System." International Legal Citation Manual Project. Washington University Global Studies Law Review. Retrieved May 25, 2005, <http://law.wustl.edu/Publications/ WUGSLR/Archives/2005Update/citationmanual.html)>.

Human Rights Internet (HRI). 1998. "For the Record 1997: The UN Human Rights System." Volume 4. <www.hri.ca/fortherecord1997/vol4/brazil.htm>.

Human Rights Watch (website). "The Honor Defense." New York, NY. Retrieved May 20, 2004, <www.hrw.org/about/projects/womrep/General-192.htm>.

International Centre for Prison Studies (ICPS). 2005. "World Prison Brief: Entire World—Prison Population Totals, Prison Brief for Brazil" and "South America—Prison Population Totals." International Centre for Prison Studies, Kings College London. Retrieved June 16, 2004, <www.kcl.ac.uk/depsta/rel/icps/worldbrief/ world_brief.html>.

International Constitutional Law (ICL). 1993. "Brazil—Constitution." Retrieved May 10, 2005, <www.oefre.unibe.ch/law/icl/br00000_.html>.

Inverso. 2005. "No hospital de custódia a reforma caminha a passos bem mais lentos." *Periodical of Commercio*, May 15, 2005. Inverso—Instituto de Convivência e de Recriação do Espaço Social. Retrieved June 2, 2005, <www.inverso.org.br/>.

Lemgruber, Julita. 2004. "The Brazilian Prison System: A Brief Diagnosis." Online article. Retrieved June 2, 2005, <www.uoregon.edu/~caguirre/lembruger_brazil.pdf>.

OECD. 2004. "Brazil: Phase 1. Review of Implementation of the Convention and 1997 Recommendation." Directorate for Financial and Enterprise Affairs. Report approved and adopted by the Working Group on Bribery in International Business Transactions on August 31, 2004. Retrieved June 2, 2005, <www.oecd.org>.

Prisoners Abroad. 2002. "Fact Sheet: Brazil Criminal Justice System." London. Retrieved May 9, 2005, <www.prisonersabroad.org.uk/publications/Brazil_criminal_justice_system.pdf>.

Scuro, Pedro. 2003. "Brazil." World Factbook of Criminal Justice Statistics. NCJ 199270. United States Department of Justice, Office of Justice Programs, Bureau of Justice Statistics. Retrieved online June 10, 2004, <www.ojp.usdoj.gov/bjs/pub/ascii/wfcjsbr.txt>.

Taborda, Jose G. V. 2001. "Criminal Justice System in Brazil: Functions of a Forensic Psychiatrist." *International Journal of Law and Psychiatry* 24: 371–86. Retrieved online June 6, 2005, <www.sciencedirect.com>, Elsevier Sciences, Ltd.

Taborda, Jose G. V., Rogério G. Cardoso, and Hilda C. P. Morana. 2000. "Forensic Psychiatry in Brazil." *International Journal of Law and Psychiatry* 23, nos. 5–6: 579–**288**. Retrieved online June 6, 2005, <www.sciencedirect.com>, Elsevier Sciences, Ltd.

Taborda, J., J. Bertolote, R. Cardoso, and Paulo Blank. 1999. "The Impact of Primary Mental Health Care in a Prison System in Brazil." *Canadian Journal of Psychiatry* 44. Retrieved online May 24, 2005, <www.cpaapc.org/Publications/Archives/CJP/1999/Mar/taborda.htm>.

United States Department of State. 2003. "Background Note: Brazil." Washington, D.C.: U.S. Department of State. Retrieved online June 14, 2004, <www.state.gov/r/pa/ei/bgn/1972.htm>.

Winslow, Robert. 2005. "Brazil" from *Crime and Society: A Comparative Criminology Tour of the World*. Retrieved May 24, 2005, <www.rohan.sdsu.edu/faculty/rwinslow/index.html>.

Part IV

WESTERN EUROPE

6

France

THE REPUBLIC OF FRANCE, HOME TO 60.6 million inhabitants throughout twenty-two regions, borders the Bay of Biscay and the English Channel (CIA 2005). Ninety-two percent of the population is French (a mix of Celtic, Latin, Germanic and Slavic origin), 3 percent are North African, and 2 percent are German. The remainder are Slavic, Indochinese, and Basque. Over 80 percent of the population is Roman Catholic, although other religious groups practice Protestantism (2 percent), Judaism (1 percent), and Islam (5 to 10 percent). French is the official and widely spoken language, but some speak regional dialects and languages such as "Provencal, Breton, Alsatian, Corsican, Catalan, Basque, and Flemish" (CIA 2005).

The French legal system was accusatorial until the sixteenth century, after which it was inquisitorial (Borricand 1993). Following the French Revolution (1789–1799), a judicial system was created. A Code of Criminal Instruction was created in 1808 and later replaced by the Code of Criminal Procedure of 1958. A Penal Code was enacted in 1810 and categorized various offenses into *crimes, misdemeanors,* and *violations* (Borricand 1993). This categorization still remains in the Penal Code of 1994. However, today's penal code uses the terms *felony, misdemeanor,* and *petty offense.*

Under Article 2 of its 1946 Constitution, France is an "indivisible, secular, democratic, and social Republic" (ICL 1992). Another constitution was drafted in 1958 and later amended several times, the most recent change occurring in 2000 when the presidential term of office was reduced from seven to five years (CIA 2005).

The president of France, who is chief of state, is elected every five years (CIA 2005). The National Assembly nominates a prime minister who is then appointed by the president. Cabinet members are appointed by the president as well. France has a bicameral Parliament with 321 Senate members who serve nine-year terms, as well as a National Assembly whose 577 members are elected for five-year terms. Within the judicial branch are the Supreme Court of Appeals, the Constitutional Council, and Council of State. The judges in the Supreme Court of Appeals are appointed by the president while the Constitutional Council consists of nine members, of whom three are appointed by the president, three by the president of the National Assembly, and three by the president of the Senate.

Legislation, which is passed by Parliament, establishes offenses, punishments, and criminal procedure (Title IV, Article 34) (ICL 1992). Courts can hear both criminal and civil cases (Borricand 1993). Offenses are labeled as attacks against persons, property, or public security; intentional homicide; intentional violence; and rape.

Background

The first contemporary legal code in France was the Code Napoléon of 1804 (CEE 2005). Derived from Roman and Germanic law, the Code Napoléon enumerated "the private law of France" (CEE 2005) and has influenced the legal systems of numerous nations throughout the world. The Code of Civil Procedure was enacted in 1806, followed by the Code of Criminal Instruction in 1808, and the Napoleonic Penal Code of 1810, which stated: "Crime cannot be constituted by actions committed by persons finding themselves in a state of dementia at the moment of commission, or who were motivated by a force which they were unable to resist"[1] (cited in Traverso, Ciappi, and Ferracuti 2000: 498). In 1830, Algiers was conquered by the French who, in 1838, mandated that all lunatics be interned "at public expense in every French department" (Keller 2001: 312).

Today's penal code adheres to principles of the classical school of criminology in that it treats individuals as if they have free will and are rational decision-makers (Clavier 1997).

Individuals who are accused of offenses cannot plead guilty and are prosecuted by the Public Minister (Borricand 1993). Correctional Courts hear cases for which sentences can be up to ten years in prison. Cases in which the defendant can be sentenced to life in prison are handled by Assize Courts. Judges determine the outcome of the case.

Felonies can be punishable by life sentences of up to thirty years, with a ten-year minimum.[2] Misdemeanor offenders can receive sentences entailing prison (a maximum of ten years), fines, day-fines, and community service.[3] Prison sentences for misdemeanors are specified on a scale of two months, six months, one year, two years, three years, five years, seven years, and ten years.[4] Capital punishment was abolished in 1981 (Borricand 1993).

French penal facilities consist of central houses for inmates with sentences of more than one year, detention centers where inmates may be re-socialized, stop houses for offenders with sentences of less than one year, penitentiaries for either long- or short-term offenders, and semi-liberty centers for inmates who are permitted to leave the facility for various reasons, such as schooling, work, or medical treatment (Borricand 2003).

In 2002 there were 185 penal facilities. In 2004, there were 55,025 prisoners in metropolitan France (including pre-trial and remand prisoners) (ICPS 2005). The incarceration rate was 91 per 100,000 national population and females accounted for 3.8 percent of the prison population.

Legal Criteria

The French penal code, according to Clavier (1997), views individuals as rational beings and therefore does not take into account external circumstances that may have influenced one's choice. But it does recognize that mental illness may sometimes render a person less responsible for a decision.

Article 121-3[5] of the Penal Code[6] states that intent must be present for an individual to commit a felony or misdemeanor. An offender is not considered "criminally liable" if the crime was committed "under a force or constraint which he could not resist."[7] The Penal Code reads:

> A person is not criminally liable who, when the act was committed, was suffering from a psychic or neuropsychic disorder which destroyed his discernment or his ability to control his actions.[8]

However, an offender who suffered from a "psychic or neuropsychic disorder" resulting in a diminution of "discernment" or self-control can still be punished. In such cases, the offender's mental state is taken into consideration when the court determines the sentence.

Burden of Proof

The burden of proof is not clearly described.

Form of Verdict

A mentally ill offender may be found not guilty by reason of insanity.

Who Decides?

Sentences are determined by judges (Winslow 2005; Borricand 2003).

Role of Experts

Though the court makes sentencing decisions, it is heavily influenced by expert witnesses (Winslow 2005). In general, the court will follow the witnesses' recommendations. Article 722[9] of the Code of Criminal Procedure states that the post-sentencing judge "attached to" each penal facility determines "the main terms of penitentiary treatment" after an offender has been convicted. Dispositions include: "noncustodial postings, semi-detentions, remissions, divisions and suspensions of penalties, permission for escorted leave, temporary leave, parole, postings under electronic supervision, or he refers the case to the competent court to adapt the enforcement of the sentence." The judge generally renders a decision after hearing from the post-sentencing commission when determining whether to grant sentence remissions or escorted or temporary leaves. Except in cases of "sentence remissions which do not lead to an immediate release and permissions for escorted leave," the aforementioned "enumerations" cannot be granted for persons "sentenced for the murder or assassination of a minor, accompanied by rape, torture or acts or barbarity, or convicted for one of the offences listed in articles 222-23 to 222-32 and 227-25 to 227-27 of the Criminal Code" without the opinion of a psychiatric expert. In cases of the "murder, assassination or rape" of a child less than fifteen years old, the court must hear from three experts.

Article 763-4[10] of the Code of Criminal Procedure states:

> Where the person sentenced to socio-judicial surveillance entailing a medical treatment injunction must undergo this measure after serving a custodial sentence, the post-sentencing judge may order a medical expert examination of the person concerned before he is released. Such an expert opinion is compulsory if the sentence was imposed more than two years previously.
>
> The post-sentencing judge may also, at any stage of the socio-judicial surveillance and notwithstanding the provisions of article 763-6, order on his own motion or upon the application of the district prosecutor, any expert opinion necessary to inform him of the medical or psychological state of the person convicted.

The expert opinions provided for by the present article are given by a single expert, unless the post-sentencing judge makes a reasoned decision to the contrary.

What Happens to the Defendant?

If the defendant is found to be insane, then he or she undergoes further examination to determine whether he or she is mentally ill and dangerous at the present time. The defendant so found is sent either to a prison or to a hospital, where he or she remains until both the medical experts and the civil authorities give approval for release. A defendant may appeal a negative release decision to a special judicial tribunal, which can release him or her over the objections of the medical and civil authorities.

Under Article 131-36-1[11] of the Penal Code,[12] courts may order an offender to undergo socio-judicial probation for up to ten years for a misdemeanour or twenty years for a felony conviction. In such cases, the offender must follow "measures of supervision and assistance designed to prevent recidivism." Treatment may be a component of socio-judicial probation, as ordered by a trial court after hearing from medical experts.[13] For severe crimes, the court must hear from two experts.[14] The defendant cannot undergo treatment without consent; refusing treatment can lead to imprisonment. In some cases, the offender may undergo treatment while incarcerated.

Article 763-7 [15] of the Code of Criminal Procedure states:

Where a person sentenced to socio-judicial surveillance entailing an injunction to undergo medical treatment must serve a custodial sentence, he serves the sentence in a prison provided for in the second paragraph of article 718, which guarantees him the appropriate medical and psychological surveillance.

He is immediately informed by the post-sentencing judge of the possibility of receiving medical treatment. If he does not consent to treatment, this information is repeated at least once every six months.

The obligations of socio-judicial surveillance apply in the event of a suspension or division of the penalty, or of a noncustodial posting or semi-detention measure.

Notes

1. Article 64.
2. Penal Code Article 131-1.
3. Penal Code Article 131-3.

4. Penal Code Article 131-4.

5. Act no. 1996-393 of 13 May 1996, Article 1, Official Journal of 14 May 1996; Act no. 2000-647 of 10 July 2000, Article 1, Official Journal of 11 July 2000.

6. Penal Code, First Part (Enacted Parts), Book 1 (General Provisions), Title 2 (Of Criminal Liability), Chapter 1 (General Provisions).

7. Article 122-2.

8. Article 122-1, Chapter 2: Grounds for Absence of Attenuation of Liability.

9. Law no. 72-1226 of 29 December 1972, Article 37, Official Journal of 30 December 1972; Law no. 78-788 of 28 July 1978, Article 25-i and 25-ii, Official Journal of 29 July 1978; Law no. 78-1097 of 22 November 1978, Article 2, Official Journal of 23 November 1978; Law no. 81-82 of 2 February 1981, Article 36-i and 86-ii, Official Journal of 3 February 1981; Law no. 83-466 of 10 June 1983, Article 6-i and 6-ii, Official Journal of 11 June 1983, in force 27 June 1983; Law no. 94-89 of 1 February 1994, Article 8, Official Journal of 2 February 1994, in force 2 February 1994; Law no. 97-1159 of 19 December 1997, Article 1, Official Journal of 20 December 1997; Law no. 98-468 of 17 June 1998, Article 29 and 30, Official Journal of 18 June 1998; Law no. 2000-516 of 15 June 2000, Article 125 and 140, Official Journal of 16 June 2000, in force 1 January 2001; Law no. 2002-1138 of 9 September 2002, Article 44, Official Journal of 10 September 2002.

10. Inserted by Law no. 98-468 of 17 June 1998, Article 8, Official Journal of 18 June 1998.

11. Inserted by Act no. 1998-468 of 17 June 1998, Article 1, Official Journal of 18 June 1998.

12. Penal Code, Title 3 (Of Penalties), chapter 1 (Of the Nature of Penalties), section 1 (Penalties Applicable to Natural Persons), subsection 6 (Of Sociojudicial Probation).

13. See Penal Code, article 131-34-4.

14. "This examination is carried out by two experts in the case of a prosecution for the murder of a minor preceded or accompanied by rape, torture or acts of barbarity."

15. Inserted by Law no. 98-468 of 17 June 1998, Article 8, Official Journal of 18 June 1998.

References

Bégué, Jean-Michel. "Un siècle de psychiatrie francaise en Algérie, 1830–1939" (CES Mémoire, Université Pierre et Marie Curie, Paris, 1989). I cite the version located at the Bibliothèque Médicale Henry-Ey, Centre Hospitalier Sainte-Anne, Paris. Readers may find a summary of the thesis in Jean-Michel Bégué, "French Psychiatry in Algeria (1830–1962): From Colonial to Transcultural," *History of Psychiatry* 7, no. 28 (1996): 533–48.

Borricand, Jacques. 1993. "France." World Factbook of Criminal Justice Statistics. Institut de Sciences Penales et de Criminologie. Grant no. 90-BJ-CX-0002 from the Bureau of Justice Statistics to SUNY at Albany. Retrieved July 5, 2005, <http://www.ojp.usdoj.gov/bjs/pub/ascii/wfbcjrus.txt>.

Central Intelligence Agency (CIA). 2005. "France." The World Factbook. <www.odci .gov/cia/publications/factbook/geos/fr.html>.

Clavier, Sophie M. 1997. "Perspectives on French Criminal Law." Paris, France, and San Francisco, Calif.: Online article. Retrieved June 1, 2005, <http://userwww.sfsu.edu/ ~sclavier/research/frenchpenalsystem.doc>.

Code of Criminal Procedure (CCP). <www.legifrance.gouv.fr/html/codes_traduits/ liste.htm>.

Columbia Electronic Encyclopedia, The (CEE). 2005. "Code Napoléon." Columbia University Press. Retrieved June 2, 2005, <www.infoplease.com>.

International Centre for Prison Studies (ICPS). 2004. "World Prison Brief: Entire World—Prison Population Totals, Prison Brief for France." International Centre for Prison Studies, Kings College London. Retrieved May 10, 2005, <www.kcl.ac.uk/ depsta/rel/icps/worldbrief/world_brief.html>.

International Constitutional Law (ICL). 1992. "France—Constitution." A. Tschentscher, ed. Retrieved May 11, 2005, <www.oefre.unibe.ch/law/icl/info.html>.

Keller, Richard. 2001. "Madness and Colonization: Psychiatry in the British and French Empires, 1800–1962." *Journal of Social History* 35, no. 2: 295–326. Retrieved July 14, 2004, from the Project Muse website, <http://must.jhu.edu.proxyau.wrlc .org>.

Ministère de la justice. 2001a. "Criminal Justice: Activity of Public Prosecutor's office in 1998." From Records of Public Prosecutor's Office, SDSED (Provisional data). Retrieved May 17, 2005, <www.justice.gouv.fr/anglais/chiffres/penale.htm>.

———. 2001b. "Criminal Justice in 1997: Activity of Public Prosecutor's office in 1997." From Records of Public Prosecutor's Office, SDSED (Provisional data). Retrieved May 17, 2005, <www.justice.gouv.fr/anglais/chiffres/penale.htm>.

Nationmaster.com. 2005. "Encyclopedia: Jacques Chirac." Retrieved online June 2, 2005, <www.nationmaster.com/encyclopedia/Jacques-Chirac>.

Penal Code. <www.legifrance.gouv.fr/html/codes_traduits/liste.htm>.

Winslow, Robert. 2005. "France" from *Crime and Society: A Comparative Criminology Tour of the World.* Retrieved May 24, 2005, <www.rohan.sdsu.edu/faculty/rwinslow/ index.html>.

7

Germany

FOUNDED IN 1949, GERMANY IS a democracy with a population of 83 million in sixteen states (Winslow 2005). Located in central Europe east of the Netherlands, Belgium, Luxembourg, and France, west of Poland and the Czech Republic, northwest of Austria, north of Switzerland, and south of Denmark, it also borders the Baltic Sea in the northeast and the North Sea in the northwest (CIA 2005). Within the republic, there is a population of 82.4 million, of whom 91.5 percent are German, 2.4 percent Turkish, and 6.1 percent Greek, Russian, Polish, Italian, Spanish, and Serbo-Croatian (CIA 2005). The official language is German, protestants and Roman Catholics each make up 34 percent of the population, Muslims comprise 3.4 percent, and the remaining 28.3 percent are of other religions or are unaffiliated (CIA 2005).

The Federal Republic of Germany and the German Democratic Republic were unified on October 3, 1990 as set forth under Article 23 of the F.R.G. Basic Law (U.S. Department of State 2004). Germany's Constitution (*Bundesrepublik Deutschland*) was adopted on May 23, 1949 and subsequently updated on July 18, 2003. The German government consists of executive, legislative, and judicial branches. The president and chancellor titles fall under the executive branch and the bicameral parliament makes up the legislative branch. An independent Federal Constitutional Court comprises the judicial branch. Article 74 of the Constitution, titled "Concurrent Legislation," includes criminal law and punishment, the organization of the courts, and economic laws (Tschentscher 2002: 53).

Background

Prior to the 1960s, the mentally ill fared poorly in Germany (Rössler, Salize, and Riecher-Rössler 1996). Prussia's mental hospitals increased by 400 percent from 1880 (27,000) to 1910 (140,000), thus reflecting the growing need for more psychiatric care. Needless to say, mental institutions were not too overcrowded during the Nazi era when 90,000 to 140,000 mentally ill individuals were killed.

The conditions of mental hospitals, which were considered "crude and inhumane" (Deutscher Bunderstag 1973),[1] came to the attention of the German government in the late 1960s (Rössler et al. 1996). A 1975 publication, in which various reforms were suggested, "marked a turning point for mental health care in Germany" (Deutscher Bunderstag 1973: 392). Despite these changes, "mentally ill offenders were largely neglected" (Deutscher Bunderstag 1973: 406).

When East and West Germany united, the former adopted the latter's legal system (Rössler et al. 1996: 395). Today, federal laws, as set forth by the German Federal Constitution, take precedent over the state laws of each of Germany's sixteen states (Aronowitz 1993). Each state has its own constitution. However, there is no centralized mental health system.

Civil law provides the basis of the German criminal justice system (Library of Congress [LOC] 1995). The revised Code of Criminal Procedure and Federal Prison Acts were set forth in West Germany in the 1970s, a decade that brought about great change in Germany's criminal law (Hollweg 1998). The Criminal Code (Strafgesetzbuch, StGB[2]) was promulgated in 1998 and the Criminal Procedure Code (Strafprozeβordnung, StPO[3]) was promulgated in 2002 (Federal Ministry of Justice).

Today, offenders can be tried in local, regional/land courts, and appellate land courts (LOC 1995). The Federal Court of Justice is the highest court in Germany. Serious crimes are tried by a judge and two lay judges, while lesser crimes are tried by a single judge. In more extreme cases, an offender may be tried by three judges and up to six lay judges within the land court. Crimes are defined as felonies and misdemeanors, the former of which may result in incarceration. Misdemeanor offenders may be sentenced to short-term imprisonment with or without fines, or just fines (LOC 1995). The death penalty in West Germany was abolished in 1987. Following the reunification of East and West Germany, East Germany adopted the criminal code of West Germany.

Since 1933, preventive detention has been used in Germany to increase public safety and to rehabilitate by detaining offenders who are dangerous and likely to recidivate (Connelly and Williams 2000: 76). Preventive detention is served after the imposed sanction. Dangerous offenders who are likely to recidivate, such as sex offenders, are given "preventive detention" (Connelly and Williams 2000: 7). Offenders who are "dangerous and insane" (Connelly and Williams 2000 80) can be committed to psychiatric facilities. Connelly and Williams report that since the 1970s preventive detention has been ordered less than thirty times per year (78).

Generally, crime rates are higher in the eastern and northern areas of Germany. Recorded crime in Germany fell by 6 percent from 1996 to 2000 (Barclay and Tavares 2002: 1) but has been increasing since. Oberwittler and Höfer (2005) report that while violent crime is rare in Germany, it has been slightly increasing since the mid-1990s. From 1998 to 2000, there were 259 homicides in Berlin (Barclay and Tavares 2002: 4). In 1991, only 100,000 out of 600,000 convicted offenders were sentenced to prison, of whom 80 percent were given terms of less than one-year incarceration (LOC 1995). Only 1 percent of the 100,000 convicted offenders received sentences of five to fifteen years. In 2004, there were 237 prison facilities in Germany and 79,329 inmates (including pre-trial and remand) (ICPS 2005). The 2004 prison population rate was 96 per 100,000 national population. Between 1990 and 2000, there was a 56 percent increase in the prison population but no change between 1999 and 2000 (Barclay and Tavares 2002: 7).

Legal Criteria

Section 20 of the Criminal Code (StGB) of the Federal Republic of Germany states:

> A person is not criminally responsible if at the time of the act, because of a psychotic or similar serious mental disorder, or because of a profound interruption of consciousness or because of feeblemindedness or any other type of serious mental abnormality, he is incapable of understanding the wrongfulness of his conduct or of action in accordance with his understanding.

Burden of Proof

The burden of establishing the defense of insanity rests on the defense. To succeed, the defense must rebut the presumption of sanity by discharging the evidential burden on a balance of probabilities. The defense must adduce sufficient evidence proving insanity.

Form of Verdict

A defendant may be found not guilty by reason of insanity.

Who Decides?

The judge decides.

Role of Experts

An expert witness may examine relevant parties, including witnesses, or observe while the accused is undergoing examination (sections 80 and 80a of the Criminal Procedure Code [CCP]). During the preliminary phase, experts are able to prepare their opinions if it seems likely that the defendant will be sent to a psychiatric or substance abuse treatment facility. During a criminal hearing, an expert might be asked to render an opinion on the appropriate treatment:

> An expert shall be examined at the main hearing on defendant's condition and his treatment prospects if it is expected that the defendant's committal to a psychiatric hospital, an institution for withdrawal treatment or preventive detention will be ordered. If the expert has not previously examined the defendant, he is to be given the opportunity to do so before the main hearing (Section 246a)

The Criminal Procedure Code specifies that the expert falls under the auspice of the judge: "The judge shall guide the experts' participation, so far as he deems this necessary."[4] In addition, Criminal Procedure Code states that when the offender's mental state is in question and after hearing from both the defense and an expert, the court can order a defendant to be evaluated in a public psychiatric hospital for up to six weeks.[5]

What Happens to the Defendant?

The defendant by order of the court is committed to a psychiatric hospital. The committal order is revoked if the conditions for the committal no longer exist. The defendant is released.

TABLE 7.1
Number and Percentage of Offenders Convicted, Found to Have Diminished Responsibility or Irresponsibility, and Admitted

Year	Convictions	Diminished Responsibility	Irresponsibility	Admissions
1967	628,751	6,047 (0.96%)	656 (0.10%)	295 (0.05%)
1970	631,923	5,935 (0.94%)	649 (0.10%)	259 (0.04%)
1975	655,971	7,356 (1.16%)	312 (0.04%)	300 (0.05%)
1980	735,170	11,452 (1.56%)	435 (0.06%)	355 (0.05%)
1985	741,861	13,556 (1.83%)	455 (0.06%)	427 (0.06%)
1990	756,285	14,246 (1.88%)	521 (0.07%)	446 (0.06%)
1994	820,831	14,274 (1.74%)	582 (0.07%)	512 (0.06%)

Source: Board for Criminological Statistics, Wiesbaden, Germany; statistics of convictions in Germany (West) of adult offenders.

Frequency of Use

Table 7.1 shows how many offenders in West Germany were convicted, found to have diminished responsibility, found irresponsible, and compulsorily admitted from 1967 through 1994.

Types of Offenses (e.g., Violent, Property)

Müller-Isberner (1996: 83, table 3.) examined 123 patients who were discharged from the Haina Forensic Psychiatric Hospital from 1989 to 1991[8]. Table 7.2 shows the "initial delinquency" that led to the individual's commitment and the percentage of patients who received subsequent forensic outpatient care.

TABLE 7.2
Percentage of Discharged Patients
Who Received Patient Care, 1989–1991

	Forensic Outpatient Clinic	
	Yes (N = 67)	No (N = 56)
Killing	21%	23%
Physical Injury	15%	15%
Violent Sex Offense	15%	23%
Nonviolent Sex Offense	9%	7%
Violent Property Crime	10%	14%
Nonviolent Property Crime	12%	2%
Fire Setting	15%	14%
Other	3%	2%

Notes

1. Cited in Rössler et al. 1996: 391.
2. StGB = Criminal Code or Penal Code.
3. StPO = Criminal Procedure Code.
4. Code of Criminal Procedure (StPO), Section 78.
5. CCP (StPO), Section 81.

References

Aronowitz, Alexis A. 1993. "Germany." World Factbook of Criminal Justice Statistics. Grant no. 90-BJ-CX-0002 from the Bureau of Justice Statistics to SUNY at Albany. Retrieved online June 10, 2004, <www.ojp.usdoj.gov/bjs/pub/ascii/ wfbcjger.txt>.

Aschaffenburg, Gustav. 1941. "Psychiatry and Criminal Law." *Journal of Criminal Law and Criminology (1931–1951)* 32, no. 1 (May–June 1941): 3–14. Retrieved from JSTOR on May 18, 2005, <www.jstor.org>.

Barclay, Gordon, and Cynthia Tavares. 2002. "International Comparisons of Criminal Justice Statistics 2000." Issue 05/02. Retrieved June 15, 2004, <www.homeoffice.gov/ uk/rds/pdfs2/hosb502.pdf>.

Central Intelligence Agency (CIA). 2005. "Germany." The World Factbook. <www.odci .gov/cia/publications/factbook/geos/gm.html>.

Connelly, Clare, and Shanti Williams. 2000. "A Review of the Research Literature on Serious Violent and Sexual Offenders." *Scottish Executive, Central Research Unit.* Retrieved May 23, 2005, <www.scotland.gov.uk/cru/kd01/green/s-off-02.htm>.

Criminal Code (Strafgesetzbuch, StGB). 2001. Translated by the Federal Ministry of Justice. Retrieved June 8, 2005, <www.iuscomp.org/gla/statutes/StGB.htm>.

Criminal Procedure Code (Strafprozeßordnung, StPO). 2001. Translated by the Federal Ministry of Justice. Retrieved June 10, 2004, <www.iuscomp.org/gla/statutes/ StPO.htm>.

Darby, Joseph J. 1987. *Penal Code of the Federal Republic of Germany.* The American Series of Foreign Penal Codes 28. Edward M Wise, ed. Buffalo, N.Y: Fred B. Rothman & Co. Retrieved May 20, 2004, <http://wings.buffalo.edu/law/bclc/Germind.htm>.

Deutscher Bundestag. 1973. *Enquête über die Lage per Psychiatrie in der Bundesrepublik Deutschland: Zwischenbericht der Sachverständigenkommission zur Erabeitung der Enquête über die Lage der Psychiatrie in der Bundesrepublik Deutschland. Drucksache* 7/1125. BonnL Deutscher Bundestag.

Deutsches Strafgesetzbuch/German Penal Code (German/English). Updated 1998. Joseph J. Darby, trans.; Edward M. Wise, ed. 1987. <http://wings.buffalo.edu/law/ bclc/StGBframe.htm>.

Hollweg, Matthias. 1998. "Modification of Criminal Law and Its Impact on Psychiatric Expert Opinions." *International Journal of Law and Psychiatry* 21, no. 1: 109–16. Retrieved June 7, 2005, <www.sciencedirect.com>, Elsevier Sciences, Ltd.

International Centre for Prison Studies (ICPS). 2005. "World Prison Brief: Entire World—Prison Population Totals, Prison Brief for Germany." International Centre for Prison Studies, Kings College London. Retrieved May 10, 2005, <www.kcl.ac.uk/depsta/rel/icps/worldbrief/world_brief.html>.

Library of Congress. 1995. "Germany: Criminal Justice." *Library of Congress Country Studies.* Washington, D.C.: Library of Congress. Retrieved June 25, 2004, <http://memory.loc.gov/frd/cs/>.

Müller-Isberner, Rüdiger. 1996. "Forensic Psychiatric Aftercare Following Hospital Order Treatment." *International Journal of Law and Psychiatry* 19, no. 1: 81–86. Retrieved June 7, 2005, <www.sciencedirect.com>, Elsevier Sciences, Ltd.

Müller-Isberner, Rüdiger, Roland Freese, Dieter Jöckel, and Sara Gonazlez Cabeza. 2000. "Forensic Psychiatric Assessment and Treatment in Germany." *International Journal of Law and Psychiatry* 23, nos. 5–6: 480–2000. Retrieved June 7, 2005, <www.sciencedirect.com>, Elsevier Sciences, Ltd.

Nedopil, Norbert. and Karin Banzer. 1996. "Outpatient Treatment of Forensic Patients in Germany." *International Journal of Law and Psychiatry* 19, no. 1: 75–79. Retrieved June 7, 2005, <www.sciencedirect.com>, Elsevier Sciences, Ltd.

Oberwittler, Dietrich and Sven Höfer. 2005. "Crime and Justice in Germany: An Analysis of Recent Trends and Research." *European Journal of Criminology* 2, no. 4: 465–508. Sage Publications, Ltd. and European Society of Criminology. Retrieved July 13, 2005, <http://www.iuscrim.mpg.de/forsch/onlinepub/obi_hoefer.pdf>.

Riecher, A. and W. Rössler. 1992. "Die Zwangseinwesung psychiatrischer Patienten im nationalen und internationalen Vergleich—Häufigkeiten und Einflußfaktoren." *Fortschritte der Neurologie und Psychiatrie* 60: 375–82.

Rössler, Wulf, Hans-Joachim Salize, and Anital Riecher-Rössler. 1996. "Changing Patterns of Mental Health Care in Germany." *International Journal of Law and Psychiatry* 19, nos. 3–4: 391–411. Retrieved June 7, 2005, <www.sciencedirect.com>, Elsevier Sciences, Ltd.

Seifert, Dieter, Karen Jahn, Stefanie Bolten, and Markus Wirtz. 2002. "Prediction of Dangerousness in Mentally Disordered Offenders in Germany." *International Journal of Law and Psychiatry* 25: 51–66. Retrieved June 7, 2005, <www.sciencedirect.com>, Elsevier Sciences, Ltd.

Spitzer, Carsten, Heike Liss, Manuela Dudeck, Stefan Orlob, Michael Gillner, Alfons Hamm, and Harald J. Freyberger. 2003. "Dissociative Experiences and Disorders in Forensic Inpatients." *International Journal of Law and Psychiatry* 26: 281–88. Retrieved June 7, 2005, <www.sciencedirect.com>, Elsevier Sciences, Ltd.

Tschentscher, Axel. 2002. "The Basic Law (Grundgesetz): The Constitution of the Federal Republic of Germany (May 23, 1949)." Last updated July 18, 2003. Jurisprudentia Verlag, Würzburg. <www.jurisprudentia.de/jurisprudentia.html>.

United States Department of State. 2004. "Background Note: Germany." Washington, D.C.: U.S. Department of State. Retrieved online June 14, 2004, <www.state.gov/r/pa/ei/bgn/3997.htm>.

Winslow, Robert. 2005. "Germany" from *Crime and Society: A Comparative Criminology Tour of the World.* Retrieved May 24, 2005, <www-rohan.sdsu.edu/faculty/rwinslow/index.html>.

8

Great Britain

GREAT BRITAIN IS LOCATED IN Western Europe. It is between the North Atlantic Ocean and the North Sea, and is northwest of France. The population is 60,094,648 (estimate from July 2003). The ethnic groups are English (81.5 percent), Scottish (9.6 percent), Irish (2.4 percent), Welsh (1.9 percent), Ulster (1.8 percent), West Indian, Indian, Pakistani, Black Caribbean, Black African, and other (2.8 percent). The religions are Anglican and Roman Catholic (40 million), Muslim (1.5 million), Presbyterian (800,000), Methodist (760,000), Sikh (500,000), Hindu (500,000), and Jewish (350,000). The languages spoken are English, Welsh, and Gaelic (The Columbia Electronic Encyclopedia, 6th ed. © 2004, Columbia University Press).

Great Britain is a constitutional monarchy and the monarch is the Sovereign Head of State and Head of Government. The government is comprised of the Legislature (Parliament), the Executive, and the Judiciary. Parliament consists of the House of Lords and House of Commons. Most of the work of Parliament is conducted in the House of Commons at Westminster. The prime minister is the active head of the government. The official language of instruction and use is English.

Background[1]

As far back as the thirteenth century mentally ill offenders were identified and perceived differently than the common criminal. Lord Bracton of England set forth the notion of "mental deficiency in human behavior" (Menninger 1968,

cited in Gado 2004) in which an offender who does not know what he is
doing cannot be held technically guilty due to a lack of intent or malice
(Gado 2004; see Melton et al. 1997). Equating such an individual to a wild
beast (see Melton et al. 1997), an insanity standard was established where defendants had to prove their level of understanding to be equivalent to that of
a wild animal or an infant (Gado 2004). Used until the infamous *M'Naghten*
case in 1843 (Gado 2004), this "wild beast standard" was applied in the trial
of Edward Arnold, in which he was deemed "totally deprived of his understanding and memory, and does not know what he is doing, no more than an
infant, than a brute, or a wild beast, such a one is never the object of punishment" (Hucker 2004).

Originally, an asylum was a place where criminals or politically persecuted
individuals could seek shelter from the legal system, but its meaning broad-
ened in the eighteenth century as asylums became known as a "place for
refuge" (Roberts 2001).

In the 1800s, the notion of diminished responsibility first emerged in Scotland (LRC 1997a). The defense was introduced as a means of bypassing a
murder conviction of those who could not meet the criteria for the insanity
defence but who did have a form of mental impairment (LRC 1997a).

The Criminal Lunatics Act of 1800 was enacted to provide safe custody for
defendants who were :

a) charged with treason, murder or felony, or who were acquitted on the
   grounds of insanity
b) indicted and found insane at the time of the arraignment
c) brought before any criminal court to be discharged for want of prosecution who appeared insane
d) apprehended under circumstances denoting a derangement of mind
   and a purpose to commit an indictable offense
e) appearing to be insane and endeavouring to gain admittance to the
   royal presence by intrusion on one of the royal residences. (Roberts 2001;
   see 1844 Report, p. 196)

The 1840 Insane Prisoners Act was applied to mentally ill offenders who
had committed misdemeanors so that they too could be placed into an asylum. It was not applied to civil prisoners (Roberts 2001).

The *M'Naghten* rules (1843) resulted from the *M'Naghten* case. It was determined by Law Lords that

the jurors ought to be told in all cases that every man is to be presumed to be
sane, and to possess a sufficient degree of reason to be responsible for his crimes,
until the contrary to be proved to their satisfaction; and that to establish a de-

fence on the ground of insanity, it must be clearly proved that, at the time of committing of the act, the party accused was labouring under such a defect of reason, from disease of the mind, as not to know the nature and quality of the act he was doing; or, if he did know it, that he did not know he was doing what was wrong. (Roberts 2001)

In an 1844 report, the "Suggestions for the Amendment of the Law" section set forth that a "proper and convenient Hospital" should be available for the "insane poor of every county" and provided guidelines for the administration and regulations of such hospitals (Roberts 2001). The report differentiated the different forms of insanity found in lunatic asylums. These are (Roberts 2001):

1. Mania
    a. Acute mania/raving madness
    b. Ordinary mania, acute chronic madness
    c. Periodical or remittent mania with comparatively lucid intervals
2. Dementia, or decay and obliteration of the intellectual faculties
3. Melancholia
4. Monomania
5. Moral insanity
6. Congenital idiocy
7. Congenital imbecility
8. General paralysis of the insane
9. Epilepsy

The 1883 Trial of Lunatics Act stated that a "special verdict" should be given to a person who committed an offense but was insane. This was later amended by the Criminal Procedure (Insanity) Act of 1964. A person with this verdict would be committed to a hospital for an unspecified amount of time but with "restrictions on discharge" (Walton). The Criminal Procedure Act of 1991 amended this and provided the courts with more flexibility in sentencing when the special verdict was handed down.

The 1913 Mental Deficiency Act defined four levels of "mental defective" which were applicable only to those who had had mental problems since birth or early childhood (Roberts 2001). The act defined *idiots* as persons "so deeply defective in mind as to be unable to guard against common physical dangers." *Imbeciles* were different from idiots but were "incapable of managing themselves or their affairs, or, in the case of children, of being taught to do so." *Feeble-minded* was defined as a condition that rendered adults incapable of providing their own "care, supervision, and control for their own protection or the protection of others." As applied to children, *feeble-minded* referred to mental deficiencies that are "so pronounced that they by reason of such defectiveness appear to be personally incapable of receiving proper benefit from instruction in ordinary schools." Finally, *moral defectives* were those who had "some permanent mental defect coupled with strong vicious or criminal propensities on which punishment had little or no effect" since childhood (Roberts 2001).

The 1987 Mental Health Act, section 37[2] states that courts could send mentally ill offenders to hospitals, rather than prison, if there is clinical evidence of a mental disorder "for which compulsory treatment in hospital is appropriate, and on the court's view that it is the most suitable disposable" (Chiswick 1996). Mental health review tribunals or clinicians could release individuals at their own discretion. In 1996, the British government stated, "the public has a right to expect to be protected from dangerous offenders" (Chiswick 1996; see Home Office press release 130/96). If it is believed that it is necessary to protect the public from "serious harm," a judge may order an offender to a hospital indefinitely. A mental health tribunal may later discharge such patients, but psychiatrists alone may not. This gave courts more options when sentencing mentally ill offenders in cases where treatment did not decrease the danger posed by the offender to the public, and where a "punitive element" was deemed necessary in order to "reflect the offender's whole or partial responsibility" (Chiswick 1996; see Home Office 1996).

In the Crime Sentences Bill, Clause 36[3], an offender may be sent to a hospital and then later to prison after treatment, which Chiswick (1996) labels as a "hybrid of imprisonment and treatment" and "runs contrary to modern concepts of psychiatric care for mentally disordered offenders." This option will apply to psychopathic disordered offenders in England and Wales, while in Scotland it may apply to any offender who falls under the provisions set forth in the Mental Health (Scotland) Act of 1984.

Court Cases

In *Bratt v A-G* (Northern Ireland), Lord Denning asserted:

> No act is punishable if it is done involuntarily: and an involuntary act in this context—some people nowadays prefer to speak of it as "automatism"—means an act which is done by the muscles without any control by the mind, such as a spasm, a reflex action or a convulsion; or an act done while suffering from concussion or whilst sleep-walking. (Ridgway 1996: section 7)

A landmark case in the use of the insanity defense was the trial of James Hadfield (see Hucker 2004). In 1800, Hadfield attempted to shoot King

George III at the Drury Lane Theatre in London. Various individuals testified that Hadfield was prone to bouts of insanity and was therefore found to be insane (from <www.exclassics.com>).

In 1840, Edward Oxford attempted to shoot Queen Victoria. In addressing the jury, the attorney general, stated:

> It appears to me that if the prisoner was at the time accountable for his actions, there can be no doubt of his guilt. I now come to the question whether the prisoner was accountable for his actions at the time when the offence was committed. And I will at once admit, under the law of England, that if he was then of unsound mind—if he was incapable of judging between right and wrong—if he was labouring under any delusion of insanity, so as not to be sensible of his crime, or conscious of the act which he committed—if at the time when that act was committed he was afflicted with insanity, he will be entitled to be acquitted on that ground. I have a duty to discharge to the Crown and to the public, and I must say that, so far as I have yet learned, there is no reason to believe that the prisoner at the time he committed this crime was in a state of mind which takes away his criminal responsibility for the deed. (<www.exclassics.com>; see Hucker 2004)

The defense counsel then presented evidence that Oxford was insane, and medical experts testified that he was of an "unsound state of mind." The jury acquitted the defendant for reasons of insanity and Oxford was sent to Bedlam.

Legal Criteria

According to the *M'Naghten* rule, to establish a defense of insanity it must be clearly proven that, at the time of committing the act, the party accused was laboring under such a defect of reason from disease of the mind as not to know the nature and quality of the act he was doing; or if he did know it, that he did not know that what he was doing was wrong.

Courts in Great Britain also use the rule of diminished responsibility:

> If he was suffering from such abnormality of mind (whether arising from a condition of arrested or retarded development of mind or any inherent causes or reduced by disease or injury) as substantially impaired his mental responsibility for his acts and omissions in doing or being the party to the killing. (Walton)

Burden of Proof

The Criminal Procedure (Insanity) Act of 1964 states that if a defendant claims to have been insane at the time of the commission of the offense and should not be held responsible for the offense, or if the defendant uses a diminished responsibility defense, "the court shall allow the prosecution to adduce or elicit evidence tending to prove the other of those contentions, and may give directions as to the stage of the proceedings at which the prosecution may adduce such evidence" (chapter 84, section 6).

When the rule of diminished responsibility is invoked, the burden of proof rests with the defense. If the defense brings up an insanity defense, the prosecution can "call evidence of diminished responsibility." If the prosecution "intend to show diminished responsibility, then the burden of proof is upon them to show it beyond a reasonable doubt" (Walton).

Form of Verdict

A defendant may be found not guilty by reason of insanity.

Who Decides?

The 1991 act states a jury must determine whether the defendant is fit to stand trial. The court may also delay the consideration of whether a defendant is fit to be tried until any point up to the "opening of the case for the defence" (section 4[2]). Further, "if, before the question of fitness to be tried falls to be determined, the jury return a verdict of acquittal on the count or each of the counts on which the accused is being tried, that question shall not be determined" (section 4[3]). The defendant may be tried by a jury other than the one that determined his or her fitness to stand trial if that issue was brought up at the arraignment of the defendant (section 5[a]) but if the question arises at a later time, the question "shall be determined by a separate jury or by the jury by whom the accused is being tried, as the court may direct" (section 5[b]).

Role of Experts

Under the Criminal Procedure (Insanity and Unfitness to Plead) Act of 1991, there must be oral or written evidence from at least two medical practitioners, of whom one is "duly approved" before a jury can find a defendant unfit to be tried or before a jury can acquit a defendant because of insanity (sections 1, 4).

Medical evidence is not mandatory if a defendant uses a diminished responsibility plea. The court does not have to accept medical evidence (Walton). When medical evidence is provided, courts or the prosecution generally accept 85 percent of pleas of diminished responsibility.

What Happens to the Defendant?

If a defendant is found not guilty by reason of insanity or if the jury determines that the "accused is under a disability and that he did the act or made the omission charged against him," the defendant may be admitted to a hospital (see Schedule 1 of the Criminal Procedure Act of 1991). The 1991 Act gave the court a larger range of sentencing options in the case of not guilty by reason of insanity verdicts. The court can also issue a guardianship order (see Mental Health Act 1983 [c.201]) or a supervision and treatment order (see Schedule 2 of the Criminal Procedure Act of 1991), or it may order an "absolute discharge." If a defendant is ordered to supervision and treatment, he must be under the supervision of a social worker or probation officer for two years and must undergo treatment by a medical practitioner for any length of time as ordered. The person may undergo treatment as a resident patient in a hospital or mental nursing home or as a nonresident patient.

Diminished capacity was enacted by the Homicide Act of 1957 and can be used as a defense in "unlawful killing" (Walton). Instead of the required mandatory life sentence, the defendant who successfully uses the diminished capacity defense would be found guilty of manslaughter. Defendants who are found to have diminished capacity can still be sentenced to life in prison— judges merely have more discretion in sentencing if the defendant is found guilty of manslaughter. Therapy is not mandatory if a defendant is found guilty of manslaughter as a result of a diminished capacity plea.

Frequency of Use

Between 1900 and 1949, 21.4 percent of murderers were "certified as insane" (Little 1961: 153). This figure increased to 26.5 percent from 1950 to 1959. Little concludes that 50 percent of murderers in the first half of the 1900s were either insane or committed suicide (153).

The diminished responsibility plea was successful in sixty-two cases from 1957 to 1959 (Little 1961). Between 1957 and 1959, Little suggests that 20.0 percent of all murderers and suspects were insane and 18.8 percent had diminished responsibility (153).

In England, there are approximately 600 hospital orders each year, in which a mentally disordered offender is sent to a hospital for treatment rather than to a prison (Chiswick 1996). About 250 defendants each year are hospitalized indefinitely due to the belief that the person poses a danger to society.

Notes

1. See Roberts 2001 for an extensive history of mental health, insanity, and asylums (<www.mdx.ac.uk/www/study/mhhtim.htm#1845CountyAsylumsAct>).
2. Section 37.
3. Clause 36.

References

Barclay, Gordon, and Cynthia Tavares. 2002. "International Comparisons of Criminal Justice Statistics 2000." Issue 05/02. Retrieved June 15, 2004, <www.homeoffice.gov/uk/rds/pdfs2/hosb502.pdf>.

Chiswick, Derek. 1996. "Sentencing Mentally Disordered Offenders," editorial, *BMJ* 313: 1497–1498. Retrieved July 14, 2004, <http://bmj.bmjjournals.com/cgi/content/full/313/7071/1497>.

Columbia Electronic Encyclopedia, 6th ed. © 2004, Columbia University Press.

Criminal Appeal Act [1968 c.19].

Criminal Procedure (Insanity) Act 1964, Chapter 84. Retrieved July 14, 2004, <www.markwalton.net/mdo/crim%20proc.asp?>; <www.markwalton.net/index.asp>.

Criminal Procedure (Insanity and Unfitness to Plead) Act 1991 (c. 25). Queen's Printer of Acts of Parliament, Her Majesty's Stationery Office. Prepared September 20, 2000. Retrieved July 14, 2004, <www.legislation.hmso.gov.uk/acts/acts1991/Ukpga_19910025_en_1.htm>; <www.legislation.hmso.gov.uk/acts/acts1991/Ukpga_19910025_en_2.htm>; <www.hmso.gov.uk/>.

The Ex-Classics Website. "James Hadfield." Retrieved July 6, 2004, <www.exclassics.com/newgate/ng458.htm>; <www.exclassics.com>.

———. "Edward Oxford." Retrieved July 6, 2004, <www.exclassics.com/newgate/ng630.htm; http://www.exclassics.com>.

Gado, Mark. 2004. "The Beginning of Insanity" from *All About the Insanity Defense.* Published on Courtroom Television Network, Court TV's Crime Library. Retrieved June 28, 2003, <www.crimelibrary.com/>; <www.crimelibrary.com/criminal_mind/psychology/insanity/1.html?sect=19>.

Home Office, Department of Health. 1996. "Mentally Disordered Offenders: Sentencing and Discharge Arrangements." London: Home Office, 1996.

Homicide Act of 1957.

Hucker, Stephen. 2004. "Criminal Responsibility" from ViolenceRisk.com website. Division of Forensic Psychology, McMaster University, Hamilton, Ontario, Canada. <www.violence-risk.com>.

Infanticide Act 1938.

International Centre for Prison Studies (ICPS). 2005. "World Prison Brief: Entire World—Prison Population Totals, Prison Brief for United Kingdom: England and Wales." Retrieved May 10, 2005, <www.kcl.ac.uk/depsta/rel/icps/worldbrief/world _brief.html>.

International Centre for Prison Studies, Kings College London. Retrieved June 16, 2004, <www.kcl.ac.uk/depsta/rel/icps/worldbrief/highest_to_lowest_rates.php>; <www.kcl.ac.uk/depsta/rel/icps/worldbrief/europe_records.php?code=168>.

Keller, Richard. 2001. "Madness and Colonization: Psychiatry in the British and French Empires, 1800–1962." *Journal of Social History* 35, no. 2: 295–326. Retrieved from Project Muse website July 14, 2004, <http://must.jhu.edu.proxyau.wrlc.org>.

Law Reform Commission (LRC). 1997a. "Report 82 (1997)—Partial Defences to Murder: Diminished Responsibility." Law Reform Commission Publications, Digest of Law Reform Commission References. Retrieved June 11, 2004, <www.lawlink.nsw .gov.au/lrc.nsf/pages/digest.085>.

Little, A. N. 1961. "Murder: The Exceptional Crime." *The Incorporated Statistician* 11, no. 3: 150–55. Published by the Royal Statistical Society. Retrieved July 14, 2004, <www.jstor.org/>.

Matthews, S. 2004. "Failed Agency and the Insanity Defence." *International Journal of Law and Psychiatry* 27: 413–24. Retrieved online June 6, 2005, <www.sciencedirect .com>, Elsevier Sciences, Ltd.

McCrory, P. 2001. "The Medicolegal Aspects of Automatism in Mild Head Injury." *British Journal of Sports Medicine* 35: 288–90. Retrieved July 13, 2005, <http://bjsm .bmjjournals.com/cgi/content/full/35/5/288>.

Melton, Gary B., John Petrila, Norman G. Poythress, and Christopher Slobogin. 1997. *Psychological Evaluations for the Courts: A Handbook for Mental Health Professionals and Lawyers.* New York: Guilford Press.

Menninger, Karl. 1968. *The Crime of Punishment.* New York: Viking Press.

Mental Deficiency Act, 1913: Suggestions and Plans Relating to the Arrangement of Institutions for Mental Defectives. Board of Control. Her Majesty's Stationery Office.

Mental Health Act [1983 c. 20].

Moran, Richard. 1985. "The Origin of Insanity as a Special Verdict: The Trail for Treason of James Hadfield (1800)." *Law & Society Review* 19, no. 3: 487–519.

NHS Education for Scotland. 2004. Online: <www.nes.scot.nhs.uk/>.

Ratty v. A.-G. (Northern Ireland) [1963] AC 386.

Report of the Metropolitan Commissioners in Lunacy to the Lord Chancellor. 1844. Presented to both Houses of Parliament by command of Her Majesty. Bradbury and Evans, Printers, Whitefriars.

Ridgway, Peter. 1996. "Sleepwalking—Insanity or Automatism." *Murdoch University Electronic Journal of Law* 3, no. 1. Queensland: Murdoch University. Retrieved online April 15, 2004, <www.murdoch.edu/au/elaw/issues/v3n1/ridgway.html>.

Roberts, Andrew. 2001. "Mental Health History Words." Article from the Mental Health and Disability website. Retrieved June 28, 2004, <www.mdx.ac.uk/www/ study/mhhglo.htm#LicensedHouses>; <www.mdx.ac.uk/www/study/mhhhome .htm>.

Scottish Law Commission (SLC). 2003. "Discussion Paper on Insanity and Diminished Responsibility." Discussion Paper No. 122. January, 2003. Retrieved July 14, 2005, <www.scotlawcom.gov.uk/downloads/dp122_insanity.pdf>.

United States Department of State. 2004. "Background Note: United Kingdom." Washington, D.C.: U.S. Department of State. Retrieved online June 14, 2004, <www.state.gov/r/pa/ei/bgn/3846.htm>.

Walton, Mark. "Diminished Responsibility." Retrieved July 14, 2004, from the Institute of Mental Health Practitioners website, <www.markwalton.net/mdo/Diminishedrespo.asp?css=normno&Submit=Printer+Friendly>; <www.markwalton.net/index.asp>.

———. "The Insanity Defence." Retrieved July 14, 2004, from the Institute of Mental Health Practitioners website, <www.markwalton.net/mdo/insanitydefence.asp?>; <www.markwalton.net/index.asp>.

———. "Infanticide." Retrieved July 14, 2004, from the Institute of Mental Health Practitioners website, <www.markwalton.net/mdo/infanticide.asp?>; <www.markwalton.net/index.asp>.

Ward, Tony. 2002. "A Terrible Responsibility: Murder and the Insanity Defence in England, 1908–1939." *International Journal of Law and Psychiatry* 25: 361–77. Retrieved June 7, 2005, <www.sciencedirect.com>, Elsevier Sciences, Ltd.

9

Italy

ITALY IS A PENINSULA IN SOUTHERN EUROPE that is surrounded by the Adriatic Sea to the east, the Ionian Sea in the southeast, and the Tyrrhenian Sea in the east (CIA 2005). Located in the central Mediterranean, the Republic of Italy is 301,230 square kilometers and borders Austria, France, Slovenia, and Switzerland. Italy became a nation-state in 1861 and currently has a population of 58.1 million. Its inhabitants are predominantly Italian with pockets of French-, Slovene-, German-, Albanian-, and Greek-Italians (CIA 2005). Though the population is largely Roman Catholic, there are communities of Protestants, Jews, and Muslims. Italian is the official language, although German, Slovene, and French are spoken in some areas.

Italy's government consists of an executive branch with a chief of state, prime minister, and cabinet, and a bicameral Parliament in its legislative branch that comprises a Senate and Chamber of Deputies (CIA 2005). The judicial branch contains a Constitutional Court of fifteen judges.

Background

Early Roman law treated insane offenders differently than criminals by meting out lenient punishments, since their mental illness was seen as ample punishment (see Jones 1998). Historically, the Catholic Church provided care for the mentally ill (Burti and Benson 1996), for whom the first modern hospital, St. Bonifacio, was established in 1788. Not many hospitals after St. Bonifacio were built until the late 1800s and early 1900s (Burti and Benson 1996: 374).

During this time period, more mental hospitals were built to eventually house over 50,000 patients (Burti and Benson 1996: 374).

The first penal code, the Zanardelli Penal Code of 1889, was driven by the notion of free will and rationality of the Classical School, stating that dangerously insane offenders were to be sent to civil psychiatric hospitals where they could be held indefinitely or be released by the President of the Civil Court (Traverso et al. 2000: 498).[1]

According to the Museo Criminologico, the first institution established for the criminally insane was opened in 1876 within a sixteenth-century monastery that had once been used as a penitentiary for "those of unsound mind." Inmates in this ward may have been acquitted of a crime but still posed a threat to society, or they were individuals who had psychologically deteriorated during their incarceration. Another asylum for the criminally insane opened in 1886 at Montelupo Fiorentino. Once again, it was located in a sixteenth-century villa. A third asylum, at first used to hold the "partially insane," was built in 1892 and was later used as a criminal asylum (Museo). The next asylum, established in Naples in 1923, was situated in a monastery that had previously been used as a penitentiary. And finally, an asylum at Barcellona Pozzo di Gotti in Messina was opened in 1925.

In the early twentieth century, mental hospitals would admit individuals who posed a threat to themselves or "were prone to public scandal" (Piccinelli 2002). The first nationwide law on asylums, Public Law No. 36, was passed in 1904 and allowed for involuntarily hospitalizing mentally ill patients based on assessments of dangerousness (Burti and Benson 1996: 374). The police were also able to commit an individual to a hospital if they had a "medical certificate" (Piccinelli 2002). When compulsory patients were admitted, their stay could be for an unspecified duration (Piccinelli 2002).

Past penal legislation includes the French Penal Codes of 1791 and 1795, the Napoleonic Penal Code of 1810, the Penal Code of the Kingdom of the Two Sicilies of 1819, the code of the Duchy of Parma of 1820, the Papal States of 1832, the Penal Code of 1839, the Penal Codes of Tuscany of 1853, the Codice Penal Sardo of 1859, the Penal Codes of 1889 and 1930, and the Code of Penal Procedure of 1931 (Marongiu and Biddau 1993). To adhere to the Constitution of 1948, the Penal Code has undergone several revisions.

Italian penal law (the Rocco Code) is largely based upon the legal principals set forth during the French Enlightenment (Marongiu and Biddau 1993) and the concept of responsibility-dangerousness espoused by the Third School (Traverso et al. 2000: 499). The Third School emerged out of the conflicting perspectives of Positivist thinkers and the Classical School of Criminology (Traverso et al. 2000: 499). The Rocco Code, as maintained by the Third School and present in the current code, called for punishing the "responsible criminal, while security measures were taken in accordance with the dangerousness of the criminal to society" (Traverso et al. 2000: 499). Article 42 of the Rocco Code states that punishment can only be exacted on an individual if he or she committed the act with conscience or willingness (Traverso et al. 2000: 499). In 1944, Italy abolished capital punishment (Manna and Infante 2000).

It was in 1968 when Public Law No. 431 was passed, thereby permitting voluntary admissions into public mental facilities (Burti and Benson 1996: 374). This law regulated the size of mental hospitals and also recognized the need for community-based mental health clinics that could provide outpatient care.

Prior to 1978, psychiatric practices were regulated under a law[2] (which was influenced by a legal model in France in 1838) that focused on the dangerousness of a mentally ill offender rather than treatment (Traverso et al. 2000: 494). It stated that "persons afflicted with mental alienation, resulting from any cause, and who are not or cannot be cared for outside of psychiatric hospitals must be confined to civil psychiatric institutions when they present a danger to themselves or to others, or cause public scandal" (Traverso et al. 2000: 494). Individuals labeled as "chronic quiet madmen," "harmless epileptics," "oligophrenics,"[3] and non-threatening "individuals affected by incurable mental illness" had to be admitted into special units apart from the existing civil structures (Traverso et al. 2000: 494).

In 1978, Public Law No. 180 instigated many changes within the mental health system (De Girolamo and Cozza 2000; Burti and Benson 1996). The goal of Public Law No. 180 was to phase out hospitalization in public mental institutions by providing individuals with treatment through community health mental centers (Burti and Benson 1996: 377). Inpatient hospitalization was allowed only in extreme cases and readmission was prohibited (Burti and Benson 1996: 379). If involuntary hospitalization took place, it was to occur in general hospital psychiatric wards (Burti and Benson 1996: 380). By creating a "national mental health system without the mental hospital," Law No. 180 has been called "the most radical shift in Western mental health policy in modern times" (Burti and Benson 1996: 373). Public Law No. 180 prohibited building additional public mental facilities and ceased admissions to already-existing public mental hospitals (Burti and Benson 1996: 374). Patients who had no other place to go could remain in hospitals (Burti and Benson 1996: 380). By 1989, there were only 20,000 inpatients in Italy's public mental health facilities, as opposed to 91,700 in 1965 (Burti and Benson 1996: 379). In 1998, there were 7,704 inpatient residents in thirty-nine public and eleven private mental hospitals (De Girolamo and Cozza 2000: 200).[4]

Italy's current Code of Penal Procedure was enacted in 1988 and resembles the English and American systems (Marongiu and Biddau 1993; Manna and

Infante 2000). Unlike the previous code, the current Criminal Procedure Code is accusatorial rather than inquisitorial (Manna and Infante 2000).

Section II of Italy's constitution lays forth the "Rules on Jurisdiction" (ICL 2003). Criminal proceedings are administered by public prosecutors (Article 112). The accused have the right to a fair trial before an "independent and impartial judge" (Article 111), as well as the right to be informed of the charges against them, the right to question their accusers, and the right to prepare a defense (ICL 2003).

Recorded crime in Italy fell by 9 percent from 1996 to 2000 (Barclay and Tavares 2002: 1). Between 1998 and 2000, there were 98 homicides in Rome (Barclay and Tavares 2002: 4). In 2004, there were 57,046 inmates (including pretrial and remand prisoners) in Italy, of whom 4.8 percent were female (ICPS 2005). The prison population rate in 2003 was 99 per 100,000 of national population. By year-end 2004, there were 205 penal institutions, including 163 for remand, 34 for incarcerating sentenced inmates, and 17 facilities for juveniles (ICPS 2005). Between 1990 and 2000, the prison population increased by 67 percent, yet it increased only by 2 percent between 1999 and 2000 (Barclay and Tavares 2002: 7).

Legal Criteria

A person is not considered liable for an offense if he is determined to be mentally incompetent due to mental disease, chronic intoxication from alcohol, drug abuse, or deaf-mutism (Marongiu and Biddau 1993).[5] In such a situation, according to Marongiu and Biddau, "in addition to the penal sanction, compulsory hospitalization is provided as a safe measure." The Penal Code states that for a person to be punished for a crime, he or she must have been imputable at the time of the crime (Traverso et al. 2000: 500).[6] Otherwise, he or she is not imputable. Criteria for imputability are found in Article 88, which states that "a person who, at the moment in which he/she committed a crime, was, because of an infirmity, in such a state of mind as to exclude the capacities of understanding or willing, is not imputable" (cited in Traverso et al. 2000: 500).

Furthermore, Article 89 states: "A person who, at the moment in which he/she committed a crime, was, because of an infirmity, in such a state of mind as to greatly diminish, without excluding, his/her capacities of understanding or willing, is imputable, but the sentence will be shortened" (cited in Traverso et al. 2000: 500). Offenders who suffer from a "permanently pathological state" of chronic intoxication may be assessed as totally or partially incapable (Traverso et al. 2000: 501).[7]

Form of Verdict

A defendant may be found not guilty by reason of insanity.

Who Decides?

Judges determine the guilt of the offender and the appropriate sentence (Winslow 2005).

Role of Experts

The Procedural Penal Code dictates the involvement of experts and states that their evaluations can be introduced when it is necessary to obtain specific technical, scientific, or artistic knowledge (Traverso et al. 2000: 502). What is not admitted into court is "an expert evaluation for assessing habituality or professionality in crime commission, antisocial tendencies, the character and the personality of the defendant, and more generally psychic qualities independent from pathological reasons" (Traverso et al. 2000: 502).

Forensic psychiatrists have numerous roles. They may be called upon by a judge or district attorney as an expert, or they may be retained by the prosecution or the defense to determine an individual's level of imputability during the commission of the crime and subsequent level of dangerousness (Traverso et al. 2000: 502–3). Expert witnesses for the prosecution and the offender may partake in the determination of sentencing "when an issue of mental incompetency, disease, or defect is considered in order to exclude or diminish criminal responsibility" (Winslow 2005). The judge, however, is not required to follow their suggestions (Winslow 2005).

What Happens to the Defendant?

Prior to Law 180 in 1978, offenders who were not held responsible often served time in both judicial and civil institutions (Traverso et al. 2000: 504). In the early 1980s, the Constitutional Court stated that an individual could only be hospitalized based on a prognosis of "social dangerousness" (Traverso et al. 2000: 503). Until 1982, all offenders who were declared completely or partially insane had been considered dangerous.

According to Manna and Infante (2000), an offender cannot be held liable for an offense if "the offender was unable to understand and act intentionally at the moment of the offence, due to *infirmity* (Article 88 of the Criminal Code) or other causes" (13). The offender would therefore receive no punishment unless he was rendered socially dangerous. Aside from prison farms and custodial houses, there are judicial psychiatric hospitals (Manna and Infante 2000: 45). Mentally disabled offenders can be admitted to judicial psychiatric hospitals and socially dangerous offenders may be incarcerated indefinitely (Manna and Infante 2000: 45).

When mentally disabled offenders are considered dangerous and likely to recidivate, they are subject to "safety measures" for an unspecified amount of time (Winslow 2005). These measures are "custodial, non-custodial, and patrimonial" (Winslow 2005). When custodial steps are taken, the offender may be hospitalized, imprisoned, or sent to a labor facility. Noncustodial measures generally do not involve confinement, but the offender must obey certain conditions imposed by the judge (Winslow 2005). Patrimonial safety measures refer to instances where offenders deposit money or property in return for nonconfinement (Winslow 2005).

Frequency of Use

By the end of 1987, there were 1,225 inpatients in six judicial mental hospitals (Burti and Benson 1996: 380–81). As of 1992, there were twenty-nine male and female penitentiaries, two facilities for working inmates, two mental hospitals, one semi-custody facility, four prisons for drug addicts, and one national facility where inmates may undergo psychological observation (Marongiu and Biddau 1993). Currently, most hospital admissions are voluntary (Piccinelli 2002).

Russo, Salamone, and Villa (2003) analyzed data on 265 male mentally ill individuals, of whom 125 were offenders who were admitted to the Barcellona Judiciary Psychiatric Hospital from January 1990 to January 1995. The rest were not offenders and were admitted to a hospital in Messina during the same time period. Russo et al. found that of the 125 criminal offenders, 75 (60 percent) had been found guilty of committing murder or attempted murder. Most of the other 60 (40 percent) had committed property crimes.

Notes

1. See Articles 13 and 14.
2. Law 36 on Psychiatric Hospitals and Alienated People (Legge sui manicomi e sugli alienati). Passed February 14, 1904.
3. Refers to mental retardation.

4. Also see Rothbard and Kuno 2000 for more on the deinstitutionalization of public mental hospitals.

5. Penal Code, Articles 88, 89, 95, 96.

6. Penal Code, Article 85.

7. Rocco Penal Code, Article 90.

References

Barclay, Gordon, and Cynthia Tavares. 2002. "International Comparisons of Criminal Justice Statistics 2000." Issue 05/02. Retrieved June 15, 2004, <www.homeoffice.gov/uk/rds/pdfs2/hosb502.pdf>.

Burti, Lorenzo and Paul R. Benson. 1996. "Psychiatric Reform in Italy: Developments Since 1978." *International Journal of Law and Psychiatry* 19, nos. 3–4: 373–90.

Central Intelligence Agency (CIA). 2005. "Italy." The World Factbook. <www.odci.gov/cia/publications/factbook/geos/it.html>.

De Girolamo, Giovanni, and Massimo Cozza. 2000. "The Italian Psychiatric Reform: A Twenty-Year Perspective." *International Journal of Law and Psychiatry* 23, nos. 3–4: 197–214. Retrieved online June 6, 2005, <www.sciencedirect.com>, Elsevier Sciences, Ltd.

International Centre for Prison Studies (ICPS). 2005. "World Prison Brief: Entire World—Prison Population Totals, Prison Brief for Italy." International Centre for Prison Studies, Kings College London. Retrieved May 10, 2005, <www.kcl.ac.uk/depsta/rel/icps/worldbrief/world_brief.html>.

International Constitutional Law (ICL). 2003. "Italy—Constitution." A. Tschentscher, ed. Retrieved May 11, 2005, <www.oefre.unibe.ch/law/icl/info.html>.

Jones, Richard. 1998. "Forensic Medicine for Medical Students." Retrieved July 19, 2005, <www.forensicmed.co.uk>.

Manna, Adelmo, and Enrico Infante. 2000. "Criminal Justice Systems in Europe and North America: Italy." HEUNI, The European Institute for Crime Prevention and Control, affiliated with the United Nations. Helsinki, Finland: Tammer-Paino Oy. Retrieved June 17, 2004, <www.heuni.fi/12543.htm>.

Marongiu, Pietro, and Mario Biddau. 1993. "Italy." World Factbook of Criminal Justice Statistics. NCJ 199270. United States Department of Justice, Office of Justice Programs, Bureau of Justice Statistics. Retrieved online June 10, 2004, <www.ojp.usdoj.gov/bjs/pub/ascii/wfcjita.txt>.

Munro, Robin. "Judicial Psychiatry in China and Its Political Abuses." 2000. *Columbia Journal of Asian Law* 14, no. 1: 1–128. Retrieved HeinOnline July 14, 2004, <http://heinonline.org.proxyau.wrlc.org/HOL/Index?collection=fijournals>.

Museo Criminologico website. "The Establishing of Criminal Asylums." Ministry of Justice, Department of Prison Administration. Retrieved May 12, 2005, <www.museocriminologico.it/manicomi_uk.htm>.

Piccinell, Marco. 2002. "Focus on Psychiatry in Italy." *The British Journal of Psychiatry* 181: 538–44.

Rothbard, Aileen B., and Eri Kuno. 2000. "The Success of Deinstitutionalization: Empirical Findings from Case Studies on State Hospital Closures." *International Journal of Law and Psychiatry* 23, nos. 3–4: 329–44. Retrieved online June 6, 2005, <www.sciencedirect.com>, Elsevier Sciences, Ltd.

Russo, Gaetana, Loredana Salomone, and Lucia Della Villa. 2003. "The Characteristics of Criminal and Noncriminal Mentally Disordered Patients." *International Journal of Law and Psychiatry* 26: 417–35.

Traverso, Giovanni B., Silvio Ciappi, and Stefano Ferracuti. 2000. "The Treatment of the Criminally Insane in Italy." *International Journal of Law and Psychiatry* 23, nos. 5–6: 493–508. Retrieved online June 6, 2005, <www.sciencedirect.com>, Elsevier Sciences, Ltd.

World Factbook, The. 2005. "Italy." Central Intelligence Agency. Retrieved June 9, 2005, <www.odci.gov/cia/publications/factbook/geos/it.html>.

Winslow, Robert. 2005. "Italy" from *Crime and Society: A Comparative Criminology Tour of the World*. Retrieved May 24, 2005, <www-rohan.sdsu.edu/faculty/rwinslow/index.html>.

Wylie, J. A. *Genius and Influence of the Papacy*. Book 3 in *History of thePapacy*. See chapter 3: "Influence of Popery on Government." Fundamental Baptist Institute website. Retrieved July 15, 2004, <www.fbinstitute.com/papacy/index.htm>; <www.fbinstitute.com/>.

10

The Netherlands

T HE KINGDOM OF THE NETHERLANDS, located at the mouth of the Rhine, Maas, and Meuse rivers and bordering the North Sea, Germany, and Belgium, has a population of 16.2 million (U.S. Department of State 2003). The Kingdom includes the Netherlands, as well as Aruba and the Netherlands Antilles. The population is largely Dutch (96 percent), but there are groups consisting of Moroccans, Turks, and Surinamese. Major religions practiced are Roman Catholicism (34 percent), Protestantism (25 percent), Islam (3 percent), and other (2 percent). Thirty-six percent have no religious affiliation. The official language is Dutch.

The Constitution was enacted in 1814 and 1848 (U.S. Department of State 2003). The Dutch government is a parliamentary democracy with a constitutional monarch and consists of executive, legislative, and judicial branches. The executive branch consists of a chief of state, or monarch, a prime minister who is head of the government, and a cabinet. The legislative branch is a bicameral parliament and the judicial branch contains the Supreme Court.

Background

The Dutch penal system is a "dualistic sanction system" (Boone 2002: 482) that encapsulates two approaches to punishment—retribution and maintaining public safety. *Penalties* are imposed on a defendant if the purpose of punishment is retribution, whereas a *measure* is taken if the main goal is to protect society (Boone 2002: 482). Highly influenced by European Community

Law and European treaties, Dutch criminal laws can be found in the Constitution, the Criminal or Penal Code, the Code of Criminal Procedure, and Special Acts (Roman, Ahn-Redding, and Simon 2005).

The earlier criminal code of 1881 provided for offenders of an unsound
mind who could be committed to a psychiatric hospital, but provisions for offenders "who did not lack total responsibility" were not written into law until
the 1920s (Connelly and Williams 2000: 70). Under the 1928 Psychopath Act
(Van Marle 2002), the government implemented what was called
terbeschikkingstelling van de Regering (TBR)—or "detention at the Government's pleasure" for "offenders with responsibility, but who were otherwise
lacking in development or were psychologically disturbed, at the time of the
offence" (Connelly and Williams 2000: 70). Under this legislation, judges
could impose upon offenders a penalty in addition to compulsory state care
for at least two years with no limitation on years of confinement (Connelly
and Williams 2000: 70).

Prior to the mid-1950s, forensic psychiatrists functioned under the auspices
of the Medical Inspectorate of the Ministry of Justice (Van Marle 2000: 516).
As of 2000, there were nineteen Forensic Psychiatric Services—one in each
district—employing fifty-four forensic psychiatrists (Van Marle 2000). The
districts are grouped into five courts of justice, each of which has an area co-
ordinator who helps the Forensic Psychiatric Services and the Ministry of Justice work in conjunction (Van Marle 2000: 516).

In 1988, what is known as *terbeschikkingstelling* (TBS)[1] replaced the earlier
TBR (Connelly and Williams 2000). This new provision, TBS, made the use of
what used to be TBR more difficult and "for the first time the legal position of
a person under a hospital order was regulated in the Temporary Regulation
for the Legal Status of People under a Hospital order" (528). It was at this time
that "conditional TBS" was outlawed (Van Marle 2000: 524). For a person to
be placed in an "intensive care ward", there had to be "an inherent danger and
was of limited duration, the term *imminent risk* was more closely defined"
(Van Marle 2000: 528). In addition, hospital orders were limited to four years,
except in cases of certain violent crimes in which case a person could be held
in treatment indefinitely (Van Marle 2000: 528). Another form of conditional
TBS came into existence in 1997 in which individuals could be given TBS orders "without necessitating direct admittance to a maximum-security hospital" (Van Marle 2002: 85). The purpose of TBS is to protect society from offenders rather than to exact retribution from the defendant and to prevent or
reduce recidivism (Van Marle 2002).

Recorded crime increased by 9 percent from 1996 to 2000 (Barclay and
Tavares 2002: 1). Between 1998 to 2000, there were eighty-nine homicides in
Amsterdam (Barclay and Tavares 2002: 4). In 2004, there were sixty-one pris-

ons, ten TBS psychiatric facilities, seven temporary institutions for drug smugglers, and twenty-four juvenile facilities for the Netherlands' 19,999 prisoners (including pretrial and remand prisoners) (ICPS 2005). Nearly 9 percent of the prison population is female (ICPS 2005). The prison population rate in 2004 was 123 per 100,000 of national population. Between 1990 and 2000, the prison population increased by 101 percent and by 5 percent between 1999 and 2000 (Barclay and Tavares 2002: 7).

Legal Criteria

A person who commits an offense for which he cannot be held responsible due to mental defect or mental disease is not criminally charged.

Form of Verdict[2]

A defendant may be found guilty but mentally ill.

Who Decides?

To determine an appropriate sentence, a judge may receive input from social workers, medical experts, psychiatrists, probation services, the defendant, and the defense counsel (Winslow 2005). The judge may solicit this information or it may be provided at the behest of a psychiatrist (Van Marle 2000: 526).

Role of Experts

Forensic psychiatrists generally deliver services within penitentiaries and may advise "the management, the law courts, and the Ministry of Justice about the state of mentally disturbed prisoners" (Van Marle 2000: 517). While these opinions can be requested by a number of parties involved in a case, forensic psychiatrists can also provide opinions on their own.

When an individual commits a serious crime and it is believed that the offense was related to the presence of a mental disorder, the court can order a seven-week medical evaluation prior to the trial (UK Parliament 2000). For an offender to have diminished responsibility, a disorder must have a causal relationship with the criminal offense (Van Marle 2002). The assessment is conducted by a psychiatrist, psychologist, social worker, and a lawyer. The team will make a recommendation to the court regarding the individual's account-ability. The Select Committee on Home Affairs reported that in nearly half of the assessments they examined, the team found "some degree of diminished responsibility *and* a high risk of future dangerousness" (UK Parliament 2000 website).

Forensic psychiatrists may also be asked to assess whether an offender is suit-able for detention, for which the offender must have "a mental capacity that is incapable of coping with a detention situation to such an extent that a mental disorder will develop or an existing mental state will deteriorate and this can-not be counteracted with the available means, resulting in irreparable negative effects and danger" (Van Marle 2000: 517–18). While traditionally a psychiatric role, psychologists and other experts (e.g., remedial educators) today may be involved in conducting pretrial assessments in order to determine the of-fender's state of mind during the commission of the crime (Van Marle 2000: 526). Often the assessments made by psychiatrists and psychologists are used together to better understand the defendant's mental constitution. Psychiatrists may determine "the presence or absence of psychiatric illnesses with their symptoms and the resulting limitations," while psychologists can address "de-fined deviations in character structure and behavior" (Van Marle 2000: 526).

For a court to issue a TBS order, the incarceration period for the offense must be at least four years and the assessment team must make a recommen-dation for TBS (UK Parliament 2000). Experts also assist the judge in decid-ing whether to extend compulsory treatment (Boone 2002). If a judge orders compulsory treatment, expert opinion is sought from hospitals of the Min-istry of Justice by "at least two behavioural experts, one of whom must be a psychiatrist" (Boone 2002: 483). Forensic psychiatrists will often advise psy-chologists on treatment options for offenders in prison with mental illnesses (Van Marle 2000: 518). When judges review TBS cases, their decisions are largely based on the caregivers' evaluations and prediction of risk (Nijman, de Kruyk, and van Nieuwenhuizen 2000: 79).

As of 2002, there were nine TBS hospitals in Groningen, Balkbrug, Rekken, Nijmegen, Utrecht, Amsterdam, Rotterdam, and Venray (Van Marle 2002). There were also two forensic psychiatric hospitals.

What Happens to the Defendant?

A defendant may be exempt from criminal responsibility either in whole or in part if he or she had a "defective development or a diseased disorder of men-tal faculties while committing the crime" (Boone 2002: 483). In cases of par-tial responsibility, the offender may be required to serve a sentence and then be ordered into TBS treatment if the crime was "seen as being related to a mental disorder or illness and if the specific combination of crime and disorder was considered to produce serious risk of future crimes" (Connelly and Williams 2000: 71). Such crimes, according to Connelly and Williams, might be "physical abuse, rape, child molestation, homicide" (71). In a review of Dutch TBS practices, Connelly and Williams (2000) report that over 90 percent of patients in TBS hospitals were serious violent offenders and that sexual offenders only made up approximately one-third of the population (73).

If a defendant is found to have diminished responsibility, and if the crime is severe enough to warrant at least four years of imprisonment (Nijman, de Kruyk, and van Nieuwenhuizen 2000), the court may hand down a TBS order under which they are placed in a maximum security hospital by the government (Boone 2002; Van Marle 2000). Ultimately, TBS orders are not based on whether offenders are amenable to treatment, but whether they are dangerous. Thus, TBS can only be imposed if the offender is determined to be a threat (Van Marle 2002). When this occurs, the convicted offender serves a prison sentence and is then committed to a forensic hospital (TBS hospital) to receive treatment (Boone 2002).

Prior to 2000, the Meijers Institute would evaluate TBS offenders to determine appropriate placements in TBS hospitals (Van Marle 2002). The Institute would then make a recommendation to the Ministry of Justice. Currently, hospitals make admission decisions.

Generally, a TBS order involves four additional years following the initial prison sentence. The prison sentence is based on the offender's level of responsibility (Van Marle 2002). The TBS order may be extended in cases of extreme violence and if the individual poses a threat to the public. TBS may also involve outpatient treatment, which may be combined with probation. Judges, every one or two years, will review the case to decide whether to continue TBS (Nijman, de Kruyk, and van Nieuwenhuizen 2004). An offender who is given TBS with conditions is required to meet certain criteria (e.g., being a threat to others), "while the sanction does not necessarily lead to admission to a TBS institution" (Van Marle 2000: 524). In order to extend a TBS order past six years, independent experts must be consulted. TBS orders can also be ceased for a provisional period of up to three years (Van Marle 2002).

If the individual is found not guilty, he or she may be acquitted regardless of the findings of the assessment (UK Parliament 2000). The court may order TBS with conditions for defendants who do not require closed custody (Brouwer 2002). In this case, the defendant is supervised by the probation service. The court can also order TBS with mandatory nursing in which the defendant is kept in a highly secured forensic psychiatric hospital (Brouwer 2002). If a defendant is acquitted but is believed to be a danger to himself, to others, or to property, a judge can order the individual to be detained in a psychiatric hospital for one year (Winslow 2005).[3]

Hospital treatment following incarceration usually involves education, occupational training, finance skills, and social skill training (UK Parliament 2000). These hospitals are either state-run or "particularly owned" (Boone 2002: 484). If the individual makes progress and is no longer seen as a threat to others, the court may grant release. However, the patient may remain there indefinitely (Aronowitz 1993; Boone 2002). TBS is often applied to violent sex offenders. Approximately 10 percent of the patients are deemed too dangerous to release (UK Parliament 2000). In cases where the offense was nonviolent, a defendant may only be sent to a hospital for up to two years, although that period can be extended by the Prosecution Officer (Boone 2002: 483).

The goal of the TBS hospital is to assist the patient in working towards release by emphasizing rehabilitation, encouraging family visits, and providing the patient with life and social skills (UK Parliament 2000). A TBS period is generally six years, after which a large majority of patients are released back into the community. Sexual offenders stay, on average, for 8.5 years (Connelly and Williams 2000: 73). Following the release from a TBS hospital is "supervised community treatment" (Connelly and Williams 2000: 72). Recidivism rates among those released are generally low (UK Parliament 2000). In some cases, an offender may spend more time in a TBS setting than the sentence they would have served in a prison (Van Marle 2000: 530). In other cases, as of 1997, an individual's prison sentence may be reduced by one-third or even more under certain circumstances (Van Marle 2002).

Frequency of Use

As of 2000, there were nine TBS maximum security and two forensic psychiatric hospitals (Van Marle 2000: 528). Since 1991, approximately 170 "TBS-verdicts" are imposed each year, "while every year about 80 are finished by the court" (Van Marle 2000: 528). Over the years, the number of TBS hospital orders has risen (529). Van Marle (2000) estimates that approximately 3 percent of all prisoners should be in psychiatric hospitals rather than penitentiaries (515).

Nijman et al. (2000) evaluated 128 offenders who were admitted to the Forensic Psychiatric Hospital de Kijvelanden between November 1996 and April 2001 (80). All of the offenders were male and their average age was twenty-five years. Approximately 25 percent had major psychotic disorders found in the DSM-IV, and many had Axis II disorders such as antisocial, borderline, or narcissistic personality disorders. Approximately 34 percent were hospitalized for crimes involving homicide or attempted homicide, and 26 percent for sexual crimes.

Cima et al. (2004) examined 308 males who were hospitalized in the Forensic Clinic Düren (Germany) and the Forensic Psychiatric Hospital the Kijvelanden in the Netherlands (217). The average age of the subjects was thirty-four years, and the crimes for which they had been convicted included homicide, attempted homicide, or manslaughter (33 percent); sex offenses (28 percent); "grievous bodily harm" (14 percent); and "armed robberies or arson" (75 percent). Approximately 60 percent had at least one personality disorder. Other diagnoses among the patients included psychoses (36 percent), sexual disorders (13 percent), substance abuse (51 percent) or mental retardation (8 percent).

From January 1996 to December 2001, Hildebrand and de Ruiter (2000: 235–36), studied 98 males who were hospitalized in forensic facilities. The average age of the men was 31.5 years. Fifty percent of the group had been convicted of murder or attempted murder, nearly a quarter had been convicted of sexual offenses, and the remaining 25 percent had committed other violent crimes such as arson and aggravated assault.

Van Marle (2002) states that TBS hospitals are unable to keep up with the number of individuals who are in prison awaiting TBS hospitalization (90).

Notes

1. *Terbeschikkingstelling* (TBS) means "at the discretion of the state" (Van Marle 2002).

2. According to Van Marle (2000), "Criminal law makes no distinction in the degree of diminished responsibility" (527). However, there are five levels of accountability that have been recognized, according to Van Marle (2000; 2002), that reflect the degree to which the disorder is associated with the criminal act. The first is undiminished responsibility in which an individual's free will was not compromised and therefore chose to commit an act. Severely diminished responsibility is when free will is comprised due to "a result of a severe psychiatric illness or a situationally determined exacerbation in the mental clinical picture because certain stimuli from the scene of the crime have a specific effect on the state of mind of the perpetrator, often resulting in a reality disorder that spontaneously dies off again after some time (psychotic episode), or which provokes a psychosis" (527). Other levels are somewhat diminished responsibility, diminished responsibility, and irresponsibility (527).

3. Penal Code, section 37.

References

Aronowitz, Alexis A. 1993. World Factbook of Criminal Justice Statistics. United States Department of Justice, Office of Justice Programs, Bureau of Justice Statistics. Retrieved online June 10, 2004, <www.ojp.usdoj.gov/bjs/pub/ascii/wfcjnet.txt>.

Barclay, Gordon, and Cynthia Tavares. 2002. "International Comparisons of Criminal Justice Statistics 2000." Issue 05/02. Retrieved June 15, 2004, <www.homeoffice.gov/uk/rds/pdfs2/hosb502.pdf>.

Belzen, Jacob A. 1998. "Religious Mania and Criminal Nonculpability." *International Journal of Law and Psychiatry* 21, no. 4: 433–45. Retrieved online June 6, 2005, <www.sciencedirect.com>, Elsevier Sciences, Ltd.

Blankman, Kees. 1997. "Guardianship Models in the Netherlands and Western Europe." *International Journal of Law and Psychiatry* 20, no. 1: 47–57. Retrieved online June 6, 2005, <www.sciencedirect.com>, Elsevier Sciences, Ltd.

Boone, M. M. 2002. "Imposed versus Undergone Punishment in the Netherlands." *Electronic Journal of Comparative Law* 6 (December 2002). Retrieved May 23, 2005, <www.ejcl.org/64/art64-27.html>.

Brouwer, C. 2002. "The Role of the Dutch Probation Service During TBS" in *Forensic Psychiatry and Probation in The Netherlands* (online article). Retrieved May 23, 2005, <www.ialmh.org/amsterdam2002/11.07/forensicpsychiatry.pdf>.

Cima, M., H. Nijman, H. Merckelbach, K. Kremer, and S. Hollnack. 2004. "Claims of Crime-related Amnesia in Forensic Patients." *International Journal of Law and Psychiatry* 24: 215–21. Retrieved online June 6, 2005, <www.sciencedirect.com>, Elsevier Sciences, Ltd.

Connelly, Clare, and Shanti Williams. 2000. "A Review of the Research Literature on Serious Violent and Sexual Offender." *Scottish Executive, Central Research Unit.* Retrieved May 23, 2005, <www.scotland.gov.uk/cru/kd01/green/s-off-02.htm>.

Hildebrand, Martin and Corine de Ruiter. 2004. "PCL-R Psychopathy and Its Relation to DSM-IV Axis I and II Disorders in a Sample of Male Forensic Psychiatric Patients in the Netherlands." *International Journal of Law and Psychiatry* 27: 233–48. Retrieved online June 6, 2005, <www.sciencedirect.com>, Elsevier Sciences, Ltd.

International Centre for Prison Studies (ICPS). 2005. "World Prison Brief: Entire World—Prison Population Totals, Prison Brief for Netherlands." International Centre for Prison Studies, Kings College London. Retrieved May 10, 2005, <www.kcl.ac.uk/depsta/rel/icps/worldbrief/world_brief.html>.

Nijman, Henk, Cindy de Kruyk, and Chijs van Nieuwenhuizen. 2004. "Behavioral Changes during Forensic Psychiatric (TBS) Treatment in the Netherlands." *International Journal of Law and Psychiatry* 27: 79–85. Retrieved online June 6, 2005, <www.sciencedirect.com>, Elsevier Sciences, Ltd.

Roman, Caterina Gouvis, Heather Ahn-Redding, and Rita J. Simon. 2005. *Illicit Drug Policies, Trafficking, and Use the World Over.* Lanham, Md.: Lexington Books.

United Kingdom Parliament. 2000. "The System in the Netherlands." Select Committee on Home Affairs, First Report. The United Kingdom Parliament. Retrieved June 14, 2004, <www.parliament.the-stationery-office.co.uk/pa/cm199900/cmselect/cmhaff/42/4209.htm>.

United States Department of State. 2003. "Background Note: The Netherlands." Washington, D.C.: U.S. Department of State. Retrieved online June 14, 2004, <www.state.gov/r/pa/ei/bgn/3204.htm>.

Van Emmerik, J. L. 1999. "De last van het getal; een overzicht in cijfers van de maatregel TBS." *Justitiële Verkenningen* 4/99. WODC. Gouda Quint, Deventer, 9–31.

Van Marle, Hjalmar J. C. 2002. "The Dutch Entrustment Act (TBS): Its Principle and Innovations." *International Journal of Forensic Mental Health* 1, no. 1: 83–92. Retrieved online July 21, 2005, <www.iafmhs.org/iafmhs.asp?pg=journalenglish>.

Van Marle, Hjalmar J. C. 2000. "Forensic Psychiatry Services in the Netherlands." *International Journal of Law and Psychiatry* 23, nos. 5–6): 515–531. Retrieved online June 6, 2005 (http://www.sciencedirect.com), Elsevier Sciences, Ltd.

Winslow, Robert. 2005. "Netherlands" from *Crime and Society: A Comparative Criminology Tour of the World.* Retrieved May 24, 2005, <www-rohan.sdsu.edu/faculty/rwinslow/index.html>.

11

Sweden

THE KINGDOM OF SWEDEN IS LOCATED in Northern Europe between Norway and Finland. The northeastern region borders the Gulf of Bothnia and the southeast area borders the Baltic Sea. Sweden has a population of 8.9 million residing in its twenty-one counties and 289 townships (U.S. Department of State 2003). The official language is Swedish, but there are small groups who speak Sami languages and Finnish (CIA 2005). The Swedish population includes ethnic Finns and ethnic Lapps, as well as immigrants from Finland, Bosnia, Iran, Norway, Denmark, Greece, and Turkey. Approximately 87 percent of Swedes are Lutheran. Others are Catholic, Orthodox, Baptist, Jewish, Buddhist, and Muslim.

The Swedish Constitution was passed on January 1, 1975. As a constitutional monarchy with a social-democratic government, Sweden consists of an executive, legislative, and judicial branch (U.S. Department of State 2003; SIS online; Silfverhielm and Kamis-Gould 2000). While the king is the head of state, the position only carries ceremonial duties (SIS online). The executive branch consists of a cabinet that is responsible to the parliament, while the legislative branch is a unicameral parliament. The judicial branch consists of a Supreme Court with 6 superior and 108 lower courts (U.S. Department of State 2003). The court system is hierarchical and consists of district courts, courts of appeal, and the Supreme Court (SIS online).

Background

Prior to the mid-nineteenth century, "lunatics" were sent to asylums under the belief that they were possessed. It wasn't until the late 1800s that the first facility for mentally ill individuals was constructed (Silfverhielm and Kamis-Gould 2000: 293). Recent notable mental health legislation includes: Social Services Act (1980); the Forensic Psychiatric Care Act of 1991; Swedish Health Care Act of 1982; Law on Support and Services to the Disabled in 1994 (Silfverhielm and Kamis-Gould 2000: 293).

The legal system in Sweden is accusatorial, although both prosecutors and police officers may mete out summary fines for less severe offenses, such as traffic violations (SIS online). Court proceedings fall under the Administrative Court Procedure Act (Ministry of Justice 2002). Public prosecutors choose whether to try defendants, all of whom stand trial because plea bargaining is not a part of the system (SIS online). Criminal hearings are what Moyer (1974) describes as "an informal, conversational type of hearing during which a defendant is given ample time to speak" (73).

Sweden's penal code, which categorizes crimes into subcategories, was adopted in 1962 and enacted on January 1, 1965 (Ministry of Justice 2004: 3; SIS online). The criminal code provides a list of punishments, which may include fines, imprisonment, probation, or special treatment (SIS online). In 1921, Sweden outlawed the death penalty, and in 1973, capital punishment was eliminated during times of war (SIS online). Juveniles under the age of fifteen cannot be held criminally responsible, and extenuating circumstances must exist for an offender under the age of eighteen to be incarcerated (SIS online).

In 2001, there were 5,500 beds in psychiatric hospitals, a significant decrease from the 35,000 beds available three decades ago (Arvidsson 2004).

In 1992, legislation was passed to make it more difficult for offenders to be sent to psychiatric hospitals rather than prisons (Grann and Holmberg 1999). Under the new legislation, an offender must have a severe mental disorder to be declared insane and sent to a hospital. The Psychiatric Care Reform, enacted in 1995, attempted to increase the use of social services for individuals with long-term mental illnesses (Arvidsson 2004: 8).

Between 1998 and 2000, there were sixty-three homicides in Stockholm, the capital of Sweden (Arvidsson 2004: 4). In 2003, there were 6,755 prisoners (including remand and pretrial prisoners), a prison population rate of 75 per 100,000 of national population (ICPS 2004). Between 1990 and 2000, the prison population increased by 7 percent but recorded crime decreased by 1 percent from 1996 to 2000 (Barclay and Tavares 2002: 1, 7). By April 2004, there were eighty-four prisons, of which thirty were remand facilities. Remand prisons, aside from housing suspects taken into custody, may temporarily house persons who are detained under the Compulsory Mental Care Act (Ministry of Justice 2002).

Legal Criteria

Sweden abolished the insanity defense in 1965. In its place it passed legislation applicable to all mentally ill persons, including those charged with committing criminal offenses. If a person charged with a crime is suspected of having suffered from mental illness at the time of the offense, the court can order a psychiatric evaluation of the defendant in a public facility. This examination, however, cannot be conducted unless the prosecutor has proved that the defendant has committed the criminal act or unless the defendant has confessed to the act. At the public health facility, psychiatrists will examine the defendant and submit in writing to the court their opinion as to whether the defendant was suffering from mental illness at the time of the offense. Invariably, the court accepts the opinion of the independent mental health experts concerning the defendant's mental health at the time of the offense. The defendant can appeal the court's finding to the national review board.

Role of Experts

In cases dealing with mental illnesses, a medical opinion must be rendered in order for the court to determine the outcome of the case (Moyer 1974: 79). All psychiatric assessments are handled by the Swedish National Board on Forensic Medicine (Belfrage and Fransson 2000: 510).

An offender is assessed by a forensic psychiatrist prior to sentencing (Belfrage and Fransson 2000: 10). The assessments, usually conducted by teams of psychiatrists, psychologists, and social workers, may last up to four weeks (Belfrage and Fransson 2000: 510). Ten percent of assessments are referred to the National Board of Health and Welfare which issues a second opinion (Belfrage and Fransson 2000: 510).

What Happens to the Defendant?

Criminal sanctions are determined based on the severity of the offense, the age of the offender, and the defendant's mental state (SIS online; Winslow 2005). The court can order that a defendant be evaluated by a forensic psychiatrist (Winslow 2005). If an offender is rendered mentally ill, he or she may receive compulsory psychiatric treatment (Ministry of Justice 2002) under the Forensic Mental Care Act (Ministry of Health and Social Affairs 2004) and may be sentenced to a psychiatric facility for treatment if the crime warrants more than a fine as a sentence (Wilkstrom and Dolmen 1993). As of 2000, there were five forensic psychiatric hospitals where mentally ill offenders are treated (Belfrage and Fransson 2000: 511). Drug abusers who pose a danger to themselves or others can be sentenced to such substance abuse treatment under the Care of Alcoholics and Drug Abusers Act (SIS online).

Chapter 33, sections 2 and 4 of an earlier version of the criminal code, which were repealed in 1988, stated:

> For a crime committed under the influence of mental disease, feeble-mindedness, or other mental abnormality of such profound nature that it must be considered equivalent to a mental disease, no other sanction may be given than *surrender for special care*, or . . . *fine* or *probation*. . . . The defendant shall be *free of sanction* if it is found that a sanction mentioned in the section should not be imposed. (Moyer 1974: 75)

Frequency of Use

An estimated 550 offenders are forensically evaluated each year and half meet the criteria for a severe mental disorder (Belfrage and Fransson 2000: 509; Grann and Holmberg 1999: 126). As of 2000, "Approximately 1,000 patients are subject to forensic psychiatric treatment" (Belfrage and Fransson 2000: 511).

Silfverhielm and Kamis-Gould 2000 (298: table 1) report the legal status of adult psychiatric inpatients. In 1991, 2 of the 5,684 women and 12 of the 6,004 men were in hospitals for forensic services, whereas these figures were 3 out of 2,621 women and 23 out of 3,105 men in 1997.

Kullgren, Grann and Holmberg (1996) reviewed the forensic data of 1,498 men who were prosecuted over a three-year period (196: table 4). Nearly half of the sample was diagnosed with a severe mental disorder. The number of offenses for which the men with severe mental disorders were prosecuted are as follows: assault (100), murder (72), theft (42), rape (41), arson (33), robbery (31), other sex-related offenses (28), manslaughter (11), other offenses against the person (51), other property crimes (37), and other unlisted offenses (37).

In 1993, 2.3 percent (N=372) of the 164,380 defendants who were prosecuted or sanctioned were sent to psychiatric treatment, whereas 9.6 percent (N=15,872) were sent to prison (SIS online). Nearly 68 percent (N=111,560) were given fines (Winslow 2005). By the end of the twentieth century, Van Emmerik (1999; cited in Van Marle 2002) found that approximately 96 percent of individuals under TBS orders had committed serious violent crimes or serious violent sex offenses.

References

Arvidsson, H. 2004. "After the 1996 Swedish Mental Health Care Reform—A Follow-up Study of a Group of Severely Mentally Ill." Ph.D. dissertation, Department of Psychology, Göteborg, Sweden. Retrieved July 26, 2005, <https://guoa.ub.gu.se/dspace/handle/2077/46>.

Barclay, Gordon, and Cynthia Tavares. 2002. "International Comparisons of Criminal Justice Statistics 2000." Issue 05/02. Retrieved June 15, 2004, <www.homeoffice.gov/uk/rds/pdfs2/hosb502.pdf>.

Belfrage, Henrik, and Göran Fransson. 2000. "Swedish Forensic Psychiatry: A Field in Transition." *International Journal of Law and* Psychiatry 23, nos. 5–6: 509–14. Retrieved online June 6, 2005, <http://www.sciencedirect.com>, Elsevier Sciences, Ltd.

Central Intelligence Agency (CIA). 2005. "Sweden." The World Factbook. <www.odci.gov/cia/publications/factbook/geos/sw.html>.

Grann, Martin, and Gunnar Holmberg. 1999. "Follow-Up of Forensic Psychiatric Legislation and Clinical Practice in Sweden, 1988 to 1995." *International Journal of Law and Psychiatry* 22, no. 2: 125–31. Retrieved online June 6, 2005, <www.sciencedirect.com>, Elsevier Sciences, Ltd.

International Centre for Prison Studies (ICPS). 2004. "World Prison Brief: Entire World—Prison Population Totals, Prison Brief for Sweden." International Centre for Prison Studies, Kings College London. Retrieved June 16, 2004, <www.kcl.ac.uk/depsta/rel/icps/worldbrief/highest_to_lowest_rates.php>; <www.kcl.ac.uk/depsta/rel/icps/worldbrief/europe_records.php?code=165>.

Kullgren, Gunnar, Martin Grann, and Gunnar Holmberg. 1996. "The Swedish Forensic Concept of *Severe Mental Disorder* as Related to Personality Disorders: An Analysis of Forensic Psychiatric Investigations of 1498 Male Offenders." *International Journal of Law and Psychiatry* 19, no. 2: 191–200. Retrieved online June 6, 2005, <www.sciencedirect.com>, Elsevier Sciences, Ltd.

Ministry of Justice. 2004. "The Swedish Penal Code." July 21, 2004. Retrieved May 19, 2005, <www.sweden.gov.se/sb/d/3926/a/27777>.

Ministry of Justice. 2002. "The Swedish Judicial System—A Brief Introduction." RegeringSkansliet (Government Offices of Sweden). Retrieved May 11, 2005, <www.sweden.gov.se/sb/d/2768/a/16279;jsessionid=aTgZY7X4GHYb>.

Moyer, Lloyd K. 1974. "The Mentally Abnormal Offender in Sweden: An Overview and Comparison with American Law." *The American Journal of Comparative Law* 22, no. 1 (Winter 1974): 71–106. Retrieved from JSTOR on May 18, 2005, <www.jstor.org>.

Silfverhielm, Helena, and Edna Kamis-Gould. 2000. "The Swedish Mental Health System: Past, Present, and Future." *International Journal of Law and Psychiatry* 23, nos. 3–4: 293–307. Retrieved online June 6, 2005, <www.sciencedirect.com>, Elsevier Sciences, Ltd.

Swedish Intelligence Services (SIS) (online website). "Sweden." Military Intelligence and Security Agency or Militarëns Underattelse och Sakerhetstjnst (MUST), Security Police or Saekerhets Polisen (SPO), Swedish Armed Forces Headquarters, Swedish Armed Forces Headquarters, Stockholm, Sweden. Retrieved May 12, 2005, <http://isuisse.ifrance.com/emmaf/home.html>.

United States Department of State. 2003. "Background Note: Sweden." Washington, D.C.: U.S. Department of State. Retrieved online June 14, 2004, <www.state.gov/r/pa/ei/bgn/2880.htm>.

Van Emmerik, J. L. 1999. "De last van het getal; een overzicht in cijfers van de maatregel TBS." *Justitiële Verkenningen* 4/99. WODC. Gouda Quint, Deventer, 9–31.

Van Marle, Hjalmar J. C. 2002. "The Dutch Entrustment Act (TBS): Its Principle and Innovations." *International Journal of Forensic Mental Health* 1, no. 1: 83–92. Retrieved online July 21, 2005, <www.iafmhs.org/iafmhs.asp?pg=journalenglish>.

Wikstrom, Per-Olof H., and Lars Dolmen. 1993. "Sweden." World Factbook of Criminal Justice Statistics. United States Department of Justice, Office of Justice Programs, Bureau of Justice Statistics. National Council for Crime Prevention Sweden and Department of Sociology, University of Stockholm. Retrieved online June 10, 2004, <www.ojp.usdoj.gov/bjs/pub/ascii/wfcjswe.txt>.

Winslow, Robert. 2005. "Sweden" from *Crime and Society: A Comparative Criminology Tour of the World.* Retrieved May 24, 2005, <www-rohan.sdsu.edu/faculty/rwinslow/index.html>.

Part V

EASTERN EUROPE

12

Bulgaria

B ULGARIA IS LOCATED BETWEEN Romania and Turkey. It is a country of 7.6
million in nine provinces, governed by a parliament with a president and
vice-president[1] (ICL 1991; Karadjov 2001; ICPS 2004; Bojadjieva 1993). The
country's nationality is Bulgarian. In addition to Bulgarian, Turkish (9.6 percent) and Roma (4.1) are also spoken throughout the counry (CIA 2005). The
people of Bulgaria are mostly ethnic Bulgarian (83.9 percent), but there are
small ethnic groups who are Turkish, Roma, Armenian, Macedonian, Tartar,
and Circassian (CIA 2005). Bulgarian Orthodoxy is the most common religion (82.6 percent) in addition to Islam (12.2), Christianity (1.2), and other
religions (4).

While Northern Bulgaria gained its independence from the Ottoman Turks
in 1879, the entire country was not independent until 1908 (CIA 2005). Under
Soviet influence, the nation became a People's Republic in 1946, which lasted
until 1990 when communism ended and elections were held. Bulgaria today
reflects many of its historical influences, such as the Byzantine Empire, the Ottoman Empire, the Russo-Turkish war in the late nineteenth century, and the
Treaty of Berlin (1885) (Winslow 2005).

Under the 1991 Constitution, power is relegated to legislative, executive, and
judicial bodies (Karadjov 2001: 3). The legislative branch is a 240-seat unicameral National Assembly whose members are elected every four years (CIA 2005).
Within the executive branch are the president, vice president, and the prime
minister. The Cabinet consists of a Council of Ministers whose members are
nominated by the prime minister and then elected by the National Assembly.
Within the judiciary are the following courts: Supreme Administrative Court,

Supreme Court of Cassation, and Constitutional Courts. The Supreme Judicial Council, whose members are elected every five years, consists of the Chief Prosecutor, two Supreme Court members, and twenty-two additional members who are elected by the National Assembly or judiciary.

Background

Turkish penal law, which was based on the Napoleonic Code, was in place until a few years after Bulgaria's independence (Dolaptchieff 1933: 1014). In 1896, the first modern Penal Code was created. It was heavily influenced by the Hungarian and Russian penal codes (Bojadjieva 1993) and based on the neoclassical school of thought, in which individuals are perceived as rational and calculating beings possessing free will, and whose levels of criminal responsibility should be reflected through proportionate punishments (Dolaptchieff 1933: 1014). Under this new code, for someone to be culpable of a crime they had to possess "the capacity to commit crime, the *doli-capacitas,* imputability" (Dolaptchieff 1933: 1016). Imputability referred to an individual's ability to understand the "factual nature and the meaning of his act and the capacity to guide his conduct in accordance to this understanding" (Dolaptchieff 1933: 1016). For an individual to be culpable, he must be able to understand the difference between right and wrong and be able to conform his behavior to the law (Dolaptchieff 1933: 1016). Mitigating factors that diminished culpability included

1) physical and mental underdevelopment such as age or deafmuteness,
2) mental diseases such as insanity, and
3) unconsciousness states of dream, intoxication, or hypnosis due to physiological or pathological conditions. (Dolaptchieff 1933: 1016)

The first criminal procedure code in Bulgaria was implemented in 1952 but was later replaced by a new code in 1974 (Bojadjieva 1993) and again on May 12, 2005 (SEE Security Monitor 2005). Another penal code was signed in to law in 1956 but was later replaced in 1968. This more recent penal code had a more western European influence than its earlier versions (Bojadjieva 1993). The current penal code identifies crime as "severe," in which a defendant may receive more than a five-year sentence or the death penalty, "particularly serious," in which a defendant is considered to be largely dangerous to society, and "petty," which includes minor, nonviolent offenses (Bojadjieva 1993). Offenses, which are also divided into two broader categories in court, are those of a "general type" and those of a "private type" (Bojadjieva 1993). The former category includes crimes that pose a public threat, whereas the latter are less severe offenses, such as causing mild injuries or libel (Bojadjieva 1993). The penal code also labels crimes by the following categories: crimes against the republic, crimes against persons, sex crimes, crimes against marriage, family and youth, property crimes, economic crimes, crimes against the functioning of state agencies and public bodies, false documenting, hooliganism, and those of a general nature (Bojadjieva 1993).[2] The criminal police investigate street crimes, such as murder and theft, whereas the economic police investigate crimes such as corruption and embezzlement (Bojadjieva 1993).

Defendants are innocent unless proven guilty in a court and have the right to a fair trial (ICL 1991). They have the right to know what charges have been brought against them and to actively participate in their defense (Bojadjieva 1993). Prior to a trial, a prosecutor can set into motion a pre-trial phase for "crimes of the general type, crimes committed by minors or by persons who are physically or mentally disabled and cannot defend themselves, and crimes of the private type when the victim cannot defend himself or herself" (Bojadjieva 1993). During this phase, the National Investigation Agency and other agencies investigate criminal cases while under the auspices of the prosecutor, after which the prosecutor reviews the findings and determines the next course of action, such as dismissing a case or indicting the offender (Bojadjieva 1993).

Punishments under the 1896 penal code included:

1. capital punishment;
2. life imprisonment;
3. imprisonment from one to fifteen years;
4. close confinement from one day to three years;
5. arrest;
6. fine; and
7) reprimand (only for children). (Dolaptchieff 1933: 1018)

Punishments for offenses are determined by the severity of the offense, the motive for carrying out the crime, and mitigating or aggravating circumstances.[3] The modern penal code sets forth the following punishments:

1) deprivation of liberty;
2) corrective labor without deprivation of liberty;
3) confiscation of existing property;
4) a fine;
5) compulsory domicile without deprivation of liberty;
6) deprivation of the right to hold a certain state or public office;
7) deprivation of the right to exercise a certain vocation or activity;
8) deprivation of the right to reside in certain inhabited place;
9) deprivation of the right to receive orders, honorary titles and distinctions;

10) deprivation of military rank;
11) public censure.[4]

In only the most severe cases may a person be executed.

Bulgaria's penal system is composed of prisons, labor correction facilities that are connected to prisons, and pretrial detention facilities (Kanev and Mitrev 2003: 10). In 2003, there were 9,918 prisoners (including pretrial and remand prisoners) throughout Bulgaria's fourteen penal facilities (ICPS 2004), a national incarceration rate of 127 per 100,000. Bulgaria's prison population swelled in 1998 when it reached 11,541, with an incarceration rate of 139 per 100,000, but by 2001 the figure had decreased to 8,971, an incarceration rate of 110 per 100,000.

Under civil law, an individual can be *compulsorily treated* with psychiatric care. *Involuntary psychiatric treatment* refers to situations where an offender is committed under criminal law (Amnesty International [AI] 2002: 2).[5] Compulsory treatment can be instated when: "Persons suffering from schizophrenia, paranoia, cyclophrenia, epilepsy, senility . . . who, due to their illness, are likely to perpetrate crimes constituting a serious danger to society or are dangerous to their relatives or others, or seriously threaten their own health shall be admitted for compulsory treatment in a state or municipal treatment facility under a judicial decree"[6] (AI 2002: 15). Hospitals where involuntary treatment is provided are the Lorech Neuropsychiatric Hospital and a ward within St. Nahum Specialized Neurological and Psychiatric Hospital in Sofia (AI 2002: 4).

Legal Criteria

Adults are regarded to be mentally sane and responsible, unless "because of retarded intellectual development or temporary or continuous mental derangement they could not comprehend the nature or meaning of their acts or the importance of the committed act, or could not control their actions.

Article 33(2) of the modern Penal Code states that a person cannot be held criminally responsible if "that person falls into a state of deranged consciousness, as a result of which he cannot understand the nature and meaning of his actions or manage them."[7]

Burden of Proof

During the pretrial phase, the prosecutor can raise the issue of insanity (Kanev and Mitrev 2003: 8). Sometimes evaluations are requested if the defendant is already undergoing psychiatric evaluations or if evaluators are unable to come to sound conclusions and require additional time (Kanev and Mitrev 2003: 8). In these situations prior to the trial, the prosecutor is required to raise the issue in court. However, the prosecutor must also ensure that the defendant undergoes a medical evaluation in order to determine whether he or she is dangerous to society (International Helsinki Federation for Human Rights [IHF-HR] 2005). The defendant is also required to have a lawyer. During the trial, both the defense and prosecution can raise the issue of mental health (Kanev and Mitrev 2003: 8) and "the court also may, on its own motion, commence these additional proceedings" (Kanev and Mitrev 2003: 8).

Form of Verdict

The Penal Code and Penal Procedure Code use the terms "lasting mental derangement,"[8] "state of insanity,"[9] and "penal irresponsibility."[10]

Who Decides?

During pretrial proceedings, the prosecutor can request that the offender undergo a psychiatric evaluation in a mental facility for up to thirty days.[11] The first instance court makes a decision after hearing from an expert as well as the offender.[12] If the initial thirty days is not enough time to conduct the necessary evaluation, an additional thirty days can be added.[13] However, the offender's time in a mental facility is considered time in custodial detention.[14]

Prior to a trial, a judge and two assessors determine whether to place a defendant in a psychiatric hospital if the issue has been raised (Kanev and Mitrev 2003: 8). If the trial has already commenced, the residing judge renders the decision.

Role of Experts

Prior to and during a trial, forensic evaluators play a key role in assessing the mental state of a defendant, although, as Kanev and Mitrev (2003) note, both the prosecutor and defense attorney are required to participate (8). The Penal Procedure Code states that an expert opinion must be sought if there is doubt as to the offender's level of responsibility or as to "the capability of the accused or suspect to correctly perceive facts of significance in the case, in view of his/her physical or mental status, and to give reliable explanations about them."[15]

When a defendant is sent to a psychiatric hospital for treatment, a forensic psychiatric evaluation may take place (Kanev and Mitrev 2003: 8). Further, during both pretrial and trial stages, forensic psychiatrists may testify in court.

What Happens to the Defendant?

The Penal Procedure Code[16] mandates that an offender with a "psychological disability" that renders him unable to provide his own defense is required to have a defender (Grosev and Terzieva 1998).[17] In such cases, an ex officio counsel is appointed (Kanev and Mitrev 2003: 11). Penal proceedings are stopped if "after commission of the crime, the perpetrator has fallen into lasting mental derangement, which excludes responsibility."[18] If an offender is found to be in a "state of insanity" as defined in Article 33 of the Penal Code, he or she is subject to "compulsory medical measures."[19]

A defendant may be examined in a psychiatric hospital for up to thirty days, although, as already mentioned, an additional thirty days may be approved.[20] According to Bulgaria's Penal Code, "With respect to convicts with grave psychopath, or those suffering from mental derangement which does not exclude penal responsibility, medical care shall be provided as appropriate."[21]

A defendant who is not found to be penally responsible may not be punished, although if the defendant's mental capacity is restored, he or she is subject to future punishment.[22] In such cases where the defendant lacks "penal responsibility," the court can order:

a) surrender of the person to his next-of-kin, provided they assume the obligation for his treatment under supervision by psycho-neurological dispensary;
b) compulsory treatment at ordinary psycho-neurological establishment;
c) compulsory treatment at special psychiatric hospital or at special ward in ordinary psycho-neurological establishment.[23]

A court may order involuntary treatment in cases where the defendant is a threat to public safety and is a danger to any next-of-kin.[24] After a defendant has spent six months in a hospital, the court can decide whether to end, continue, or replace the involuntary treatment.[25]

Frequency of Use

In 2000, there were 6,168 psychiatric hospital beds throughout Bulgaria, half of which were in state facilities (AI 2002: 4).[26] Eleven state psychiatric hospitals provided inpatient treatment and had the capacity to house 3,075 patients. In addition, there were "twelve psychiatric dispensaries with 1,604 beds, twelve psychiatric wards in general hospitals with 593 beds and nine psychiatric clinics and centers with a total of 896 beds." Approximately 4.4 percent of all hospitalized patients in 2000 were involuntarily or compulsorily confined (AI 2002: 4).

An IHF-FR (2005) study on Bulgarian detention facilities reported that in 2003 the Karlukovo State Psychiatric Hospital had 168 inmates who were there because of involuntary treatment orders (60). There were 190 such patients the prior year and 150 in 2001 (IHF-FR 2005: 60). None of the patients who were committed under the criminal code were there for more than seven years.

Notes

1. Chapter I, Article I of Constitution.
2. See "Classification of Crime" section.
3. Penal Code, Article 54.
4. Chapter IV, Section I, Article 37 (as amended—SG, No. 50/1995).
5. The Penal and Penal Procedure Codes both use the term "compulsory."
6. See Public Health Act.
7. As amended—SG, No. 95/1975.
8. Penal Procedure Code, Article 21.
9. Penal Code, Article 33.
10. Penal Code, Article 89.
11. Penal Procedure Code, Article 155(1).
12. Penal Procedure Code, Article 155(2).
13. Penal Procedure Code, Article 155(5).
14. Penal Procedure Code, Article 155(6).
15. Penal Procedure Code, Article 117.
16. Penal Procedure Code, Article 70.
17. See Supreme Court Judgment 419-75-II.
18. Penal Procedure Code. See Articles 21(1) and 22.
19. Penal Code, Article 34.
20. Penal Procedure Code, Article 155.
21. Penal Code, Article 40(4).
22. Penal Code, Article 33.
23. Penal Code, Article 89.
24. Penal Code, Article 90(2).
25. Penal Code, Article 91(2).
26. Data provided to Amnesty International by National Health Information Centre.

References

Amnesty International (AI). 2002. "Bulgaria Far from the Eyes of Society: Systematic Discrimination against People with Mental Disabilities." AI Index: EUR 15/

005/2002. Retrieved July 1, 2005, <http://web.amnesty.org/library/index/ENGEUR 150052002>.

Bojadjieva, Julija. 1993. "Bulgaria." World Factbook of Criminal Justice Systems. Grant no. 90-BJ-CX-0002 from the Bureau of Justice Statistics to SUNY at Albany. Bureau of Justice Statistics, Department of Justice: Washington, D.C. Retrieved online July 5, 2005, <www.ojp.usdoj.gov/bjs/pub/ascii/wfbcjbul.txt>.

Central Intelligence Agency (CIA). 2005. "Bulgaria." The World Factbook. <www.odci .gov/cia/publications/factbook/geos/bu.html>.

Dolaptchieff, N. 1933. "The Criminal Law in Bulgaria." *Journal of Criminal Law and Criminology* (1931–1951) 23, no. 6 (March–April 1933): 1012–19. Retrieved from JSTOR May 17, 2005, <www.jstor.org>.

Grosev, Yonko, and Vessela Terzieva. 1998. "Access to Legal Aid for Indigent Criminal Defendants in Central and Eastern Europe, Country Report: Bulgaria." *Parker School Journal of East European Law* 5: 1–2.

International Centre for Prison Studies (ICPS). 2004. "World Prison Brief: Entire World—Prison Population Totals, Prison Brief for Bulgaria." International Centre for Prison Studies, Kings College London. Retrieved June 16, 2004, <www.kcl.ac.uk/ depsta/rel/icps/worldbrief/highest_to_lowest_rates.php>.

International Constitutional Law (ICL). 1991. "Bulgaria—Constitution." A. Tschentscher, ed. Retrieved May 11, 2005, <www.oefre.unibe.ch/law/icl/info.html>.

International Helsinki Federation for Human Rights (IHF-HR). 2005. "Places of Detention in Bulgaria." *Report from the Visit of the Delegation of Human Rights NGOs to Places of Detention in Bulgaria on 27 and 28 September 24.* Published April 2005, Sofia, Vienna. Retrieved May 12, 2005, <www.ihf-hr.org/viewbinary/viewdocument .php?doc_id=6257>.

Kanev, Krassimir, and Georgi Mitrev. 2003. "Access to Justice Country Report: Bulgaria." From *Access to Justice in Central and Easter Europe: Country Reports.* Public Interest Law Initiative/Columbia University Budapest Law Center; Bulgarian Helsinki Committee; Polish Helsinki Foundation for Human Rights. Retrieved May 12, 2005, <www.pili.org/publications/CEE%20Conference_CountryReports/PDF/ Bulgaria.pdf>; <www.pili.org/publications/CEE%20Conference_CountryReports/ country_reports.html>.

Karadjov, Ventsislav. 2001. TI Bulgaria Programme Director. "National Integrity Systems Country Study Report: Bulgaria 2001." Retrieved May 12, 2005, <http:// unpan1.un.org/intradoc/groups/public/documents/UNTC/UNPAN012403.pdf>.

Penal Code. Ministry of Justice. Retrieved May 12, 2005, <www.umt.edu/lawinsider/library/lawbyjur/bulgarpc.htm>; <http://ials.sas.ac.uk/links/Bulgaria/NK.doc>.

Penal Procedure Code. Retrieved from <http://ials.sas.ac.uk/links/Bulgaria/NPK.doc>.

SEE Security Monitor. May 12, 2005. "Bulgaria." From BBC Monitoring/BTA website, Sofia, <www.csees.net/?page=news&news_id=43391&country_id=3>.

Winslow, Robert. 2005. "Bulgaria" from *Crime and Society: A Comparative Criminology Tour of the World.* Retrieved May 24, 2005, <www-rohan.sdsu.edu/faculty/ rwinslow/index.html>.

13

Hungary

THE REPUBLIC OF HUNGARY, located in central Europe, is a parliamentary democracy with a population of 10.1 million. Hungary is bordered by Slovakia in the north, the Ukraine in the northeast, Romania in the southeast, Serbia and Montenegro in the south, Croatia and Slovenia in the southwest, and Austria to the northwest. Approximately 92 percent of the population is Hungarian and 2 percent Roma (CIA 2005). Hungarian is the official language. The majority of Hungarians are Roman Catholic (51.9 percent), while other religions that are practiced include Calvinism, Lutheranism, Greek Catholicism, and other denominations of Christianity (CIA 2005).

Until the mid-1800s, the Hungarian legal system was based on common law written in 1517. Today's criminal justice system was developed during the late 1800s. The first code of criminal law was created in1878 and the first criminal proceedings code was enacted in 1896. Prior to World War I, Hungary was part of the Austro-Hungarian Empire (CIA 2005). Hungary's legal system became socialist in 1948 and was based on two codes of criminal law from 1961 and 1978 and three codes of criminal procedure in 1951, 1962, and 1973. A new code of criminal procedure was enacted in 2003 (IHF-HR 2004).

Hungary's Constitution was enacted in 1949 but underwent revisions in 1972, 1989, and 1997 (CIA 2005). The executive branch of the Hungarian government consists of a prime minister and the Council of Ministers, which is elected by the National Assembly (CIA 2005). The National Assembly, whose members are also elected, is the legislative branch and elects judges. The most recent election was in April 2002. Hungary became a member of the North Atlantic Treaty Organisation (NATO) in 1999 and joined the European Union in 2004 (CIA 2005).

Background

The court system in Hungary consists of local courts, county courts, and the Supreme Court (Pusztai 1993). The criminal justice system categorizes offenses as either felonies or misdemeanors. An offense must be intentional to be considered a felony and must be punishable by at least two years in prison. There is no jury system today; cases are tried by judicial panels or individual judges. The death penalty was abolished in 1990. The main purpose of punishment in the Hungarian legal system is specific and general deterrence, as well as public safety.[1]

In 2005, Hungary's prison population was 16,543, a rate of 164 per 100,000 national population (ICPS 2005). Women make up 5.8 percent of the prison population. There are thirty-three correctional institutions, including national prisons, maximum/medium level prisons, medium/minimum level prisons, a juvenile correctional facility, two health institutions, and county institutions (ICPS 2005; Pusztai 1993).

Legal Criteria

To meet the legal criteria for insanity, the defendant must suffer from an "insane mental state such as lunacy, imbecility, dementia, cognitive or personality disorder which makes him unable to recognize the consequences of the act or to act in accordance with this recognition."[2]

Burden of Proof

The burden of proof is on the prosecutor to prove intention on the part of the accused. The defendant need not prove his innocence.

Form of Verdict

Defendants may be found not guilty by reason of insanity.

Who Decides?

A judge renders a decision in insanity cases.

Role of Experts

If an accused displays "directly menacing" behavior that is preventable through treatment, the "physician detecting the danger" must have the individual transferred to a hospital (Kádár et al. 2002: 20). The court must be notified within twenty-four hours by the head of the psychiatric institution. If an offender displays behavior that is not "directly menacing," the psychiatrist can order compulsory treatment through the court, which has fifteen days to make a decision (Kádár et al. 2002: 20). When a case is brought before the court—whether or not the offender is "directly" menacing—the patient, the head of the psychiatric hospital, and an independent forensic psychiatrist are heard (Kádár et al. 2002: 20).

What Happens to the Defendant?

The defendant is subjected to forced medical treatment in a closed institution, particularly in cases of "violent crimes against the person or punishable acts causing public danger." The forced medical treatment may be terminated when the need for it ceases.

Note

1. See Criminal Code (1978), section 37.
2. See Criminal Code (1978), section 24(1).

References

Central Intelligence Agency (CIA). 2005. "Hungary." The World Factbook. Retrieved June 28, 2005, <www.cia.gov/cia/publications/factbook/geos/hu.html>.

Criminal Code. 1978. Act IV of 1978 on the Criminal Code.

International Centre for Prison Studies (ICPS). 2005. "World Prison Brief: Entire World—Prison Population Totals, Prison Brief for Hungary." International Centre for Prison Studies, Kings College London. Retrieved June 16, 2004, <www.kcl.ac.uk/depsta/rel/icps/worldbrief/world_brief.html>.

International Helsinki Federation for Human Rights (IHF-HR). 2004. *Hungary.* Based on the report by the Hungarian Helsinki Committee to the IHF, *Human Rights in Hungary 2003*, February 2004. Retrieved online June 28, 2005, <www.ihf-hr.org/viewbinary/viewdocument.php?doc_id=5521>.

Kádár, András, Márta Pardavi, and Zsolt Zádori. 2002. "Access to Justice Country Report: Hungary." Hungarian Helsinki Committee, Project on Promoting Access to

Justice in Central and Eastern Europe. European Forum on Access to Justice, December 5–7, 2002, Budapest.

Pusztai, Laszlo. 1993. "Hungary." World Factbook of Criminal Justice Statistics. NCJ 199270. United States Department of Justice, Office of Justice Programs, Bureau of Justice Statistics. Retrieved online June 10, 2005, <www.ojp.usdoj.gov/bjs/pub/ascii/wfcjsbr.txt>.

14

Poland

POLAND IS LOCATED IN CENTRAL EUROPE, east of Germany and west of the Russian Republic. The Republic of Poland has a population of 39 million, of whom 98 percent are Poles. The remaining 2 percent are German, Ukrainian, Belarusian, and Lithuanian (U.S. Department of State 2004). Nearly 98 percent speak Polish, which is the national language. While 90 percent of Poles are Roman Catholic, other religions that are practiced include Eastern Orthodox, Uniate, Protestantism, and Judaism.

Following the second World War, Poland was under the control of the Soviet Union for approximately fifty years (Ciszewski and Sutula 2000: 547). Russian troops were not completely gone until 1993. In 1989, Poland had its first noncommunist government and began a transformation from a totalitarian country to a democracy (Ciszewski and Sutula 2000).

Poland held its first parliamentary elections in 1991 (Ciszewski and Sutula 2000: 547). The current Polish Constitution was approved in 1997 and provides for a president, prime minister, and parliament. Further, it emphasizes judicial review and the legislative process (U.S. Department of State 2004).

Within the Polish government, there are three branches: the executive, legislative, and judicial (U.S. Department of State 2004). The executive branch consists of a president and prime minister while the legislative branch is composed of a bicameral National Assembly with a lower and upper house. The judicial branch contains a Supreme Court, provincial and local courts, and a constitutional tribunal (U.S. Dept. of State 2004).

Poland joined the North Atlantic Treaty Organisation (NATO) in 1999 (Ciszewski and Sutula 2000: 547).

Background

Poland's current criminal code was enacted in 2003. The death penalty remained until 1998 (Ciszewski and Sutula 2000).

Sentencing remains discretionary, yet limits are found in Article 50 of the Polish Penal Code, which provides recommendations for sentences. The sentences may reflect differing purposes of sanctions, such as just desert, general deterrence and specific deterrence (Adamski 1997).

The sanctions that may be handed down by the courts include immediate imprisonment, a conditional suspension of incarceration, the limiting of liberty, fines, the death penalty (which was outlawed), and accessory penalties (Adamski 1997). The most common form of punishment is the conditionally suspended deprivation of liberty. In 1995, 54 percent of offenders received this sentence, 33 percent of whom were under probationary supervision (Adamski 1997). Fines, which were imposed upon 25 percent of all offenders, were the second most common punishment in 1995 (Adamski 1997). Fines may also be added to a sentence of deprivation of liberty and generally range from 100 to 25,000 zlotys (Adamski 1997). Nearly 17 percent of offenders in 1995 were given sentences that usually ranged from three months to fifteen years, with an average sentence of two years (Adamski 1997). Of the 32,324 individuals incarcerated, twenty-eight were given sentences of twenty-five years (Adamski 1997). The sentence of limitation of liberty was introduced in 1969 and was intended to replace short-term sentences of incarceration (Adamski 1997). In 1995, it was imposed upon 4 percent of offenders. Individuals given this sentence are not incarcerated but remain under court evaluation for up to two years (Adamski 1997). These individuals are given work assignments or may be ordered to pay up to 25 percent of their salaries.

Finally, until 1998, the death penalty could be imposed on heinous crimes, including high treason, armed robbery and terrorism (Adamski 1997). Between 1970 and 1995, 211 individuals received the death penalty. The use of capital punishment in Poland has decreased, as sentences may be commuted. The use of accessory penalties may be used to limit individuals' rights, such as those involving parenting, driving, and working (Adamski 1997).

Poland has an above average incarceration rate (Ciszewski and Sutula 2000: 548). Poland's 156 penal institutions hold approximately 79,807 inmates (including pretrial and remand prisoners) (ICPS 2004). In 2004, the prison population rate was 209 per national population. Women made up nearly 3 percent of inmates. Between 1990 and 2000, the prison population in Poland increased by 40 percent, and between 1999 and 2000, the population rose by 19 percent (Barclay and Tavares 2002: 7).

In 2000, there were approximately eight hundred "mentally disturbed criminal offenders" among Poland's forty thousand patients in psychiatric hospitals (Ciszewski and Sutula 2000: 548).

Before the Mental Health Act of 1994, but under the auspices of the Ministry of Health, "the psychiatrist at the hospital admission room" would generally make the decision to involuntarily commit an individual in a hospital (Ciszewski and Sutula 2000: 549). Article 23 of the Mental Health Act of 1994 states that involuntary commitment can only occur when an individual's "behavior to date indicates that the person poses an imminent danger to his own life or to the life or health of others" (cited in Ciszewski and Sutula 2000: 549). Article 29 also allows involuntary hospitalization of a mentally ill person if, without hospitalization, the mental illness is predicted to "cause considerable deterioration of that person's mental health," if the person could not "self-sufficiently" take care of his or her basic needs, and if treatment is believed to improve the individual's mental state (cited Ciszewski and Sutula 2000: 549). The Penal Code of 1998 and the Mental Health Act of 1994 provide guidelines for forensic psychiatry (Ciszewski and Sutula 2000: 549).

Legal Criteria

If a defendant's sanity is questionable, he or she must be appointed a defense counsel.[1] Psychiatrists who examine mentally disturbed offenders may assess whether "this insanity seriously limited or ruled out their capacity to recognize the meaning of the crime or to control their behavior" (Ciszewski and Sutula 2000: 550).

Intent must be present for a crime to be committed.[2] Article 31 of Chapter III in the 1998 Penal Code states, "Whoever, at the time of the commission of a prohibited act, was incapable of recognising its significance or controlling his conduct because of a mental disease, mental deficiency or other mental disturbance, shall not commit an offense." Furthermore, Article 31 continues to state, "If at the time of the commission of an offence the ability to recognise the significance of the act or to control one's conduct was diminished to a significant extent, the court may apply an extraordinary mitigation of the penalty."

Form of Verdict

An individual can be held "unaccountable" for their actions or have "seriously limited accountability" (Ciszewski and Sutula 2000: 550). Article 94 of the

Penal Code of 1998 also states that an offender "in a state of irresponsibility" can be sent to a psychiatric hospital.

Who Decides?

In general, judges and lay persons vote on sentences after deliberating a case (Adamski 1997). Three factors are examined in determining the appropriate sentence: evidence, science, and personal experience (Adamski 1997).

In cases of insanity where compulsory hospitalization of an "unaccountable" offender is sought, a judge renders a decision "about detention" but only after seeking the opinion of a psychologist and at least two psychiatrists (Ciszewski and Sutula 2000: 550).

Role of Experts

To involuntarily hospitalize an individual under the Mental Health Act of 1994, a court is required to seek the opinion of an expert psychiatrist other than that of the psychiatrist who initially hospitalized the patient (Ciszewski and Sutula 2000: 549). Furthermore, the Code of Criminal Procedure states, "If the determination of material facts having an essential bearing upon the resolution of the case requires some special knowledge, the court shall consult an expert or experts."[3]

If an offender is believed to have a mental illness, the court or the prosecutor may seek the expert opinions of at least two psychiatrists (Ciszewski and Sutula 2000: 550).[4] The psychiatrists may evaluate the offender on an outpatient basis or by inpatient psychiatric observation, which can last for up to six weeks,[5] to determine whether the individual is fit to participate in the legal proceedings and to determine his or her mental state at the time of the crime (Ciszewski and Sutula 2000: 550). A psychiatrist who believes an individual was insane during the commission of the crime must assess the role of the mental illness in the crime (Ciszewski and Sutula 2000: 550).

Though the court is not bound by their testimony, expert opinions are accepted within the courtroom, especially psychiatric opinions (Adamski 1997). Expert testimony may reflect the offender's "mental capabilities or potential dangerousness" (Adamski 1997).

What Happens to the Defendant?

"In cases where the defense counsel was appointed by the court because the accused had a psychological disease, his counsel is obliged to represent the client until the end of the proceedings, even if court-appointed experts have declared the accused to be in good psychological health" (Hermelinski).

Offenders considered to have limited accountability may be given less severe sanctions (Ciszewski and Sutula 2000: 550).[6] But they are sent to prison, not to a psychiatric hospital. In prison they can receive treatment. As of 2000, the psychiatric wards in six of Poland's prison hospitals held three hundred beds (Ciszewski and Sutula 2000: 552). A majority of the beds were occupied by those awaiting trial or being evaluated for the court. Other patients included those who developed mental illnesses while in prison.

If a person is declared unaccountable for their actions, they are not held responsible (Ciszewski and Sutula 2000: 550). If the offender's crime was "socially harmful" (Ciszewski and Sutula 2000: 550) and recidivism is thought to be possible, the Penal Code calls for a "protective measure," which is compulsory hospitalization, even if the individual was found unaccountable (Ciszewski and Sutula 2000: 550). Under Article 93 of the Penal Code of 1998, "the court may impose a preventive measure . . . which involves committing to a closed medical institution only when necessary to prevent repeated offending, by the perpetrator, of a prohibited act connected with mental disease, mental impairment or addiction to alcohol or other narcotic drugs." Before taking these preventive measures, a psychiatrist and psychologist must be consulted. The hospital will update the court on the individual's case every six months. The length of hospitalization is not set, but the patient can be discharged if additional hospitalization is not needed. However, for five years after discharge the person can be recommitted if the court believes that he or she will recidivate (Ciszewski and Sutula 2000: 550).

The National Psychiatric Board for Protective Measures decides which offenders should be placed in which psychiatric hospitals (Ciszewski and Sutula 2000: 552). Because the board makes decisions regarding security, it "takes responsibility for the consequences of a wrong decision" (Ciszewski and Sutula 2000: 552). An offender may be sent to a psychiatric hospital with basic security or, if believed to be dangerous, to a reinforced-security or a maximum-security hospital (Ciszewski and Sutula 2000: 551). As of 2000, the Regional Forensic Psychiatry Centre in Gostynin was Poland's only maximum-security psychiatric hospital.

Notes

1. Code of Criminal Procedure 1998, Chapter 8, Article 79.
2. Penal Code 1998, Article 8.
3. Code of Criminal Procedure 1998, Chapter 22, Article 193.
4. Code of Criminal Procedure 1998, Chapter 22, Article 202.

5. Code of Criminal Procedure 1998, Chapter 22, Article 203.
6. Penal Code, Article 31.

References

Adamski, Andrzej. 1997. "Criminal Justice Profile of Poland." Retrieved May 19, 2004, <www.law.uni.torun.pl/publikacje/aadamski/raport/>.

Barclay, Gordon, and Cynthia Tavares. 2002. "International Comparisons of Criminal Justice Statistics 2000." Issue 05/02. Retrieved June 15, 2004, <www.homeoffice.gov/uk/rds/pdfs2/hosb502.pdf>.

Ciszewski, Leszek, and Ewa Sutula. 2000. "Psychiatric Care for Mentally Disturbed Perpetrators of Criminal Acts in Poland." *International Journal of Law and Psychiatry* 23, nos. 5–6: 547–54. Retrieved online June 6, 2005, <www.sciencedirect.com>, Elsevier Sciences, Ltd.

Code of Criminal Procedure. Act of 6 June 1997. Effective 1998.

Hermelinski, Wojciech. 1998. "Access to Legal Aid for Indigent Criminal Defendants in Central and Eastern Europe, Country Report: Poland." *Parker School Journal of East European Law* 5: 1–2. Retrieved May 25, 2005, <www.pili.org/publications/jeel1998/poland.htm>.

International Centre for Prison Studies (ICPS). 2005. "World Prison Brief: Entire World—Prison Population Totals, Prison Brief for Poland." International Centre for Prison Studies, Kings College London. Retrieved May 10, 2005, <www.kcl.ac.uk/depsta/rel/icps/worldbrief/world_brief.html>.

Munro, Robin. "Judicial Psychiatry in China and Its Political Abuses." 2000. *Columbia Journal of Asian Law* 14, no. 1: 1–128. Retrieved HeinOnline July 14, 2004, <http://heinonline.org.proxyau.wrlc.org/HOL/Index?collection=fijournals>.

Penal Code. Act of June 6, 1997. Effective 1998.

Sabbatini, Renato M. E. *The History of Shock Therapy in Psychiatry*, Brain and Mind 4 (Dec. 1997–March 1998) (electronic magazine on neuroscience, found at <http://epub.org.br.cm.history_i.htm>, as of November 29, 2000).

United States Department of State. 2004. "Background Note: Poland." Washington, D.C.: U.S. Department of State. Retrieved online June 14, 2004, <www.state.gov/r/pa/ei/bgn/2875.htm>.

15

Russia

RUSSIA IS THE LARGEST COUNTRY IN the world, with an area of 17,075,200 square kilometers (6,592,800 square miles). It constitutes more than one-ninth of the world's land area and is nearly twice the size of the United States or China. It encompasses eleven time zones and stretches across two continents, from eastern Europe across northern Asia to the Pacific. Russia includes twenty-one republics, six territories know as krays; ten national areas called okrugs; forty-nine regions or oblasts; one autonomous oblast; and two cities with federal status. The population is 143.4 million, but 25 million ethnic Russians can be found throughout non-Russian republics that were once part of the former Soviet Union (Roman, Ahn-Redding, and Simon 2005). The Russian population is predominately Russian (79.8 percent) with Tartar (3.8), Ukrainian (2), Bashkir (1.2), Chuvash (1.1), and other ethnic groups (12.1) (CIA 2005). While Russian is the official spoken language, various dialects are spoken throughout its republics. Russian Orthodoxy is the main Christian faith, but Protestantism, Judaism, Roman Catholicism, and Buddhism are also practiced throughout Russia.[1]

The Russian Federation, along with fourteen other countries,[2] gained its independence after the collapse of the U.S.S.R. on August 24, 1991 (U.S. Department of State 2004; Rosenberg 2004). The Russian Constitution was passed in December 1993 and sets forth the three branches of government: the executive, judicial, and legislative (U.S. Department of State 2004). The executive branch consists of a president and prime minister. The legislative branch contains a Federal Assembly—which consists of the Federation Council and the State Duma—and the judicial branch is composed of the Constitutional

Court, Supreme Court, Supreme Court of Arbitration, and an Office of Procurator General (GSLR 2003).

The legal system in Russia is largely derived from a civil law system in which legislative acts are reviewed by the judiciary (GSLR 2003). Laws are either federal or federal constitutional, the latter of which is supreme. The main codes are the Civil Code; Code of Civil Procedure; Criminal Code; Code of Criminal Procedure; Code of Laws on Marriage, Family and Guardianship; and the Labor Code (GSLR 2003).

In 1993, a federal law entitled "On Institutions and Agencies responsible for Custodial Sentences" was adopted, as was the federal law "On the Detention in Custody of Persons suspected or accused of Criminal Offenses" in 1995 (Kalinin 2002: 6–8). Russia's criminal code became effective on January 1, 1997 (Pomorski 1996) and its correctional code became law on January 8, 1997. The Criminal Procedure Code of the Russian Federation was enacted on July 1, 2002. Aside from recognizing a presumption of innocence, it addresses changes in policies regarding search and arrest warrants, rights of the accused, prosecutorial limits, powers of defense attorneys, judicial neutrality, double jeopardy, and trial by jury.

Major laws are from the Criminal Code, the Criminal Procedure Code, Criminal Punishment Execution Code, Law on the Justice System, Law on the Militia, and Law on the Status of Judges (Nikiforov 1993). Recent changes include psychological services (Kalinin 2002: 12).

The Supreme or Higher Court of Russia is the highest court in Russia, followed by supreme courts of the republics, courts of territories and regions, and Moscow and St. Petersburg city courts. Most cases are heard at the third level which includes people's courts (Nikiforov 1993). Judges reside over civil and criminal proceedings, which are inquisitorial (GSLR 2003).

Background

Today, Russia is federative: "According to Section 71 of the Constitution of Russia, criminal and criminal-procedure law are under the exclusive jurisdiction of Federal bodies" (Nikiforov 1993).

Over 2,300 federal laws were passed within five years of Russia's joining the Council of Europe, such as the Civil Code of the Russian Federation, "On the Constitutional Court of the Russian Federation," "On the Judicial System of the Russian Federation," "On Arbitration Courts in the Russian Federation," "On the Agencies of the Judicial Community in the Russian Federation," "On State Forensic Activity in the Russian Federation," and the Arbitration Procedural Code of the Russian Federation (Kalinin 2002: 9–10). Furthermore, the administrative and institutional bodies responsible for executing punishments were transferred to the Ministry of Justice from the Ministry of the Interior in 1998 (Kalinin 2002: 10).

In 1983, the Soviet All-Union Society of Psychiatrists and Neuropathologists withdrew from the World Psychiatric Association (WPA) because of its treatment of political dissidents (Munro 2000: 3). During the 1970s and 1980s there were many dissidents in USSR's mental asylums (Human Rights Watch website; Munro 2000). Under Article 70 (anti-Soviet agitation and propaganda) or Article 190-1 (anti-state slander), political dissidents were indefinitely committed to psychiatric institutions under the Ministry of Internal Affairs (Fitzpatrick 1990: 3). Through the use of psychiatric facilities and an "unlawful criminal justice system" (Fitzpatrick 1990: 3), "troublemakers" could be indefinitely committed.

A diagnosis of "sluggish schizophrenia" was introduced in the 1930s by an American psychiatrist. This term was used and "radically developed" by Andrei Snezhnevsky, "the leading figure in Soviet psychiatry from the 1940s until his death in 1987" (Munro 2000: 19). According to Bloch:

> Characteristically, patients given this diagnosis are able to function almost normally in the social sense. The symptoms may resemble those of a neurosis or take a paranoid quality. The patient with paranoid symptoms retains some insight into his condition, but overvalues his own importance and may exhibit grandiose ideas of reforming society.... The concept of sluggish schizophrenia [thus] facilitated the application of a label of disease of the most serious kind to people whom psychiatrists in the West would regard as either normal, mildly eccentric, or at worst neurotic. In other words, it does not require much to be labeled as mad by the Snezhnevsky-trained psychiatrist. (Munro 2000: 20; see Bloch)

Other diagnoses were established and applied to political dissidents, such as paranoid psychosis, which was characterized by reformist delusions, suffering from litigation mania and overvalued/excessive religiosity, and exhibiting behaviors such as writing complaints, disseminating false information, sharing persistent ideas of reform, and showing interest in foreign fashions, art, literature, and philosophy (Munro 2000: 20; see Gluzman 1989). It is estimated that there were two hundred to three hundred political dissidents committed to psychiatric facilities prior to 1986 (Fitzpatrick 1990: 4).

In the Union of Soviet Socialist Republics (U.S.S.R.),individuals could be criminally committed following arrest after a "compulsory psychiatric examination, a determination that the defendant is not fit to stand trial for reasons of insanity, and placement by court order in a special forensic psychiatric hospital" (Fitzpatrick 1990: 5).

Under Article 9 under the "Statute on Conditions and Procedures for the Provision of Psychiatric Assistance," which went into effect on March 1, 1988:

> A person whose actions give sufficient grounds to conclude that he is suffering from a mental disorder and which disrupt social order or violate the rules of socialist community and also constitute an immediate danger to himself or others may be subjected to an initial psychiatric examination without his consent or that of his family or legal representatives, on the orders of the chief psychiatrist. (Fitzpatrick 1990: 5)

Under Article 10:

> Should doubt arise as to the mental health of a person who engages in socially dangerous activities that come under the jurisdiction of the criminal law, he must be sent for a forensic psychiatric examination in accordance with the code of criminal procedure. (Fitzpatrick 1990: 6)

In 1989, when abuses of the psychiatric system were under investigation, American psychiatrists and lawyers reported:

> According to virtually every patient and former patient questioned by the Delegation who had been hospitalized after findings of "nonimputability" [being mentally incompetent to stand trial] and "social dangerousness," the patients played no role in the criminal proceedings that resulted in their commitments. With the exception of one case, they never met with a defense attorney, even though one may have been appointed in the case. Of those interviewed on these points, only three patients reported seeing the investigative report, none reported being presented with the experts' findings, and all but one were tried *in absentia* . . . it appears that these commissions' reviews are brief [usually less than ten minutes] and *pro forma*, and do not involve independent decision making. As a practical matter, patients have no meaningful opportunity to challenge the hospital staff's decisions to retain them in the hospital. (Fitzpatrick 1990: 6)

The Delegation discovered that the prosecutor was usually the agent who ordered psychiatric investigations to justify incarceration rather than the defense who might use mental illness as a defense (Fitzpatrick 1990: 7). "Social dangerousness" is decided prior to the trial (Fritzpatrick 1990: 9). There is no "presumption of sanity" (Fritzpatrick 1990: 7).

The Delegation found and reported the following (Fitzpatrick 1990: 9–10):

- There were instances of misdiagnosis including rulings of insanity in cases of sane persons who had committed common crimes.
- Training of medical personnel is poor and psychiatric facilities are woefully inadequate.

- Soviet psychiatry is biologically based and methods such as psychoanalysis and individual and group therapy are poorly developed; emphasis is on treatment by drugs, but they are outdated and used improperly.
- Discredited theories like "creeping schizophrenia" are still widespread.
- Soviet psychiatry lacks well-disseminated ethic standards and is "punitive," that is, those who are believed to be mentally ill, or who are in fact mentally disturbed, are punished merely because they are sick. Beatings, cruelty, excessive injections of neuroleptic drugs, suspension of privileges, and other abuses are rampant.
- Although the much-publicized transfer of eleven of sixteen special psychiatric hospitals from the jurisdiction of the Ministry of Internal Affairs to that of the Ministry of Health was partially made, personnel, physical plants and practices remain unchanged. The name has been changed from "special hospital" to "strict observation hospital." Medical personnel retain their military ranks in the Ministry of Internal Affairs [MVD] and still function within a command-administration structure.
- Legal safeguards and appeals mechanisms are inadequate or not enforced, particularly in criminal commitments.

There have been many legislative changes in Russia over the past few decades. Though countries throughout the world have moved to deinstitutionalize psychiatric services, this has not happened in Russia (Ruchkin 2000). President Yeltsin approved a paper entitled "A Concept Paper for the Reorganization of the Penal System of the Ministry of the Interior of Russia" in 1996. The paper included the "introduction of individual programmes for the re-education of each prisoner based on the psychological, psychiatric and social-pedagogical diagnosis of the personality of prisoners" (Kalinin 2002: 6).

Mental health law is found in *The Law on Psychiatric Care and on Guarantees of Civil Rights During Its Provision* of 1992 (Ruchkin 2000: 555). This was the first law that moved towards a more "democratic and humanistic" form of mental health care by legally regulating psychiatry (Ruchkin 2000: 555). One of the purposes of this law was to protect society from mentally ill individuals who are dangerous (Ruchkin 2000: 556). Psychiatric care can be outpatient or inpatient (Ruchkin 2000: 556). To involuntarily hospitalize individuals, they must have a "severe mental disorder" (Ruchkin 2000: 556), and in addition, they must be a danger to themselves or others, or they must be helpless to the point that they can't care for their basic needs, or they must be in need of treatment because of a risk of harm to their health without care (Ruchkin 2000: 556–57).

Laws regarding forensic psychiatric practices are found in the Russian penal code and the "Basic Law of Russian Federation on Public Health" (Bukhanovsky and Gleyzer 2001). The following codes regulate forensic psychiatric evaluations: the Criminal Code, the Criminal-Legal Code, and the Civil-Legal Code, as well as the "Instruction for the forensic psychiatric assessment in the USSR"[3] and the "Regulation concerning the outpatient forensic psychiatric expert commission"[4]

(Ruchkin 2000: 558). The Ministry of Health Care manages the psychiatric hospitals that provide compulsory treatment under the "Temporary instruction on the order of application of compulsory and other measures of medical character towards individuals with mental disorders, who have committed publicly dangerous acts" (cited in Ruchkin 2000: 563). Correctional psychiatric hospitals, under the Corrective Labor Code of 1987, are different from the hospitals for compulsory treatment because they provide treatment to inmates (Ruchkin 2000: 563). These hospitals were under the auspices of the Ministry of Internal Affairs until the 1998 and thereafter the Ministry of Justice (Ruchkin 2000: 563).

In general, individuals who are involuntarily committed must be examined by three psychiatrists within forty-eight hours (Ruchkin 2000: 557). This commission of psychiatrists decides the disposition of the patient. If the committee feels the person should remain hospitalized on an involuntary basis, they have twenty-four hours to receive an order from the court, which, in turn, has five days to review the case (Ruchkin 2000: 557). If the court supports the decision of compulsory commitment, the individual's case is reviewed by the commission every month for six months. To prolong the hospitalization, the commission requires a court order, which can allow a one-year extension, during which the patient is examined every six months.

As of 2005, the prison population in Russia was 763,054 (including pretrial and remand prisoners) and the incarceration rate is 532 per 100,000 national population (ICPS 2005). Females make up 6 percent of Russia's prison population. There are 1,025 prisons, colonies, pretrial special isolation facilities and juvenile colonies (ICPS 2005). The prison population in Russia increased by 52 percent between 1990 and 2000, while between 1999 and 2000 it increased by 5 percent (Barclay and Tavares 2002: 7).

Legal Criteria

Under the Russian Penal Code of 1996, sanity and maturity are recognized as prerequisites for criminal responsibility. Item 21 of the Criminal Code of the Russian Federation states: "The person is not a subject for criminal liabilities if, while committing a publicly dangerous act, he/she was in a condition of criminal nonresponsibility, i.e., could not realize the actual character and public danger of the actions or to guide over them due to chronic mental disorder, temporary mental disorder, feeble-mindedness, or other unhealthy condition."

Burden of Proof

The burden of proof is on the prosecution. Any doubts or weaknesses in the prosecution's case must be construed in favor of the accused.

Form of Verdict

A defendant may be found not guilty by reason of insanity.

Who Decides?

Cases are tried either by a judge and two assessors, three judges, a jury, or a single judge (Nikiforov 1993). Jury trials for serious crimes were introduced in nine out of eighty-nine regions on an experimental basis in 1993 (Kramer 2003: 5). Individual judges may determine the outcomes in relatively minor offenses. Findings in more serious cases are determined by a majority vote of the judge and the two people's assessors. The sentence is also based on a majority vote (Nikiforov 1993).

Role of Experts

Forensic psychiatrists conduct evaluations in cases that are both criminal and civil (Bukhanovsky and Gleyzer 2001). They also provide treatment to offenders who are compulsorily hospitalized, as well as to mentally ill offenders in prison. The issue regarding competency to stand trial is not officially addressed in the penal code, but court proceedings may be temporarily halted.

In cases where the mental capacity of the offender is questioned, forensic psychiatrists are required to evaluate the individual (Ruchkin 2000: 558).[5] Generally, forensic psychiatric committees are asked by the court or coroner to make evaluations (Ruchkin 2000: 558). These committees are made up of three psychiatrists and may provide inpatient or outpatient services. Outpatient committees evaluate offenders within a single day. Opinions might be provided in criminal and civil court (Ruchkin 2000: 559–60). Inpatient committees take place within forensic psychiatric wards within psychiatric hospitals. One psychiatrist might lead the evaluation and report to the committee, who has one month to determine the "mental status and criminal responsibility of an examinee" (Ruchkin 2000: 561). Experts may be asked to determine whether the accused has a mental illness and whether he or she could control and appreciate their actions during the commission of the crime.

Forensic psychiatrists are generally not asked to determine the offender's level of dangerousness but are asked for their opinions on whether compulsory actions should be taken (Ruchkin 2000: 562–64). However, they have the legal right to be present at various stages of the proceedings if their presence can help inform their expert opinion (Bukhanovsky and Gleyzer 2001). In addition, they can "expand [on] questions posed in the initial order" if they believe it is necessary. "The expert psychiatrist is criminally responsible for the rejection or evasion of giving a conclusion in a court trial or investigation of a case" (Ruchkin 2000: 558).

What Happens to the Defendant?

If a person is found to have "reduced responsibility," the opinion is taken into consideration by the court's formulation of an appropriate punishment, and the offender may be required to undergo outpatient compulsory treatment if necessary (Ruchkin 2000: 562).

Article 21 ("Insanity") of the Criminal Code of 1996 states: "The court may impose medical treatment, as set forth in this Code, upon a person who committed a socially dangerous act while insane as contemplated in the law" (Krug 2000: 329, footnote 82).

The Criminal Code of 1997 defines "criminal nonresponsibility" for which "compulsory measures of medical character can be applied" (Ruchkin 2000: 562; Nikiforov 1993). A person who was not insane at the time of the crime but became mentally disordered and "consequently was deprived of his ability to realize the actual character and public danger of the actions or to guide over them, is not subject to punishment, as well. To such a person, as required by court, the compulsory measures of medical character can be applied, and after recovery he or she can be subjected to punishment" (Ruchkin 2000: 562).

Inpatient compulsory treatment can take place in ordinary or specialized psychiatric wards with intensive observation (Ruchkin 2000: 563). The psychiatric committee must examine an individual in inpatient compulsory treatment every six months for a year, after which they can ask for another six-month extension (Ruchkin 2000: 253). If an extension in hospitalization is given, the offender's case is reexamined annually by the court.

Notes

1. See <http://en.wikipedia.org/wiki/Russia>.
2. Other countries include Armenia, Azerbaijan, Belarus, Georgia, Kazakhstan, Kyrgyzstan, Latvia, Lithuania, Moldova, Russia, Tajikistan, Turkmenistan, Ukraine, and Uzbekistan.
3. See Ministry of Health Care of the USSR, 1970.
4. See Ministry of Health Care of the USSR, 1985.
5. See Supreme Court of Russian Federation, 1993.

References

Barclay, Gordon, and Cynthia Tavares. 2002. "International Comparisons of Criminal Justice Statistics 2000." Issue 05/02. Retrieved June 15, 2004, <www.homeoffice.gov/uk/rds/pdfs2/hosb502.pdf>.

Bloch, Sidney. 1989. "Soviet Psychiatry and Snezhnevskyism." P. 56, note 2, in *Soviet Psychiatric Abuse in the Gorbachev Era*, ed. Robert Van Voren. Amsterdam: International Association on the Political Use of Psychiatry (IAPUP).

Bukhanovsky, Alexander O., and Roman Gleyzer. 2001. "Forensic Psychiatry in the Russian Criminal Justice System." *American Academy of Psychiatry and the Law Newsletter* 25, no. 3: 14–16. Retrieved June 30, 2005, <www.emory.edu/AAPL/newsletter/N263_Russia.htm>.

Central Intelligence Agency (CIA). 2005. "Russia." The World Factbook. <www.odci.gov/cia/publications/factbook/geos/rs.html>.

Corrective-Labor Code of Russian Federation. 1987. Moscow: Juridicheskaya Literatura.

Criminal Code of Russian Federation. 1997. Moscow: Juridicheskaya Literatura.

Fitzpatrick, Catherine A. 1990. "Psychiatric Abuse in the Soviet Union" in *News from Helsinki Watch*, May: 1–22. Retrieved from Human Rights Watch website June 9, 2004, <www.hrw.org/reports/pdfs/U/USSR/USSR.905/ussr905full.pdf>.

Global Studies Law Review (GSLR). 2003. "Russian Federation, Background and Legal System." International Legal Citation Manual Project. Washington University Global Studies Law Review. Retrieved May 25, 2005, <http://law.wustl.edu/Publications/WUGSLR/Archives/2005Update/citationmanual.html>.

Gluzman, Semyon. 1989. *On Soviet Totalitarian Psychiatry* 39–44. International Association on the Political Use of Psychiatry (IAPUP).

Human Rights Watch (website). 2004. "Judicial Psychiatry in China and Its Political Abuses." New York, N.Y. Retrieved May 20, 2004, <www.hrw.org/reports/2002/china02/china00802-03.htm>.

International Centre for Prison Studies (ICPS). 2005. "World Prison Brief: Entire World—Prison Population Totals, Prison Brief for Russian Federation." International Centre for Prison Studies, Kings College London. Retrieved May 10, 2005, <www.kcl.ac.uk/depsta/rel/icps/worldbrief/world_brief.html>.

Kalinin, Yuri Ivanovich. 2002. "The Russian Penal System: Past, Present and Future." Lecture delivered at King's College, University of London, November 2002.

Kramer, Mark. 2003. "Rights and Restraints in Russia's Criminal Justice System: Preliminary Results of the New Criminal Procedural Code." *PONARS Policy Memo 289*. Harvard University. Retrieved June 14, 2004, <www.csis.org/ruseura/ponars/policymemos/pm_0289.pdf>.

Krug, Peter. 2000. "The Emerging Mental Incapacity Defense in International Criminal Law: Some Initial Questions of Implementation." *The American Journal of International Law* 94, no 2 (April): 317–35. Retrieved May 19, 2005, from ProQuest, <www.proquest.org/>.

Law on Psychiatric Care and on Guarantees of Civil Rights during its Provision. 1992. Moscow: Independent Psychiatric Association.

Ministry of Health Care of the USSR. 1985. *Regulation concerning the Out-patient Forensic Psychiatric Expert Commission (from 5 December).* Moscow: Published by author.

———. 1980. *On the Assertion of the Forms of Primary Medical Documentation in Public Health Services (order no. 1030 from 4 October).* Moscow: Published by author.

———. 1970. *Instruction for the Forensic Psychiatric Assessment in the USSR (from 27 October).* Moscow: Published by author.

Munro, Robin. "Judicial Psychiatry in China and Its Political Abuses." 2000. *Columbia Journal of Asian Law* 14, no. 1: 1–128. Retrieved July 14, 2004, from from HeinOnline, <http://heinonline.org.proxyau.wrlc.org/HOL/Index?collection=fijournals>.

Nikiforov, Ilya V. 1993. "Russia." World Factbook of Criminal Justice Statistics. Grant no. 90-BJ-CX-0002 from the Bureau of Justice Statistics to SUNY at Albany. Retrieved online June 10, 2004, <www.ojp.usdoj.gov/bjs/pub/ascii/wfbcjrus.txt>.

Pomorski, Stanislaw. 1996. "Reflections on the First Criminal Code of Post-Communist Russia." *American Journal of Comparative Law.* Review essay. On the occasion of Anatolii V. Naumov's *Rossiiskoe Ugolovnoe Pravo, Obshchaia chast'* (Russian Criminal Law. The General Part). Moscoe: Beck, 1996. Page 550. Retrieved May 19, 2004, <www.comparativelaw.org/jour-curr-4.html>.

Ribao, Renmin (People's Daily). July 14, 1964. "On Khrushchev's Phony Communism and Its World Historical Lessons" (Ninth Letter to the Soviets).

Roman, Caterina Gouvis, Heather Ahn-Redding, and Rita J. Simon. 2005. *Illicit Drug Policies, Trafficking, and Use the World Over.* Lanham, Md.: Lexington Books.

Rosenberg, Matt. 2004. "New Countries of the World." Retrieved online June 10, 2004, <http://geography.about.com/cs/countries/a/newcountries.htm>.

Ruchkin, Vladislav V. 2000. "The Forensic Psychiatric System of Russia." *International Journal of Law and Psychiatry* 23, nos. 5–6: 555–65. Retrieved online June 6, 2005, <www.sciencedirect.com>, Elsevier Sciences, Ltd.

Supreme Court of Russian Federation. 1993. "On the Forensic Practice in case of Intentional Murder (decree no. 15 of the plenum from December 22, 1992)." *Bulletin of Supreme Court of Russian Federation* 2.

U.S. Department of State. 1989. "Report of the U.S. Delegation to Assess Recent Changes in Soviet Psychiatry to Assistant Secretary of State for Human Rights and Humanitarian Affairs."

———. 2004. "Background Note: Russia." Washington, D.C.: U.S. Department of State. Retrieved online June 14, 2004, <www.state.gov/r/pa/ei/bgn/3183.htm>.

Wikipedia. 2005. "Russia" from Wikipedia, The Free Encyclopedia. Retrieved August 11, 2005, <http://en.wikipedia.org/wiki/Russia>.

Winslow, Robert. 2005. "Russia" from *Crime and Society: A Comparative Criminology Tour of the World.* Retrieved May 24, 2005, <www-rohan.sdsu.edu/faculty/rwinslow/index.html>.

Part VI
MIDDLE EAST

16

Israel

ISRAEL, ESTABLISHED IN 1948, is located on the southwestern tip of Asia, along the southwestern coast of the Mediterranean Sea. It has a population of 6.7 million inhabitants, among which 5.4 million are Jews and non-Arab Christians and 1.3 million are Arabs (U.S. Department of State 2003). Major religions that are practiced are Judaism, Islam, Christianity, and Druze. Both Hebrew and Arabic are the official languages, although Russian and English are also spoken.

The Israeli government is a parliamentary democracy that received its independence on May 14, 1948 (U.S. Department of State 2003). There is no constitution but there are separate legal systems, one being civil and the other religious, that fall within a single criminal justice system (Hooper 2004). The government consists of an executive branch, which includes a president, whose role is ceremonial, and a prime minister, a legislative branch—or Knesset—which is unicameral, and a judicial branch. The Knesset's power to pass laws exceeds that of the executive branch (GSLR 2003). The general courts are the Supreme Court, District Court, Magistrate Court, and the courts of specialized jurisdiction are the Military Tribunal, Labor Courts, and Religious Courts (GSLR 2003).

Background

Criminal law in Israel was initially found in the Mandatory Criminal Code Ordinance of 1936 (Guberman 2000). Its penal law underwent major changes in the 1950s and 1960s, during which capital punishment for murder was abolished in 1954, the Penal Law Revision of 1954 was enacted, and several penal laws[1] were amended.

Israel's legal system is adversarial and its criminal procedure falls under Criminal Procedure Law, which the Knesset adopted in 1965 (Weisman 1993; Sebba et al. 2003: 8). The criminal code is largely based on the Ottoman code and has British and American influences (Hooper 2004). In 1948, Israel became independent and adopted British Mandatory laws, which included a *M'Naghten* insanity rule. Israel's older penal code was adopted in 1977 and stated:

(18) Every person is considered sane and is considered to have been sane at the time in question, unless it has been proven to the contrary.

(19) A person shall not assume criminal responsibility for his actions or omissions if at the time of the commission he was unable, and as a result of a disease which effected his sanity or due to a defect in his intellectual capacity to understand or to know that it is forbidden to act as he acted."[2]

The Israeli Treatment of Mental Patients Law,[3] promulgated in 1991, sought to minimize restrictions imposed during treatment and created the Order for Compulsory Ambulatory Treatment (OCAT), thus allowing more patients to be treated on an outpatient basis instead of being involuntarily committed (Bar El et al. 1998: 65). To be involuntarily committed, an individual must be "suffering from an illness as a result of which their capacity for judgment or for assessment of reality is severely impaired," as well as one of the following:

1. they are likely to be an immediate physical danger to themselves or others,
2. they are likely to be a physical danger to themselves or others, but the danger does not have to be immediate,
3. they are unable or have severe difficulty taking care of their own basic needs,
4. they are the cause of the "severe mental anguish" of others and that it compromises "their orderly existence," or
5. they are "causing severe damage to property." (Bar El 1998: 65)

Israeli law has always stressed individualized attention to the offender and crime. Since the early 1990s, the lower courts have been handing down sentences that are lenient in recognition of the mental status of the offender. This has occurred despite the Supreme Court's statement that "the principle of uniform punishment, if such a thing exists, must always be secondary to the considerations which stem from the unique circumstances of the individual defendant, and to the principle of the individualization of punishment" (see Barak 1981: 203). As a result of the conflicting views of the courts, Israel passed a liberal insanity clause and a diminished capacity clause that recognizes that a mentally ill defendant can be "almost but not quite insane."

In 1994, Amendment 39 (Preliminary Part and General Part) was adopted, which essentially revised the "basic principles of criminal responsibility . . . it laid emphasis on subjective principles of culpability" (Sebba et al. 2003: 8).

A new clause was introduced to the Israeli legislature in 1995 and implemented in Israel's Penal Code in 1997 (Roe et al. 2005). Clause 300a provided for a less severe punishment in cases where the offender, who meets certain criteria, was accused of murder and would otherwise be sentenced to life in prison. The clause also defines "severe mental disorder" and "significantly restricted capacity" in determining criminal responsibility (Roe et al. 2005), thus bridging the existing gap between the legal system and the medical field.

In 2004, there were an estimated 13,602 inmates (including pretrial and remand prisoners) in Israel's twenty-four prisons (ICPS 2005). This amounted to a prison population rate of 209 per 100,000 of national population. Female prisoners made up 2.3 percent of the prison population.

Court Cases

In *Mandelbrot v. State* (1953) and *Mezan v. State* (1957), the Supreme Court declared that the insanity law at that time was too limited and decided that the defendants were not guilty by reason of insanity (NGRI) under the irresistible impulse rule. The court used medical criteria in order to make decisions on insanity and created an irresistible impulse clause, which stated:

1. At the time of the commission of the crime the defendant was unable to stop himself from behaving in the way he did
2. due to a negation or substantial reduction of his volitional capacity
3. which was resultant of a mental illness from which he was suffering at that time then
4. he will be considered inculpable and will be relieved of criminal liability.

However, in *Barazani v. State* (1958), the court ruled: "The court must use redoubled caution in applying the principle of irresistible impulse. This rule has never been passed into law and the supreme court ruling which first recognized it limited it to specific, narrowly defined cases."

In *Kesar v. State* (1985), the court ruled that the delusional disorder, paranoia, did not qualify as a legal mental disease. Patients who met the *M'Naghten* criterion could not use the insanity defense. Yet in *State v. Levi* (1991), the court also realized that the unique circumstances under which a criminal act was committed must take into account "all facets of the defendant's personality, the motives and circumstances of the crime."

Legal Criteria

Prior to 1995, the *M'Naghten* test was used to determine legal insanity. Today, however, a person is considered as not having criminal responsibility if at the time of the offense there is an illness affecting his psyche or a defect in his intellectual ability such that he is not able (1) to understand what he is doing or the wrongness or the act or (2) to refrain from doing the act.

Burden of Proof

The burden of proof is on the prosecution to prove *mens rea* or negligence.

Form of Verdict

A defendant may be found not guilty by reason of insanity.

Who Decides?

A judge renders a verdict.

Role of Experts

Clause 300a which discusses the hurdles for reduced punishment in the case of murder redefines, to an extent, the role of the medical expert in court. The psychiatric expert in his or her position as a medical expert is no longer restricted to the "psychosis test" and "level of responsibility" determination when addressing the court. As a clinician, whose major function is to diagnose and treat mental illness, the forensic psychiatrist can furnish the court with information about diagnosis, prognosis, and treatment possibilities—information that is critical for proper disposal of the mental disorder of the afflicted offender.

What Happens to the Defendant?

Sentencing takes into consideration the mental state of the offender (Hooper 2004). A mentally ill person may be incarcerated in a prison's mental health unit. Some offenders, to whom the insanity defense does not apply, may be required to carry out their prison terms and then undergo compulsory hospitalization if their mental illnesses are a danger to the public (Hooper 2004). Without the proof of negligence or mens rea, however, the individual will not be imprisoned.

Section 35a of an amendment to the Penal Code (1995) states that a mandatory sentence could be reduced because of certain circumstances. To exclude murder from Section 35a, a subsection (b) was added in which "the provisions of sub-section (a) shall not apply to the crime of murder" unless the case met the criteria for clause 300a, which stated (Roe et al. 2005):

> Not withstanding the foregoing clause 300 (which discusses the crime of murder) a more lenient punishment may be imposed in the event that the crime was committed in one of the following cases:
>
> (a) In the case where, due to severe mental disorder or deficiency in mental capacities, the defendant's ability is significantly restricted but not to the point of constituting a lack of actual ability as stated in 34H.

Again, for an individual to meet the criteria stated in 34h and therefore not be held criminally responsible, he or she must have a mental illness or defect in intellect and not be able to understand the nature of the act or refrain from committing the act.

Notes

1. See Guberman 2000. These amendments include the Penal Law Revision (Bribery) Law (1952); the Penal Law Revision (State Security) Law (1957); the Penal Law Amendment (Deceit, Blackmail, and Extortion) Law (1963); the Penal Law Amendment (Bigamy) Law (1959); the Penal Law Amendment (Prostitution) Law (1962); and the Penal Law Amendment (Prohibited Games, Lottery, and Betting) Law (1964).

2. Paragraphs 18–19.
3. Israeli Treatment of Mental Patients Law (5751-1991).

References

Barak, A. 2002. "Some Reflections on the Israeli Legal System and Its Judiciary." *Electronic Journal of Comparative Law* 6, no. 1 (April 2002). Retrieved May, <www.ejcl .org/61/art61-1.html>.

Bar El, Yair Carlos, Rimona Durst, Jonathan Rabinowitz, Moshe Kalian, Alexander Teitelbaum, and Michael Shlafman. 1998. "Implementation of Order of Compulsory Ambulatory Treatment in Jerusalem." *International Journal of Law and Psychiatry* 21, no. 1: 65–71. Retrieved online June 6, 2005, <www.sciencedirect.com>, Elsevier Sciences, Ltd.

Bazak, A. 1981. "The History of Israel's Insanity Clause." Retrieved May 18, 2004, <http://members, tripod,com/-dazc/history.htm>.

Global Studies Law Review (GSLR). 2003. "Israel, Background and Legal System." International Legal Citation Manual Project. Washington University Global Studies Law Review. Retrieved May 25, 2005, <http://law.wustl.edu/Publications/ WUGSLR/Archives/2005Update/citationmanual.html>.

Guberman, Shlomo. 2000. "The Development of the Law in Israel: The First Fifty Years." Israel Ministry of Foreign Affairs. Retrieved May 31, 2005, <www.mfa.gov.il/ mfa/history/modern%20history/israel%20at%2050/development%20of%20the%2 0law%20in%20israel-%20the%20first%2050%20yea>.

"The History of Israel's Insanity Clause." Retrieved May 18, 2004, <http://members .tripod.com/~dazc/history.htm>.

Hooper, J. F. 2004. "Israeli Forensic Psychiatry." Psychiatry and the Law, Forensic Psychiatry Resource Page. University of Alabama. Retrieved May 16, 2005, <http:// bama.ua.edu/~jhooper/israel.html>.

International Centre for Prison Studies (ICPS). 2005. "World Prison Brief: Entire World—Prison Population Totals, Prison Brief for Israel." International Centre for Prison Studies, Kings College London. Retrieved May 10, 2005, <www.kcl.ac.uk/ depsta/rel/icps/worldbrief/world_brief.html>.

Penal Law of Israel (626/1996). 1996. "Penal Law—Draft Proposal and New Code," 30 Israel Law Review 5-27. Retrieved May 20, 2004, <http://wings.buffalo.edu/law/ bclc/israeli.htm> or <http://wings.buffalo.edu/law/jlsa/resources/penal.htm>.

Roe, David, Ya'ir Ronen, Jossef Lereya, Shmuel Finnig, and Silvana Fennig. 2005. "Reduced Punishment in Israel in the Case of Murder: Bridging the Medico-legal Gap." *International Journal of Law and Psychiatry* 28, no. 3: 222–30. Retrieved online June 6, 2005, <www.sciencedirect.com>, Elsevier Sciences, Ltd.

Sebba, Leslie, Manachem Horovitz and Ruth Geva. 2003. "Criminal Justice Systems in Europe and North American: Israel." HEUNI, The European Institute for Crime Prevention and Control, affiliated with the United Nations. Helsinki, Finland: Yliopistopaino. Retrieved June 17, 2004, <www.heuni.fi/12543.htm>.

U.S. Department of State. 2003. "Background Note: Israel." Washington, D.C.: U.S. Department of State. Retrieved online June 14, 2004, <www.state.gov/r/pa/ei/bgn/3581.htm>.

Weisman, Gloria. 1993. "Israel." World Factbook of Criminal Justice Statistics. United States Department of Justice, Office of Justice Programs, Bureau of Justice Statistics. Israeli Ministry of Justice, Retrieved online June 10, 2004, <www.ojp.usdoj.gov/bjs/pub/ascii/wfcjisr.txt>.

17

Turkey

LOCATED IN SOUTHEASTERN EUROPE and southwestern Asia, Turkey borders both the Black Sea to the north and the Mediterranean Sea to the south (CIA 2005). To the east Turkey is surrounded by Georgia, Armenia, Iran, Iraq, and Syria, while to the west it borders Bulgaria and Greece. Founded in 1923 after the fall of the Ottoman Empire, Turkey is a parliamentary democracy with a population of 69.6 million (Infoplease 2004; CIA 2005). The capital, Ankara, has a population of over 3.5 million. Approximately 80 percent of the country's population is Turkish, with Kurds making up the other 20 percent, though they are not officially recognized as a minority group (Infoplease 2004). An estimated 99.8 percent of the population practices Islam, while 0.2 percent are Christian or Jewish (CIA 2005). The official language in Turkey is Turkish, although other spoken languages are Kurdish, Arabic, Greek and Armenian (CIA 2005).

Turkish history stretches back to its occupation by the Indo-European Hittites in 1900 B.C. and to the rise and fall of the Persian, Roman, Byzantine and Ottoman Empires (Infoplease 2004).

Turkey joined the United Nations in 1945 and became a member of the North Atlantic Treaty Organisation (NATO) in 1952 (CIA 2005). It is in the process of becoming a member of the European Union. The executive branch consists of a president, a prime minister who is appointed by the president, and a cabinet. The last presidential election was held in 2000. The judiciary consists of several courts, such as the Constitutional Court, the High Court of Appeals, Council of State, Court of Accounts, and the Military High Administrative Court (CIA 2005).

Background

During the fifteenth century, Mehmed the Conqueror established an asylum in Istanbul called Bimarhane-i-Ebulfeth Sultan Mehmed (Songar 2002). The first mental asylum under the Ottoman Empire, the Mosque of Sultan Bayazit II in Edime, opened in 1915. The second, the Haseki Sultan Asylum,[1] was established in Istanbul and is the first in which forensic psychiatry was practiced.

The Turkish criminal justice system is largely influenced by European models and its laws are heavily influenced by the Swiss (Library of Congress [LOC] 1995; Embassy of the Republic of Turkey [Embassy] 2002b). Until 1839, the legal system was based on Islamic Law and crimes were handled by religious courts (Embassy 2002b). In 1881, a new set of laws and regulations emerged, such as the Charter of Gulhane and the Ferman of Reforms (Embassy 2002b). The Civil Code, adopted from the Swiss, was enacted in 1926. The 1926 Criminal Code was adopted from Italy's 1899 Penal Code and the Code of Criminal Procedure of 1929 was adopted from Germany's Code of Criminal Procedure of 1877 (Embassy 2002b; Komurcu 2002). The most recent Penal Code (TCK) came into effect in June of 2005 (TurkishPress.com 2005).

Turkey's Constitution, which was adopted in 1982, recognizes that no one can be rendered guilty unless proven so in court.

Crimes are categorized as misdemeanors or felonies. Punishments for felonies may include heavy fines, strict imprisonment, ordinary imprisonment, and the death penalty, which was last used in 1984 prior to a moratorium. However, it wasn't formally abolished (during peacetime) until 2002 (BBC News 2004). Offenders ordered to strict imprisonment may be sentenced to hard labor for one year to life, whereas ordinary imprisonment may include hard labor but can only extend to twenty years. Solitary confinement is still used in cases of repeat offenders.

Offenders may be tried in criminal courts or commercial courts (LOC 1995). Penal Courts of the Peace, of which there are 840 throughout the republic, are the lowest penal courts and are resided over by one judge and have jurisdiction over penal misdemeanors recognized in the Criminal Code, the Criminal Procedure Code, and the Code on the Application of the Criminal Code (Embassy 2002b). There are nearly 900 Penal Courts of the First Instance, which handle "the essential local criminal law" (Embassy 2002b). The Central Criminal Courts have jurisdiction in cases where the sentence could be over five years of incarceration and have a "presiding judge and two members with a public prosecutor" (Embassy 2002b). Juries are not used in Turkey.

In 2004, the prison population was 67,772 (including pretrial and remand prisoners) with an incarceration rate of 95 per 100,000 national population

(ICPS 2004). There are at least 500 penal institutions throughout Turkey. The occupancy level in 2002 was 83.5 percent. Females make up 3.5 percent of the prison population.

Diminished responsibility has been used in the past by men to get reduced sentences for honor killings, although recent legal decisions have moved to ban the use of this defense (Majid 2004).

Legal Criteria

Anyone afflicted with a mental disease that causes a complete lack of conscience or freedom of action at the time of the commission of the act shall not be punished. Mentally ill criminals may he held in custody and treated.

Article 13 of the Law on the Duties and Competences of the Police was amended by the Turkish National Grand Assembly in 2002 to state: "The police shall apprehend and carry out the necessary procedures on . . . mentally disturbed persons who may pose a threat to the society for the purpose of treatment, training and rehabilitation at an institution, in accordance with the provisions of the relevant laws and the implementing regulation of this Law" (Secretariat General for European Union Affairs 2002).

Burden of Proof

The burden of proof rests with the defense.

Form of Verdict

A defendant may be found not guilty by reason of insanity.

Who Decides?

A judge renders a decision.

Role of Experts

Medical experts testify in court as to the defendant's mental state at the time he or she committed the criminal act.

What Happens to the Defendant?

A defendant who is found to be not guilty by reason of insanity can be committed to a mental institution. The defendant's release from the mental institution is made by the court on the basis of a report from the hospital board of the institution in which the defendant was a patient. The report must state that the patient has recovered and must give its opinion about whether the defendant should be examined on a regular basis to be sure that his or her symptoms have not recurred. The prosecution has the responsibility for carrying out and checking on the defendant's compliance with these requirements. Should there be signs of mental illness, the defendant must be recommitted.

Note

1. Later known as the Haseki Medical Observation Centre.

References

BBC News. 2004. "Turkey Agrees to Death Penalty Ban." BBC News World Edition. January 9, 2004. Retrieved June 30, 2005, <http://news.bbc.co.uk/go/pr/fr/ /2/hi/europe/3384667.stm>.

Central Intelligence Agency (CIA). 2005. "Turkey." The World Factbook. <www.cia.gov/cia/publications/factbook/geos/tu.html>.

Embassy of the Republic of Turkey. 2002a. "Government and Politics." Washington, D.C. Retrieved June 28, 2005, <www.turkishembassy.org/governmentpolitics/index.htm>.

———. 2002b. "The Judiciary Branch." Washington, D.C. Retrieved June 28, 2005, <www.turkishembassy.org/governmentpolitics/politicsjdcourt.htm#system>.

Gürelli, Nevzat. 1965. *The Turkish Criminal Code*. With an introduction by Nevzat Gürelli. The American Series of Foreign Penal Codes 9. South Hackensack, N.J.: Fred B. Rothman, ca. 1965. Pages xviii, 190.

Infoplease. 2004. "Turkey." *Pearson Education*. Retrieved June 25, 2004, <www.infoplease.com/ipa/A0108054.html>.

International Centre for Prison Studies (ICPS). 2005. "World Prison Brief: Entire World—Prison Population Totals, Prison Brief for Turkey." International Centre for Prison Studies, Kings College London. Retrieved May 10, 2005, <www.kcl.ac.uk/depsta/rel/icps/worldbrief/world_brief.html>.

International Constitutional Law (ICL). 2002. "Turkey Constitution." A. Tschentscher, ed. Retrieved May 11, 2005, <www.oefre.unibe.ch/law/icl/info.html>.

Library of Congress. 1995. "Turkey: Crime and Punishment." *Library of Congress Country Studies.* Washington, D.C.: Library of Congress. Retrieved June 25, 2004, <http://memory.loc.gov/frd/cs/>.

Komurcu, Mehmet. 2002. "Reforms in the Turkish Legal System: From the Islamic Legal Tradition to the Civil Law Tradition." University of Wisconsin Law School, University of Wisconsin. KOLSA Publications. Online article retrieved June 28, 2005, <http://students.law.wisc.edu/kolsa/publication.htm>.

Majid, Sa'ad Abdul. 2004. "Turkey Tightens Measures Against Honor Killings." Islam-Online.net, July 8, 2004. Retrieved online June 28, 2005, <www.islamonline.net/English/News/2004-07/08/article02.shtml>.

Prisoners Abroad. 2000. "Fact Sheet: Turkey Criminal Justice System." London. Retrieved May 9, 2005, <www.prisonersabroad.org.uk>.

Secretariat General for European Union Affairs. 2002. "Harmonization Law (3) (Law Amending Various Laws): Unofficial Translation." Retrieved online June 28, 2005, <www.byegm.gov.tr/on-sayfa/uyum/uyum-ing-3.htm>.

Songar, Ayhan. 2002. "Socio-psychiatric Institutions in Old Turks Under Islamic Tradition." Al Yusra website. Retrieved June 30, 2005, <www.positive-action.net/al-yusra/artile%20turkey.htm>.

TurkishPress.com. 2005. "New Turkish Penal Code Goes Into Effect Today." June 1, 2005. TurkishPress.com, Anatolia.com Inc. Retrieved June 28, 2005, <www.turkishpress.com/news.asp?id=43021>.

Part VII
ASIA

18

China

CHINA IS BORDERED BY THE EAST CHINA SEA, Korea Bay, Yellow Sea, and South China Sea. It is between North Korea and Viet Nam. The other border countries are Afghanistan, Bhutan, Burma, India, Kazakhstan, Kyrgyzstan, Laos, Macau, Mongolia, Nepal, Pakistan, Russia, and Tajikistan. The People's Republic of China has a population of 1.3 billion inhabitants. While 91.9 percent of the population is Han Chinese, other ethnic groups include Zhuang, Manchu, Hui, Miao, Uygur, Yi, Mongolian, Tibetan, Buyi, and Korean. China is a communist state that was established on October 1, 1949 (U.S. Department of State 2004) and is composed of provinces, autonomous regions, and municipalities (Guo et al. 1993). Officially, China is an atheist republic, although Taoism, Buddhism, Islam and Christianity are practiced. Aside from many regional dialects, the main language is Mandarin.

When the communist government devised new laws after its establishment in 1949, it annulled six laws of the Kuomintang regime: constitutional law, civil law, commercial law, criminal law, civil procedure law, and criminal procedure law (Guo et al. 1993). Thus, a new socialist legal system was formulated. In 1954, the People's Republic of China (PRC) adopted a Constitution at the National People's Congress. However, through the Cultural Revolution of 1966 to 1978, focus on legal construction waned (Guo et al. 1993). Afterwards, there was "great emphasis on the institutionalization and legislation of the socialist democracy and on the stability, continuity and authority of law" (Guo et al. 1993). Changes to the Constitution were enacted on December 4, 1982 (Guo et al. 1993).

The government consists of an executive branch, with a president, vice president, state council, and premier, while its legislative branch is a unicameral

National People's Congress. The judicial branch is the Supreme People's Court. Major PRC codes are the Criminal Code, Criminal Procedure Code, General Principles of Civil Law, Civil Procedure Code, and Contract Law (GSLR 2003).

For the first time in 1986, crime-based statistics were made public. As of 2003, China had nearly 1.55 million sentenced prisoners (including pretrial and remand prisoners) and an incarceration rate of 118 per 100,000 national population (ICPS 2005). About 4.6 percent of prisoners are female. In 2004, there were 679 penal institutions, of which 30 were for juveniles.

Background

The Chinese legal system is largely based on "the old Soviet model" in which there is a "complete network of public security bureaus" (Prisoners Abroad 2001: 1). The other three levels of criminal courts include the Highest People's Courts, the Intermediate People's Courts, and the Primary People's Courts. Members of the People's Procurate, a separate branch of the criminal justice system, are responsible for prosecution. The People's Mediation of Disputes informally handles privately prosecuted cases (Guo et al. 1993). In nonprivate prosecution, cases are initially tried by a panel of one judge and two people's representatives who decide whether the offender is guilty and what sentence is warranted.

Over the past two thousand years, there have been accounts of individuals who committed violent offenses but who were treated with leniency or pardoned because of mental illness (Munro 2000: 15). Those who were deemed mentally ill and who committed murder were often exempt from the death penalty. The defendant could, however, be given the death penalty if a victim was a grandparent or if the defendant committed serial homicides (Munro 2000: 26).

The Ch'ing government, which was in power from 1644 to 1911,

> came to grips with the problem of criminal insanity soon after the consolidation of its rule in the late seventeenth century. It initially relied on the voluntary efforts of the families and neighbors of insane persons to keep them under control, but this soon gave way to the more interventionist measure of registration and confinement, designed to isolate the insane from the rest of society. Mandatory confinement of all insane persons was soon followed by the introduction of prison sentences for insane killers. (Ng 1980, cited in Munro 2000: 15)

Family members could be punished with forty blows of a bamboo stave if they assumed legal responsibility for a mentally ill offender who subsequently committed another crime (see Bodde and Morris 1967).

In 1911, China became a republic with a new law stating that punishments for crimes committed by mentally ill individuals could be withheld or lessened (Munro 2000: 16). The first mental hospital in China was built in Guangzhou in 1898. Additional hospitals were later built in Beijing (1906), Suzhou (1929), Shanghai (1935), and in Nanjing (1947) (Munro 2000: 16). "Psychopathic hospitals" were also established, the first of which was in Guangzhou, "where opium addiction, syphilis, vagabondage and concubinage were among the more common social causes of crime-related mental illness" (Munro 2000: 16). Psychopathic Hospitals were established to provide medical treatment rather than to merely detain (Munro 2000: 17). Offenses for which individuals were committed included, according to Munro, "killing mother with an axe," "attempted suicide," "appearing naked in public," and "burning of incense" (17; see Hsu 1939).

In 1932, the Institute of Forensic Medicine was created and run by Lin Ji. Another facility, the Peiping (Beijing) Municipal Psychopathic Hospital, housed 250 criminally insane individuals among its mentally ill population in 1935 (Munro 2000: 16). Patients in this hospital stayed anywhere from one to eighteen months (Munro 2000: 17).

Post-1949 psychiatrists were highly influenced by the Soviets, who were also committing political dissidents to mental hospitals. In the 1930s, an American psychiatrist introduced the diagnosis of "sluggish schizophrenia." Andrei Snezhnevsky, "the leading figure in Soviet psychiatry from the 1940s until his death in 1987" (Munro 2000: 19), later "adopted and radically developed" this diagnosis. The Chinese also adopted this diagnosis, called "qianyinxing jing-shenfenliezheng." They also applied to political dissidents labels such as paranoid psychosis and litigious mania (Munro 2000: 22).

Chinese psychiatrists were required to read Russian forensic psychiatry textbooks starting in the 1950s. Soviet influence on the Chinese could be seen by the psychiatric diagnoses given to dissidents "who were perceived by the police as displaying a puzzling 'absence of instinct for self-preservation' when staging peaceful political protests, expressing officially banned views, pursuing legal complaints against corrupt or repressive officialdom, etc." (Munro 2000: 26).

Chinese mental patients in the 1960s were punished with insulin coma treatment and electroconvulsive shock therapy (ECT), which was developed in Europe during the 1920s and 1930s (Munro 2000: 24). Prefrontal lobotomies were also conducted from 1949 to 1955 in Tianjin, Nanjing, Shanghai, Beijing, and Xian (Munro 2000: 25). The case of Chen Lining, a critic of President Liu Shaoqi, is a prime example of the treatment afforded to political dissidents. Chen was admitted to mental hospitals seven times, during which, he reported:

> I was subjected to numerous bouts of drug interrogation, given electro-convulsive therapy more than 40 times and insulin-coma shock therapy altogether 29 times,

and was fed large quantities of chlorpromazine. They treated me like an experimental object and it was all a disguised form of physical torture. It was extremely painful, and by the end, I was left trembling and sweating all over and my memory had started to go. (Cited in Munro 2000: 31)

Wei Jingsheng was a political activist who sought democratic and humanitarian reforms. He spent seventeen years in prison and described his time spent in Qincheng Prison, and reported:

The most common form of torture is simple beating. The prisoner is summoned and surrounded by a group of men who slug and kick until he is bruised, bloody, and completely breathless. Even more common is for prisoners to be so heavily drugged that they become mentally unstable. The justification for administering these drugs is to cure "mental illness." Sometimes people are sent to the hospital for further "treatment." One person who had received the treatment recalls that after taking the medication he had talked to himself constantly for days on end. Naturally, such monologues were recorded for use during the next interrogation. Among the hospitals that participate in such practices are the Fuxing Hospital, Hospital 301, and Anding Hospital. (Cited in Munro 2000: 36; see Jingsheng 1980)

Political dissidents who were arrested were subject to the death penalty. If a prisoner was later deemed "normal," he or she could be executed. Therefore, many feigned mental illness so they would be sent to a mental hospital. One such prisoner, Mr. C, was considered insane because he had declared himself as sane, thus subjecting himself to the possibility of execution (see Human Rights Tribune 1990). To the wardens, no "sane" person would do such a thing.

In the 1990s, political dissidents were being admitted to psychiatric hospitals indefinitely (HRW 2002; Munro 2000). For example, Wang Wanxing was another political activist initially arrested in the 1970s. After his release he participated in the Tiananmen Square protest and was re-arrested. He was sent to a mental institution for criminally insane individuals and was deemed "paranoid psychotic" until 1999 (HRW 2002: 36). After his release, he attempted to share his story with international journalists and was again arrested and indefinitely placed back into in the same psychiatric institution.

While there were facilities for criminally insane offenders in the 1960s, facilities for "dangerously mentally ill offenders" were established throughout China in 1987 (HRW 2002: 40; Munro 2000). They are called Ankang (Peace and Health) and were operated by the Ministry of Public Security. Political prisoners evaluated by state forensic psychiatrists are often deemed the most serious and dangerous of the mentally ill population and are institutionalized in these Ankang facilities.

The 1979 Criminal Law stated:

> A mentally ill person who causes dangerous consequences at a time when he is unable to recognize or unable to control his own conduct is not to bear criminal responsibility; but his family or guardian shall be ordered to subject him to strict surveillance and arrange for his medical treatment. A person whose mental illness is of an intermittent nature shall bear criminal responsibility if he commits a crime during a period of mental normality. An intoxicated person who commits a crime shall bear criminal responsibility. (see HRW 2002: 97)

However, most individuals who were "aged, weak, sick and disabled or mentally ill prisoners" were set free through government amnesty in 1979 (Munro 2000: 44; see "Joint Directive" 1979 and *Jiancha Gongzuo Shouce* 1980). Approximately 4,600 were given amnesty that year, most of whom were over eighty years old, but many were still kept in solitary confinement (see Huai 1996).

This was updated in a 1997 revision of the Criminal Law, which stated that the government can force a defendant to receive medical treatment (Munro 2000: 55). Further, the law stated that offenders who commit crimes without the complete absence of control, and are therefore still held criminally responsible, may be given a mitigated punishment (Munro 2000: 55).

A 1983 textbook on forensic psychiatry, produced by the Ministry of Public Security, still retained the use of abusive practices among political dissidents (HRW 2002; also see Liu 1983). One section, titled "Manifestations of Counterrevolutionary Behavior by the Mentally Ill," reads:

> As Article 90 of the [1979] Criminal Law points out: "All acts carried out with the aim of overthrowing the political power of the dictatorship of the proletariat and the socialist system, and which endanger the People's Republic of China, are crimes of counterrevolution." (HRW 2002: 90)

However, some individuals may engage in behavior that threatens the "proletarian dictatorship and socialist state" due to psychological disorders. These types of counterrevolutionary offenders are most often marked by delusions of grandeur or persecution (HRW 2002: 90). An individual with a delusion of grandeur may believe himself to be a "leading political figure" and devise new governmental policies. For example:

> In one case, a mentally ill person proclaimed himself as a "peasant revolutionary leader" and called for a new political party to be set up in order to carry out a second revolution, and he openly drew up a manifesto and handed out leaflets. (HRW 2002: 91)

Such individuals are grandiose in the sense that they believe themselves to be of more importance than they truly are. The disordered aspect of this behavior stems from the belief that mentally healthy individuals would find such desire to be "quite unimaginable." Those with delusions of persecution may "harbor feelings of suspicion towards the Party organization, government departments and certain leading officials, may adopt all kinds of retaliatory measures against them, thereby occasioning counterrevolutionary behavior" (HRW 2002: 91). Mentally ill offenders who engage in counterrevolutionary behavior, according to the text, may have personality disorders or cognitive disorders leading them to "try to interpret and understand the present political situation [in China] from the standpoint of pure theory" (HRW 2002: 91).

The textbook also discusses specific means of identifying among the mentally disordered those who are engaging in "counterrevolutionary behavior" (HRW 2002). Such behavior, according to the textbook, is qualitatively different from individuals carrying out actual counterrevolutionary behavior. A mentally ill person engaging in such behavior is described as one with no history of political ideology that could explain his or her current behavior. Another indicator of mental illness is the "groundless" suspicion of and therefore "resentment upon the entire Party organization," for this belief is not "logical reasoning." Mentally ill political dissidents were also described in the textbook as those who openly carry out counterrevolutionary behavior without "scruples or misgivings." Often, their behavior is marked by handing out literature in public, making public speeches, or writing anonymous letters that are actually products of "mental impairment":

> For example, a person suffering from mental illness wrote a letter to all Military Regions in the country and to the Central Committee, signing his name as "Chen Zhenli" ["Chen the Truth"]; this was not his real name, but he still wrote his actual address on the envelope. After the case was cracked and he had been caught, the person was asked why he had written this anonymous letter. He replied that it was actually an open letter: he'd used the name "Chen Zhenli" because he had the truth on his side and the viewpoints he expressed were all "true." (HRW 2002: 92)

In addition:

> The most important grounds for ascertaining the commission of counterrevolutionary behavior by the mentally ill is where, necessarily, a correspondence exists between the particular manifestation of mental abnormality and the mental illness in question. A detailed investigation of the person's background and medical history may reveal additional psychiatric symptoms, and the counterrevolutionary behavior will then be seen as simply one manifestation or symptom of mental illness. (HRW 2002: 93)

A more recent textbook further distinguished paranoiacs from political dissidents (HRW 2002: 93; Long 1994).[2] Political dissidents, it claims, have specific "dissenting opinions" rather than disagreeing with everything and will intentionally select "the time, place, and audience for expressing his views" (HRW 2002: 94). Their sound opinions have "a certain capacity to spread to [literally: 'infect'] others" (HRW 2002: 94). On the other hand, those with paranoid psychosis (pianzhixing jingshenbing), or "document crazies" (wen fengzi), are described as having deficiencies in their political reasoning. They often believe that their perspectives on social problems are the correct views, yet their "political theory and their political stance are mutually contradictory; although they oppose the [government's] general line and policies, they also support Marxism-Leninism and materialism." Their beliefs are therefore not conducive to the transmission to others. The text maintains that a paranoiac will "peddle his views, without regard to time, place, or audience" (HRW 2002: 94). In addition, paranoiacs' beliefs surpass their level of "education, reading, and status" (HRW 2002: 94).

For example,

> an old retired worker with only three years of elementary school education who worked untiringly to write a "Manifesto of Scientific Communism." He bought a typewriter and printer with his own money and sent his "work" out everywhere. Neither his wife nor his children could convince him to stop. The acts and views of political dissidents are consistent with their learning and their status; moreover they generally have better sense than to pursue something in complete disregard of the [legal] consequences. (HRW 2002: 94–95)

In 1999, the Falun Gong group was targeted by the Chinese government (Munro 2000). It has been estimated that up to six hundred members of this spiritual group were admitted to mental hospitals. At least three members have died while in mental asylums.

Historically, the criminal justice system was operated by administrative officials and criminal laws reflected the current dynasty. For example, there were the Yuxing Criminal Laws of the Xia Dynasty, the Tandxing Criminal Laws of the Shang Dynasty, and later, the Daminglu Criminal Code of the Ming Dynasty (Guo et al. 1993).

China's current correctional system falls under the auspices of the Ministry of Justice (Guo et al. 1993). The Supreme People's Procuratorate is China's highest prosecutorial body (ICL 2004). Its legal system is highly Marxist and largely perceived by legislators as a social control system through which the ruling class can control the lower class (Guo et al. 1993). However, there is a checks-and-balances system bridging the public security branches, the People's Procurates, and the People's Courts to ensure the effective implementation and administration of law (Guo et al. 1993). The Fifth National People's Congress adopted the Criminal Law of the People's Republic of China and the Criminal Procedure Law of the People's Republic of China in July of

1979 (Guo et al. 1993). These new laws provided boundaries on the power of criminal judges for the first time.

Today, crimes are classified as crimes of counterrevolution (i.e., treason, espionage); crimes of endangering public security or people's well-being (i.e., arson, explosions, causing traffic accidents); crimes of undermining the socialist economic order (i.e., smuggling, illegally chopping down trees); crimes of infringing upon the rights of individuals and the democratic rights of citizens (i.e., homicide, rape); crimes of property violence (i.e., robbery, corruption, swindling); crimes of disrupting social order (i.e, gambling, hiding stolen goods); crimes of disrupting marriage and family (i.e., abandonment, bigamy, abuse); and crimes of dereliction of duty (i.e., bribery or abusing prisoners) (Guo et al. 1993; Prisoners Abroad 2001: 1). Under the Criminal Procedure Law, crimes are considered Crimes of Public Prosecution or Crimes of Private Prosecution (Prisoners Abroad 2001: 1).

In some cases, arrestees are held in administrative detention without trial for up to three years (Prisoners Abroad 2001: 1). However, the 1982 constitution states that court cases should be public and that the accused has the right to a defense (Section VII, Article 125) (ICL 2004). Penalties may range from Guanzhi (similar to probation in the United States) and Juyi (sentence served in a detention house rather than prison) to the death penalty, which is administered by shooting. There are five types of penal facilities: prisons, reform-through-labor institutions, reform houses for juveniles, Juyi houses (criminal detention), and Kanshou houses (pretrial detention facilities) (Guo et al. 1993). As of 2000, there were approximately twenty Ankang facilities in operation in China (Munro 2000).

Legal Criteria

Persons who have no capacity to take criminal responsibility are usually the mentally ill so determined and recognized through legal procedures because they are unable to recognize or control their own conduct. Persons who have limited capacity to take criminal responsibility include those who are mentally ill who have not yet completely lost their ability to recognize or control their own conduct. They may be given a lesser or mitigated punishment.

Section 75 of the Criminal Procedure Ordinance recognizes that some defendants may not be fit to plead in court. It states:

1. Where on the trial of a person the question arises (at the instance of the defence or otherwise) whether the accused person is under disability, the following provisions shall have effect.

2. The court, if having regard to the nature of the supposed disability is of the opinion that it is expedient so to do and in the interests of the accused person, may postpone consideration of the said question (hereinafter referred to as "the question of fitness to be tried") until any time up to the opening of the case for the defence, and if before the question of fitness to be tried falls to be determined the jury returned a verdict of acquittal on the count or each of the counts on which the accused person is being tried that question shall not be determined.

Chapter 3 of the 1997 Homicide Ordinance (Persons Suffering from Diminished Responsibility) reads[1]:

Where a person kills or is a party to the killing of another, he shall not be convicted of murder if he was suffering from such abnormality of mind (whether arising from a condition of arrested or retarded development of mind or any inherent causes or induced by disease or injury) as substantially impaired his mental responsibility for his acts and omissions in doing or being a party to the killing.

Under Chapter 136, section 51, of the Mental Health Ordinance (1999):

If a court or magistrate is of the opinion that any person who is charged before the court or magistrate with an offence, including a person in respect of whom any information or change for an indictable offence is being heard or has been heard . . . or who has been convicted but not sentenced of an offence being, in the case of a conviction by a magistrate, an offence punishable on summary conviction by imprisonment or an indictable offence of which the magistrate has convicted the accused summarily, may be or is alleged to be mentally incapacitated, the court or magistrate may remand such person to a mental hospital, prison, training center, or detention facility[2]: The magistrate or court may also admit the person to bail.

Burden of Proof

Under the Homicide Ordinance (1997),[3] the defendant bears the burden of proving diminished responsibility in homicide cases.[4]

Form of Verdict

The Homicide Ordinance (1997) uses the term "diminished responsibility" in section 2. The Criminal Procedure Ordinance states that a "'verdict of acquittal' does not include a special verdict that the accused person is not guilty by reason of insanity."[5] The term "under disability" as defined in the Criminal Procedure Ordinance "means under any disability such that apart from this ordinance it would amount to a bar to his being tried"[6] (see Justice Patrick Chan in *R v. Leung Tak Choi* [1995] 5 HKPLR 379).

Who Decides?

The Criminal Procedure Ordinance states that the question of fitness is determined by a jury and

a. where it falls to be determined on the arraignment of the accused person, then if the trial proceeds the accused person shall be tried by a jury other than that which determined that question;
b. where it falls to be determined at any later time it shall be determined by a separate jury or by a jury by whom the accused person is being tried, as the court may direct.[7]

Role of Experts

In 1989, the Temporary Regulations for Judicial Appraisal of the Mentally Ill set forth procedures for the provision of expert psychiatric "appraisals" in criminal, civil, and administrative courts (Munro 2000: 60). The regulations also established Psychiatric Judicial Appraisal Committees at different echelons of the government. The committees would consist of "responsible officials and experts" from "courts, procuracy, and public security, judicial administration and health departments" (Munro 2000: 61). The appraisers were charged with determining whether an offender was mentally ill when the offense was committed. They had to also specify the "specific nature" and "severity" of the mental illness and determine the level of responsibility of the defendant (Munro 2000: 61). The appraisers would evaluate the following:

> overall legal responsibility for criminal acts committed; capacity to distinguish between right and wrong actions; ability to control one's behavior and actions; capacity to stand trial (capacity for litigation); to serve a sentence or undergo other punishment; to testify or provide evidence; and (in the case of mentally ill victims of alleged sexual assault) to exercise either self-defense or sexual consent. (Munro 2000: 61)

As of 2000, the 1989 Temporary Regulations were still in place.

Under the Mental Health Ordinance, at least one of the registered medical practitioners who presents evidence to the court or magistrate should be a medical officer.[8]

What Happens to the Defendant?

If an accused person is "under disability," the proceedings are ceased. The Mental Health Ordinance (1997) states[9]:

> . . . the Chief Executive may order that a person not guilty by reason of insanity be detained in custody. . . .[10]

Under the Criminal Procedure Ordinance[11]:

1. Where—
    b. a finding is recorded that the accused person is under disability, the court shall make an order that the accused person be admitted to the Correctional Services Department Psychiatric Centre or such mental hospital as may be specified by the Governor.
2. The provisions in that behalf of the Fourth Schedule shall have effect in relation to orders for admission to the Correctional Services Department Psychiatric Centre or a medical hospital made under this section.
3. Subject to the provisions of the Fourth Schedule, if while a person is detained in a mental hospital in pursuance of an order under subsection (1)(b) the Governor, after consultation with the medical superintendent, is satisfied that the said person can properly be tried, the Governor may by order direct such person be remitted to prison or to a training center established under section 3 of the Training Centres Ordinance (Cap 280) for trial at the court where but for the order he would have been tried; and on his arrival at the prison or training center the order under subsection (1)(b) shall cease to have effect.
4. Subject to the provisions of the Fourth Schedule, if the Governor, after consultation with the Commissioner of Correctional Services, is satisfied that a person detained in the Correctional Service Department Psychiatric Centre in pursuance of an order under subsection (1)(b) can properly be tried—
    a. The Governor may by order direct that such person be detained in the custody of the Commissioner of Correctional Services for trial at the court where but for the order under subsection (1)(b) he would have to be tried; and
    b. The order under subsection (1)(b) shall cease to have effect if the Governor makes an order under paragraph (a).

Part IV of the Mental Health Ordinance of 1999 is entitled "Admission of Mentally Disordered Persons Concerned in Criminal Proceedings, Transfer of Mentally Disordered Persons Under Sentence and Remand of Mentally Incapacitated Persons." [12] Under this ordinance, a court or magistrate can admit a convicted offender to the Correctional Services Department Psychiatric Centre or hospital for a period that is no longer than the sentence the offender would have otherwise received. To do so, the court or magistrate must be presented with written or oral evidence from two medical practitioners stating:

(i)   such person is a mentally disordered person; and
(ii) the nature or degree of the mental disorder from which the person is suffering warrants his detention in the Correctional Services Department Psychiatric Centre or a mental hospital for treatment.

If a person who has been hospitalized no longer needs mental health treatment, he or she can be sent to prison for a time period that is not longer than the time set forth by the hospital order. The Criminal Procedure Ordinance states:

1(1) An order for admission to the Correctional Services Department Psychiatric Centre or to a mental hospital under section 76(1) may be sufficient authority for—
       a. in the case of admission to the Correctional Services Department Psychiatric Centre, the Commissioner of Correctional Services; or
       b. in the case of admission to a mental hospital, any person acting under the authority of the Governor,
       to take the person to whom the order relates and convey him at any time within the period of 28 days (beginning with the day on which the order was made) to the Correctional Services Department Psychiatric Centre or the mental hospital specified by the Governor.
1(2) The court by which any such order as aforesaid is made may give such directions as it thinks fit for the conveyance of a person to whom the order relates to a place of safety and his detention therein pending his admission to the Correctional Service Psychiatric Centre or the mental hospital within the said period of 28 days.
1(3) Where a person is admitted within the said period to the Correctional Services Department Psychiatric Centre or the mental hospital specified by the Governor under section 76(1), such order shall be sufficient authority for the Commissioner of Correctional Services or the medical superintendent to detain him therein in accordance with section 45 of the Mental Health Ordinance (Cap. 136) as applied by paragraph (2) of this Schedule.
2.   A person who is admitted to the Correctional Services Department Psychiatric Centre or a mental hospital in pursuance of an order under section

76(1) shall be treated for the purposes of the Mental Health Ordinance (Cap. 136) as if he had been so admitted in pursuance of a hospital order made on the day of the order under section 76(1) under section 45 of the Ordinance without an endorsement under subsection (1A) of that section.

The Homicide Ordinance (1997) section entitled "Persons Suffering from Diminished Responsibility" states: "A person who but for this section would be liable, whether as principal or as accessory, to be convicted of murder shall be liable instead to be convicted of manslaughter."[13]

Frequency of Use

It has been estimated that in 1982, 20.7 percent of murder, injuries, arson, poisoning, and explosions in an area in China was due to mental illness (see Li Tianfu et al. 1988, cited in Munro 2000: footnote 9).

Between 1978 and 1987, 386 schizophrenic offenders were evaluated in Beijing and Tianjin. Approximately 97.5 percent of these offenders were deemed "not legally responsible" for their behavior (Munro 2000: 22; see Li Congpei 1987). Of the estimated 10 million people in China who are mentally ill, it has been said that 10 to 20 percent are a danger to society (Munro 2000; see Li Congpei 1992).

Types of Offenses

In the 1970s and 1980s when political dissidents were being admitted to psychiatric hospitals, "reactionary speeches," "sticking up posters with absurd content," and "shouting reactionary slogans" (Munro 2000: 22) were among the behaviors considered to be associated with mental illness (see Xinchen 1983).

Tian et al. examined 961 forensic-psychiatric evaluations at Anding Hospital in Beijing from 1983 to 1987 (cited in Munro 2000: 96–97; see Tian et al. 1988). Approximately 32 percent of the defendants examined had an "impaired ability to recognize" their actions and 33 percent had an "impaired ability to control" their actions. Nearly 35 percent had "no impairment of legal capacity."

In 1987, the Hangzhou No. 7 People's Hospital reported:

According to this hospital's statistics, cases of antisocial political speech and action accounted for 54 percent of all cases [examined] during the year 1977;

currently, the proportion of such cases has fallen to a level of 37 percent. This shows that the present situation of stability and unity in China has resulted in a marked fall in the number of cases arising from such factors. (Munro 2000: 45; see Zhong et al. 1987)

Between the years 1973 and 1986, offenders who received forensic psychiatric evaluations at the Hangzhou No. 7 People's Hospital were examined. Among the 654 offenders who were evaluated, 103 had committed political crimes, of which "forty cases involved the making of political statements, twenty-five involved [the display or distribution of] political slogan-banners or leaflets, twenty-one cases involved acts of political propaganda; and seventeen cases involved [the writing and sending of] letters" (cited in Munro 2000: 88; see Shen et al. 1988). Of the 103 offenders who had committed political crimes, 15 percent were deemed not to have a mental illness. Those found to be mentally ill could be admitted to a hospital, whereas those without a mental illness could be criminally prosecuted. Of the one hundred political offenders who had been accused of "disturbing social order," thirteen were not deemed mentally ill. The other eighty-seven were considered not legally responsible (Munro 2000: 89).

Zhang Junxian's (1986) study of eighty-three schizophrenics who had committed crimes found that 13.3 percent of the offenses were political in nature (cited in Munro 2000: 87). Murder and injury accounted for 55.4 percent of the cases, and hooliganism and sexual offenses made up 10.8 percent of the cases. Another study from 1982 to 1989 examined 111 cases of criminal defendants who received forensic psychiatric evaluations. It was found that 39 percent of the cases involved murder, 13 percent were for rape, 13 percent were for theft, 6 percent were for arson, 14 percent were for injury, 8 percent were for writing political letters, 4 percent were for shouting political slogans, and 4 percent were for suicide (cited in Munro 2000: 88; see Zhang Xinzhi 1993).

A study of eleven schizophrenics (Zhou 1987) who had committed "antisocial acts or statements" revealed that "six involved the writing of slogan-banners in public places, three involved the shouting of slogans amidst crowds of people, and two involved the sending of openly signed letters by post" (cited in Munro 2000: 87).

Shen et al. (1988) examined 222 schizophrenics, of whom 66 (29.7 percent) had committed crimes resulting in murder or serious injury, 55 had committed political crimes, and 48 had committed social disturbances, thus amounting to 79.1 percent of all 222 cases (cited in HRW 2002: 135). This led the authors to conclude that schizophrenics posed a danger to the political and social order.

With the more recent persecution of Falun Gong followers, thousands have been arrested and subjected to judicial abuses. The following is one account of a man's experience at a mental treatment facility (see Zhou et al. 2000):

> On the afternoon of July 25, the local police and officers from the Civil Affairs Bureau asked Chen Zhong to go for interrogation. Without any due legal procedure, he was then taken to the Treatment Center for Mental Diseases in No. 102 Hospital, Changzhou, for examination. Without any attempt at disguise, they said, "If you continue to practice Falun Gong, we can make you crazy even if you are not." But he did not give in.
>
> On the afternoon of September 28, again using interrogation as an excuse, the police took Chen Zhong to the Mental Hospital of the No. 3 People's Hospital in Wujin County. He was forcibly hospitalized and made to take medicines normally used for mental patients. Chen Zhong refused to take the medicine, so they proceeded to electrocute him. They later did so again (altogether five times) and then forced him to take the medicines. This went on for more than ten days.
>
> In an audiocassette tape, he said, "I am feeling very cold as I only have a T-shirt on me. My family does not know my whereabouts. I do not have a change of clothes, nor can I shave. In fact, the hospital, which calls itself a 'humanitarian hospital,' is detaining many people who appealed to the government for various injustices they have received. This hospital is an even worse place than the [police] detention centers, with many more cruel mental and physical tortures. I am a Falun Dafa practitioner and also a law-abiding citizen. I practice 'Truthfulness, Compassion and Tolerance,' which is beneficial to both the State and society. Why am I being treated like this?" (cited in Munro 2000: 113)

A 1999 governmental publication stated:

> According to doctors at the Beijing University of Medical Science, since 1992 the number of patients with psychiatric disorders caused by practicing "Falun Gong" has increased markedly, accounting for 10.2 percent of all patients suffering from mental disorders caused by practicing various *qigong* exercises. In the first half of this year, the number rose further, accounting for 42.1 percent. (cited in Munro 2000: 114)

One claim was made that 30 percent of all mental patients in China are Falun Gong members (cited in Munro 2000: 114; see Chinese Government 1999).

Table 18.1 below lists the various crimes appraised by forensic psychiatrists in ten Chinese journals from 1976 to 1995 (Munro 2000). Interestingly, 5.52 and 2.06 percent of the appraisals made during the time periods of 1976 to 1990 and 1991 to 1995, respectively, were under the "Politics" category. Over the course of 1976 to 1995, 3.78 percent of the appraisals fell under this category.

TABLE 18.1

Forensic Psychiatric Appraisals Listed in Ten Chinese Journals by Number of Offenses and Percentages, 1976–1995

Period	Murder and Injury	Theft	Arson	Sexual Crime	Sexual Victims	Obstructing Social Order	Politics	Hooliganism	Other	Total
1976–1990	2,016 (40.9%)	617 (12.52%)	129 (2.62%)	465 (9.43%)	373 (7.57%)	591 (11.99%)	272 (5.52%)	81 (1.64%)	385 (7.81%)	4,929 (100%)
1991–1995	1,841 (36.85%)	605 (12.11%)	172 (3.44%)	612 (12.25%)	1,178 (23.58%)	331 (6.63%)	103 (2.06%)	88 (1.76%)	66 (1.32%)	4,996 (100%)
Total	3,857 (38.86%)	1,222 (12.31%)	301 (3.03%)	1,077 (10.85%)	1,551 (15.63%)	922 (9.29%)	375 (3.78%)	169 (1.70%)	451 (4.54%)	9,925 (100%)

Source: Munro 2000, table 2, page 91.

Notes

1. Cf. 1957 c. 11 s. 2 U.K.
2. Amended 46 of 1988 s. 19; 81 of 1997 s. 58.
3. Cf. 1957 c. 11 s. 2 U.K.
4. Chapter 339, section 3.
5. Section 75.
6. Sections 75 and 76.
7. Section 75.
8. Chapter 136, section 46.
9. Chapter 136, section 57.
10. Replaced 34 of 1972 s. 22. Amended 60 of 2000 s. 3.
11. Section 76.
12. Chapter 136, section 45, part IV.
13. Chapter 339, section 3. Cf. 1957 c. 11 s. 2 U.K.

References

1979 Criminal Law, Article 15.

Bodde, Derk, and Clarence Morris. 1973. *Law in Imperial China.* Philadelphia: University of Pennsylvania Press. Page 77.

Chinese Government. 1999. Falun Gong—Cult of Evil (CD-ROM).

Columbia Encyclopedia, Sixth Edition. "Ch'ing." 2001. Retrieved online July 18, 2004, <www.bartleby.com/65/ch/Ching.html>.

Global Studies Law Review (GSLR). 2003. "China, Background and Legal System." International Legal Citation Manual Project. Washington University Global Studies Law Review. Retrieved May 25, 2005, <http://law.wustl.edu/Publications/WUGSLR/Archives/2005Update/citationmanual.html>.

Guo, Jianan, Guo Xiang, Wu Zongxian, Xu Zhangrun, Peng Xiaohui, and Li Shuang-shuang. 1993. "China." World Factbook of Criminal Justice Statistics. Grant No. 90-BJ-CX-0002. United States Department of Justice, Office of Justice Programs, Bureau of Justice Statistics. Retrieved online June 14, 2004, <www.ojp.usdoj.gov/bjs/pub/ascii/wfbcjchi.txt>.

Homicide Ordinance, Chapter 339, Section 3, "Persons Suffering from Diminished Responsibility." Version Date 30/06/1997. Cf. 1957 c. 11 s. 2 U.K. Downloaded from Bilingual Laws Information System on June 16, 2004, <www.justice.gov.hk/eng/home.htm>.

HKSAR v. Leung Wai Chung. 1999. 2 HKC 471, Criminal Appeal No 85 of 1998. Downloaded from Hong Kong Cases on LexisNexis on June 9, 2004, http://web.lexis-nexis.com>.

Hsu, Francis L. K. 1939. "A Brief Report on the Police Co-operation in Connection with Mental Cases in Peiping." Pages 202–30 in R. Lyman et al., eds., *Social and Psychological Studies in Neuro-Psychiatry.* Beijing: Henri Vetch.

Huai, Lin, ed. *Jingshen Jibing Huanzhe Xingshi Zeren Nengli He Yilliao Jianhu Cuoshi* (Capacity of Mental Illness Sufferers for Criminal Responsibility and Measures for Their Medical Guardianship). Beijing: Renmin Fayuan Chubanshe. Page 67.

Human Rights Tribune 16, no. 1. 1990. "Shanghai Detention Center for the Mentally Disordered: An Interview with Mr. C." Page 5.

Human Rights Watch (HRW). 2002. "Dangerous Minds: Political Psychiatry in China Today and its Origins in the Mao Era." Human Rights Watch, Geneva Initiative on Psychiatry. Retrieved July 11, 2005, <http://hrw.org/reports/2002/china02/>.

International Centre for Prison Studies (ICPS). 2005. "World Prison Brief: Entire World—Prison Population Totals, Prison Brief for China." International Centre for Prison Studies, Kings College London. Retrieved May 9, 2005, <www.kcl.ac.uk/depsta/rel/icps/worldbrief/world_brief.html>.

International Constitutional Law (ICL). 2004. "China Constitution." A. Tschentscher, ed. Retrieved May 11, 2005, <http://www.oefre.unibe.ch/law/icl/info.html>.

Jiancha Gongzuo Shouce [A Handbook of Procuratorial Work], vol. 1. 1980. Kunming: Yunnan Sheng Renmin Jianchayuan. Pages 281–83.

Jingsheng, Wei. 1980. "A Twentieth-Century Bastille." Page 217 in James D. Seymour, ed., *The Fifth Modernization: China's Human Rights Movement, 1978–1979.* New York: Earl M. Coleman Enterprises.

"Joint Directive of the Supreme People's Court, Supreme People's Procuratorate and Ministry of Public Security Concerning the Clearing Out of Aged, Weak, Sick and Disabled or Mentally Ill Prisoners," April 16, 1979.

Li Congpei et al. 1987. "An Analysis of Forensic Psychiatric Evaluations in Cases of Schizophrenia." *Chinese Journal of Nervous and Mental Diseases* 20, no. 3: 135–38.

———, ed. 1992. *Sifa Jingshenbingxue* (Forensic Psychiatry). Beijing: Renmin Weisheng Chubanshe. Page 381.

Li Tianfu et al. 1988. *Fanzui Tongjixue* [Criminal Statistics]. Beijing: Qunzhong Chubanshe. Page 45.

Liu Anqiu, ed. 1983. *Sifa Jingshenbingxue Jichu* Zhishi (Basic Knowledge in Forensic Psychiatry). Beijing: Qunzhong Chubanshe. Pages 18–19.

Long Qingchun, ed. 1994. *Sifa Jingshen Yixue Jianding Zixun Jieda* (Consultative Questions and Answers for Forensic-Psychiatric Medical Evaluations). Beijing: Chinese University of Politics and Law Publishing House. Pages 58–59.

Mental Health Ordinance, Chapter 136, Section 45, "Powers of Court or Magistrate to Make a Hospital Order." Version Date 1/02/99. Cf. 1959 c. 72 s. 60 U.K. Downloaded from Bilingual Laws Information System on June 16, 2004, <www.justice.gov.hk/eng/home.htm>.

Mental Health Ordinance, Chapter 136, Section 46, "Requirement as to Medical Evidence." Version Date 01/01/1999. Cf. 1959 c. 72 s. 62 U.K. Downloaded from Bilingual Laws Information System on June 16, 2004, <www.justice.gov.hk/eng/home.htm>.

Mental Health Ordinance, Chapter 136, Section 51, "Remand." Version date 01/02/99. Downloaded from Bilingual Laws Information System on June 16, 2004, <www.justice.gov.hk/eng/home.htm>.

Mental Health Ordinance, Chapter 136, Section 57, "Persons Ordered to be Admitted to a Mental Hospital under Criminal Procedure Ordinances." Version date

01/07/1997. Downloaded from Bilingual Laws Information System on June 16, 2004, <www.justice.gov.hk/eng/home.htm>.

Munro, Robin. 2000. "Judicial Psychiatry in China and its Political Abuses." *Columbia Journal of Asian Law* 14, no. 1: 1–128. Retrieved July 14, 2004 from HeinOnline, <heinonline.org.proxyau.wrlc.org/HOL/Index?collection=fijournals>. Table reprinted with permission from the *Columbia Journal of Asian Law.*

Ng, Vivien W. "Ch'ing Law Concerning the Insane: An Historical Survey." *Ch'ing Shi Wen-t'i* (Problems in Ch'ing History) 4, no. 4 (December 1980): 84.

Prisoners Abroad. 2001. "Fact Sheet: China Criminal Justice System." London. Retrieved May 9, 2005, <www.prisonersabroad.org.uk>.

R v. Leung Tak Choi. 1995. 5 HKPLR 379, Criminal Case No 457 of 1995. Retrieved from Hong Kong Public Law Reports on LexisNexis on June 9, 2004, <http://web.lexis-nexis.com>/

Shen Muci, Jin Wei, Cai Jianhua, and Han Baojin. 1988. "Sifa Jingshen Yixue Jianding 654 Li Fenxi" (An Analysis of 654 Cases of Forensic-Psychiatric Medical Evaluation). *Chinese Journal of Nervous and Mental Diseases* 21, no. 3: 168.

Tian Zu'en, Yu Qingbo, Qi Wei, Wang Ping, Chen Lifeng, and Yu Tian. 1988. "Jingshenbingren de Xingshi Falu Nengli" (Criminal Legal Capacity of the Mentally Ill). *Chinese Journal of Nervous and Mental Diseases* 21, no. 3: 169–71.

United States Department of State. 2004. "Background Note: China." Washington, D.C.: U.S. Department of State. Retrieved online June 14, 2004, <www.state.gov/r/pa/ei/bgn/18902.htm>.

Xinchen Wu. 1983. "An Exploration of the Hallmarks of Criminal Behavior Among Schizophrenics." *Chinese Journal of Nervous and Mental Diseases* 16, no. 6: 135–38.

Zhang Xinzhi. 1987. "A Preliminary Analysis of 50 Cases of Crime by the Mentally Ill." Page 417 in Shou Yingde, ed., *General Theory of Criminal Investigation: Reference Materials.* Beijing.

———. 1993. "Jingshenbingren Fanzui 111 Li Qianxi" (A Preliminary Analysis of 111 Cases of Crimes by the Mentally Ill). Pages 556–61 in Zhai Jian'an, ed., *Forensic Medical Practice in China* (Zhongguo Fayi Shijian). Beijing: Police Officers' Educational Publishing House.

Zhong Xingsheng et al. 1987. "A Preliminary Analysis of 210 Cases of Forensic Psychiatric Medical Assessment." *Chinese Journal of Nervous and Mental Disease* 20, no. 3: 139–41.

Zhou Shiyu et al., eds. August 2000. "A Report on Extensive and Severe Human Rights Violations in the Suppression of Falun Gong in the People's Republic of China—August 2000 Update." *Report on Extensive and Severe Human Rights Violations in the Suppression of Falun Gong in the People's Republic of China—August 2000 Update.* Golden Lotus Press. Pages 65–82. Available at <http://hrreport.fldf.net> as of December 4, 2000.

19

India

INDIA IS LOCATED IN SOUTHERN ASIA. It is bound on the north by Afghanistan, China, Nepal and Bhutan, on the east by Bangladesh, Myanmar, and the Bay of Bengal; on the south by the Palk Strait, the Gulf of Mannar and the Indian Ocean; and on the west by the Arabian Sea and Pakistan. It is the world's seventh largest country in area. India occupies more than three million square kilometers. With more than one billion inhabitants, India ranks second only to China among the world's most populous countries. It is home to 16 percent of the world's population. India is divided into twenty-six states and six union territories.

English is spoken by as many as 5 percent of Indians, and various Dravidan languages are spoken by about 25 percent. Hindi is the language of the majority of the people. Most people in India practice Hinduism (83 percent) with Islam a distant second (11 percent). Other practiced religions include Christianity (2 percent), Sikhism (2 percent), Buddhism (0.7 percent), and Jainism (0.4 percent).

India has had a federal political system and democratic government for more than fifty years. The country is a member of the Commonwealth of Nations, an association of political entities that once gave or currently give allegiance to the British monarchy. India is a federal republic, governed under a constitution and incorporating various features of the constitutional systems of the United Kingdom, the United States, and other democracies. The powers of the government are separated into three branches: executive, legislative, and a judiciary headed by a Supreme Court. Like the United States, India is a union of states, but its federalism is slightly different. The central government has power over the states, including the power to redraw state boundaries. But the states, many of which have large populations sharing a common language, culture and history, have an identity that is in some ways more significant than that of the country as a whole.

Background

Historically, gender was significant in the evaluation of the mentally ill (Keller 2001). Failure to meet certain gender roles was considered a cause of madness among certain women, and madness among men was attributed, for example, to not being able to meet military standards (Keller 2001: 301).

Traditionally, the Indian system was designed to contain mentally ill persons rather than to provide them with treatment (Banerjee 2002). The first mental hospital is believed to have been built in Bombay in 1745 (Ganju 2000). Other eighteenth-century institutions were built in Calcutta (circa 1787) and in Bihar (1795). These institutions were created for Europeans in India during the 1700s and as such, they were restricted to soldiers fighting for the British (Ganju 2000).

In the early 1800s, mental illnesses among Europeans in India were attributed to the "tropical climate" (Banerjee 2002). Many of these patients were sent to England if their conditions did not remit within six months. An asylum in Calcutta in 1817 was reported to house "between fifty to sixty European patients with clean surroundings and a garden . . . excited patients were treated with morphine and opium, and were given hot baths and sometimes leeches were applied to suck their blood" (Sharma and Chadda 1996; cited in Ganju 2000: 395). The term "asylum" was used until 1920 when the term "mental hospital" was adopted (Ganju 2000: 395).

Several acts were passed, such as the Asylum Act of 1808, the Lunatic Care Treatment Act of 1883, the Lunatic Asylums Act of 1853, the Lunacy Act of 1858, the Lunatic Asylums Act of 1858, the Military Lunatics Act of 1877, the Lunatic Asylums Act of 1886, and the Lunatic Asylums Act of 1889. The Lunatics Removal Act was passed in 1851 but not enacted until 1891 (Banerjee 2002).

The Lunacy Act, promulgated in 1858, established guidelines for mental asylums, which were designed to hold the dangerously insane, and regulated the process of admission and treatment (Ganju 2000: 395). As set forth through the Lunacy Act of 1912, mental hospitals were placed under the auspices of Civil Surgeons rather than the Inspector General of Prisons, psychiatrists were hired as full-time officers, and mental asylums were centrally controlled (Ganju 2000: 395).

In 1987, India passed the Mental Health Act, which annulled the Indian Lunacy Act of 1912 and the Lunacy Act of 1977 (Health and Family Welfare Department). Under this new act, the mentally ill are required to be treated only in licensed private asylums (Dhanda 2005: 165).[1] This act also recognized the difference between individuals with mental retardation and those with mental illnesses for the first time (Ganju 2000: 397). Among other intentions, the Act was designed to "protect society from the presence of mentally ill persons who have become or might become a danger or nuisance to others . . . [and] to provide for legal aid to mentally ill persons at State expense in certain cases" (Ganju 397).

A descendant of the British system, the Indian criminal justice system is set forth through the Indian Penal Code and the Code of Criminal Procedure of 1973 (Library of Congress [LOC] 1995). The Penal Code was promulgated in 1953, while the original Code of Criminal Procedure dated back to 1898 (LOC 1995). Correctional administration falls under the Prisons Act of 1894, the Prisoners Act of 1900, and the Transfer of Prisoners Act of 1950 (LOC 1995). The Supreme Court is the highest court in India, under which fall eighteen high courts that have "supervisory authority over all subordinate courts within their jurisdiction" (LOC 1995). Each subordinate criminal court has executive and judicial magistrates.

Crimes in India are designated as cognizable or noncognizable and are categorized as: "crimes against the state, the armed forces, public order, the human body, and property; and crimes relating to elections, religion, marriage, and health, safety, decency, and morals" (LOC 1995). Punishments include fines and loss of property, imprisonment, imprisonment with hard labor, imprisonment for life, and death, which is carried out by hanging (LOC 1995). Children may be imprisoned with their parents.

In 2003, there were 313,635 prisoners (including pretrial and remand prisoners) in India's 1,119 penal facilities, 3 percent of whom were female (ICPS 2004, 2005). With a national population of 1,065.5 million, the prison population rate was 29 per 100,000 of national population. In 2003, the prison system was 35.5 percent over capacity. Sometimes "non-criminal lunatics" (LOC 1995) are placed in prison because mental institutions are scarce. Generally they are subject to harsher conditions than convicted inmates.

Currently, there are approximately 1,500 psychiatrists in India and 42 mental hospitals throughout the country that can hold approximately 22,000 beds (Dhanda 2005; Ganju 2000). Some hospitals hold 1,000 to 2,000 patients, while others hold 200 to 500 or even less than 100 (Ganju 2000: 399). Maharashtra contains approximately 33 percent of the hospitals. Some prisons embrace rehabilitation as a philosophy of punishment. Upper-class offenders, or those from high castes, are generally separated from lower-class inmates (LOC 1995).

Legal Criteria

The defendant must not know the nature of the act, or not know that it was wrong or illegal, due to unsoundness of the mind (Code of Criminal Procedure, Section 334).

Burden of Proof

The burden of proof rests with the defendant. There is a presumption of sanity.

Form of Verdict

A defendant may be acquitted due to unsound mind.

Who Decides?

A judge renders a verdict.

Role of Experts

According to the 1973 Code of Criminal Procedure, in a "case of accused being lunatic,"[2] a magistrate holding an inquiry may order an examination of a defendant who is suspected of being unable to aid in his defense due to an unsound mind. The defendant will be examined by a medical professional, who will then be asked to serve as a witness in court. If the defendant is found unfit to aid in his defense, as determined by a civil surgeon or medical officer, the proceedings are ceased and postponed.

What Happens to the Defendant?

The 1973 Code of Criminal Procedure states that "if at the trial of any person ... it appears to the Magistrate or Court that such person is of unsound mind and incapable of making his defence,"[3] the magistrate or court must "try the fact of such unsoundness and incapacity." Furthermore, "the trial of the fact of the unsoundness of mind and incapacity of the accused shall be deemed to be part of his trial before the Magistrate or court."[4] Those found to be unable to aid in their defense (under sections 328 and 329) may be released if they pose no danger to themselves or others and are sure to reappear in court when called upon, or they may be held in custody (section 330). The Code of Criminal Procedure states:

> If such person is detained under the provisions of sub-section (2) of Section 330, and in the case of a person detained in a jail, the Inspector General of Prisons, or, in the case of a person detained [in] a lunatic asylum, the visitors of such asylum, or any two of them shall certify that, in his or their opinion, such person is capable of making his defence, he shall be taken before the Magistrate or Court.[5]

Based on section 337, if an individual previously found unfit to aid in his defense at an inquiry or trial is later found to be of sound mind, the proceedings may continue (Code of Criminal Procedure section 331).

A person who was found to be of unsound mind who is deemed not to be a danger to himself or others, as determined by the inspector general or visitors, can be released by the state government, detained, or transferred to a public lunatic asylum.[6] If a transfer is ordered, a Commission made up of "a Judicial and two medical officers" makes "a formal inquiry into the state of mind of the person." This information is reported to the state government, which may release the individual or continue his or her detention.

If a person is acquitted of an act due to an unsound mind, "the finding shall state specifically whether he committed the act or not" (section 334) and the individual may be ordered by the Magistrate or Court to be placed in safe custody (in accordance with the Indian Lunacy Act 1912) or with relatives or close friends who must ensure that the individual will be cared for and prevented from committing further harms to himself or others and must appear as ordered by the state government (section 335). For safety reasons, section 335 also allows offenders who are acquitted due to insanity to be confined indefinitely (Dhanda 2005: 167).

Notes

1. Mental Health Act of 1987, sections 82 and 83.
2. Code of Criminal Procedure, chapter XXV, section 328.
3. Code of Criminal Procedure, section 329.
4. Code of Criminal Procedure, section 329(2).
5. Code of Criminal Procedure, section 337.
6. Code of Criminal Procedure, section 338.

References

Banerjee, Guaranga. 2002. "The Law and Mental Health: An Indian Perspective." Retrieved 11/7/04, <www.psyplexus.com/excl/lmhi/html>.

Central Intelligence Agency (CIA). 2005. "India." The World Factbook. Retrieved online June 8, 2005, <www.cia.gov/cia/publications/factbook/geos/in.html>.

Code of Criminal Procedure, 1973. Retrieved online June 9, 2005, <www.indialawinfo.com/bareacts/crpc.html>.

Dhanda, Amita. 2005. "The Right to Treatment of Persons with Psychosocial Disabilities and the Role of the Courts." *International Journal of Law and Psychiatry* 28: 155–70. Retrieved online June 6, 2005, <www.sciencedirect.com>, Elsevier Sciences, Ltd.

Ganju, Vijay. 2000. "The Mental Health System in India." *International Journal of Law and Psychiatry* 23, nos. 3–4: 393–402. Retrieved online June 6, 2005, <www.sciencedirect.com>, Elsevier Sciences, Ltd.

Health and Family Welfare Department website. "The Mental Act, 1987." Government of Tamil Nadu. Accessed June 8, 2005, <www.tnhealth.org/mha.htm>.

Indian Bare Acts, Code of Criminal Procedure, 1973. Chapter XXV, Provisions as to Accused Persons of Unsound Mind. Retrieved online July 14, 2004, <www.helplinelaw.com/bareact/index.php?dsp=code-criminal-pro>.

International Centre for Prison Studies (ICPS). 2004. "World Prison Brief: Entire World—Prison Population Totals, Prison Brief for India." International Centre for Prison Studies, Kings College London. Retrieved June 16, 2004, <www.kcl.ac.uk/depsta/rel/icps/worldbrief/highest_to_lowest_rates.php>.

———. 2005. "World Prison Brief: Entire World—Prison Population Totals, Prison Brief for India." International Centre for Prison Studies, Kings College London. Retrieved May 10, 2005, <www.kcl.ac.uk/depsta/rel/icps/worldbrief/world_brief.html>.

Keller, Richard. 2001. "Madness and Colonization: Psychiatry in the British and French Empires, 1800–1962." *Journal of Social History* 35, no. 2: 295–326. Retrieved from Project Muse website July 14, 2004, <http://must.jhu.edu.proxyau.wrlc.org>.

Library of Congress (LOC). 1995. "A Country Study: India." *Library of Congress Country Studies.* Washington, D.C.: Library of Congress. Retrieved June 8, 2005, <http://lcweb2.loc.gov/frd/cs/intoc.html>.

"The Mental Health Act, 1987." May 22, 1987. Retrieved 7/15/04, <www.indianngos.com/issue/disability/overall/legal/acts3a.html>.

Sharma, S., and R. K. Chadda. 1996. *Mental Hospitals in India: Current Status and Role in Mental Health Care.* Delhi, India: Institute of Human and Allied Sciences.

20

Japan

JAPAN IS AN ARCHIPELAGO IN EAST ASIA, located in the North Pacific Ocean off the coast of Asia. Japan, with a population of 127.4 million, is composed of four main islands, Honshu, Hokkaido, Kyushu, and Shikoku, in addition to more than thirty thousand smaller ones. Ethnic Japanese account for 99 percent of the population while the remaining 1 percent includes Koreans, Chinese, Brazilians, and Filipinos. Japanese, the official language of Japan, has a number of regional dialects that at times are incomprehensible to speakers of other dialects. Ainu is Japan's only other indigenous language. Korean and Chinese residents of Japan usually speak Japanese as their first language. Many Japanese study foreign languages, most commonly English.

Japan is a primarily secular society in which religion is not a central factor in most people's daily lives. Yet, certain religious practices help define the society. Most Japanese people profess at least some religious affiliation. The dominant religions are Buddhism and Shintoism, a religion that originated in Japan. There is a small Christian minority (1 percent). Today, about two-thirds of Japan's Christians are Protestants, and about one-third are Roman Catholics. Small communities of other faiths are present in Japan as well.

Japan's older Meiji Constitution of 1889 was replaced in 1947. Today, Japan is a parliamentary democracy with a prime minister and a cabinet whose members are appointed by the prime minister. An emperor acts as the formal head of state, although his official status under the Constitution is the "symbol" of the Japanese nation and its people. Japan is a unitary state, in which the authority of the central government is superior to that of the country's prefectural governments. The legislature is a bicameral Diet with a House of Councillors and a

House of Representatives. The judicial branch consists of a Supreme Court. But Japan's forty-seven prefectures and several thousand city, town, and village governments enjoy a significant degree of autonomy over local affairs.

Background

Japan's first publicized set of legal codes, modeled after the French system, were published in the Penal Code of 1880 and the Code of Criminal Instruction of 1880 (Library of Congress [LOC] 1994). In 1907 the Penal Code was revised and heavily influenced by the German legal system. The 1907 code was replaced in 1947 with few changes (LOC 1994). The criminal justice system falls under the jurisdiction of the Ministry of Justice. All judicial power rests in the Supreme Court and inferior courts, as stated in Article 79 of the Japanese Constitution (United Nations Asian and Far East Institute [UNAFEI] 2004: 6). The national judicial system is broken down into five types of courts: Supreme Court, High Court, District Court, Family Court, and Summary Court (UNAFEI: 6). Correctional services fall under the auspices of the Correction Bureau of the Ministry of Justice.

The 1948 Code of Criminal Procedure (CCP) and the Rules of Criminal Procedure of 1949 govern Japanese criminal procedures (UNAFEI 2004: 16). Under the CCP, the accused are afforded various rights (LOC 1994). The Constitution also provides many safeguards for suspects' rights. For example, Article 34 states that "no person shall be detained or confined without being at once informed of the charge against him or without the immediate privilege of counsel" (UNAFEI 2004: 16). Furthermore, a suspect cannot be convicted if there is reasonable doubt. Arrestees are not guaranteed a defense attorney until they are indicted, after which those with limited financial means are appointed a defense lawyer by the court (Prisoners Abroad 2004: 1). Offenders are prosecuted by public prosecutors and defended by a defense attorney (Prisoners Abroad 2004). Trials are public and the court's findings and sentences are rendered at the same time. However, there are no jury trials in Japan (Prisoners Abroad 2004). A panel of three judges decides the outcome of a case (Prisoners Abroad: 2). If there is a reasonable doubt among the panel that the offender is guilty, they must deliver a verdict of innocent. In such cases, the defendants are compensated for the time for which they were detained (Prisoners Abroad: 2).

Modern psychiatry in Japan can be traced back to the mid-1800s (Nakatani 2000). As early as 1880, criminal law set forth that a person who could not be held criminally responsible, and who therefore could not be punished, is one who "was unable to discriminate right and wrong because of loss of mental capacity at the time of committing the crime" (Nakatani 2000: 594).

In 1990, the Law for the Custody of Insane Persons, the first law for the mentally ill, was enacted (Nakatani 2000). The law addressed custody issues (most people with mental illnesses lived at home) and set in place administrative regulations (Nakatani 2000). At that time, half of Japan's psychiatrists were in Tokyo where the country's only public mental institution was located. In 1900, there were 2,000 psychiatric beds in Japan (Nakatani 2000). Attempts were made through the Mental Health Law of 1919 to increase the number of mental hospitals, but due to financial constrictions related to the recent war this was not actualized. However, the number of private hospitals did increase (Nakatani 2000).

The Mental Hygiene Law of 1950 replaced the Law for the Custody for Insane Persons of 1900. This new law mandated that each prefectural government construct mental hospitals, legally define mental disorders, create the Mental Hygiene Committee, and initiate community mental health treatment (Nakatani 2000).

In 1961, a draft of a revision to the criminal law was drawn up by the Council for Legislation (Nakatani 2000). The council addressed ways to deal with mentally ill offenders by focusing less on public security and more on treatment (Nakatani 2000: 595). They proposed that for treatment to take place there must be evidence of a psychological disorder, a crime must have been committed that would normally be punished with imprisonment, and there must be evidence suggesting that hospitalizing the offender would be in the best interest of public safety. In such cases, the individual could only be institutionalized for a year, and this period could only be renewed once for one year. While the number of hospital beds increased in the 1950s and 1960s, so too did the number of involuntary admissions ordered by prefectural governors (Nakatani 2000). In 1997, there were 359,778 public and private hospital beds available, and 336,475 people were actually hospitalized (Nakatani 2000: 593).

The Mental Health Law of 1988 focused on assisting mentally ill patients rather than incapacitating them. This was later replaced by the Mental Health and Welfare Law of 1995 (Nakatani 2000). The purpose of the current law is to increase the mental health of individuals and all of society. The goal is to medically treat and rehabilitate mentally ill individuals and provide ways to assist them. The law guides the selection of physicians under the auspices of the Minister of Health and Welfare, establishes guidelines for liability in cases of domestic care, and sets forth different forms of commitment (e.g., voluntary). The prefectural governor must order involuntary admissions if two or more physicians deem it necessary due to likely self-injury. A medical examination can be instigated by a police officer, prosecutor, head of the probation office or of a correctional institute, or the superintendent of a mental hospital (Nakatani 2000: 593).

The Japanese Civil Liberties Union (JCLU) indicates that due to several recent crimes committed by individuals with histories of mental illness, the public is becoming less forgiving of mentally ill offenders (2002). Much of this public opinion stems from the sensationalization of certain crimes. In 2002, the "Law Concerning Medical Treatment and Observation of People Who Have Committed Grave Acts Against Others While in a State of Insanity" (a.k.a. "The New Law") was drafted, and in 2003 it was adopted (JCLU 2002). The New Law states that offenders who were mentally ill at the time of the offense can be hospitalized for an indefinite period of time (JCLU 2002). This law has been met with criticism and concern. According to Kitamura (JCLU 2002), the New Law is intended to apply to criminally insane individuals who commit crimes such as arson, rape, homicide, homicide with consent, injury, robbery, and forcible indecency.

On July 10, 2003, the House of Representatives passed the Act for Observation of Insane Persons Charged with Offences Bill (Semba 2003). According to Semba (2003), president of the National Association of Psychiatric Hospitals, "this is the first legislation to deal with persons found not guilty by reason of insanity." At the time during which the bill was passed, facilities did not exist that were capable of housing dangerous patients.

In 1970, there were over 1,700,000 penal code offenders (UNAFEI 2004: 14). By 1998, the figure had decreased to 1,006,804. In the same year, the number of reported penal code offenses were: 1,388 homicide, 3,425 robbery, 1,789,049 larceny, 65,380 embezzlement, 48,279 fraud, and 656,721 traffic professional negligence. In 1998, the Public Prosecutors Office reported 1,068,427 penal code offenses. The most common penal code violation was "professional negligence causing injury/death" (70.6 percent). Other categories included larceny (15.1 percent), bodily injury (3.7), embezzlement/breach of trust (3.9), fraud (1.1), intrusion upon habitation (0.53), indecency through compulsion/rape (0.36), gambling (0.36), and homicide (0.13). There were an additional 1,496,802 special law offenses, which were categorized as: violations of stimulant drug control law; road traffic law violations; and others.

Between 1998 and 2000, there were 440 homicides in Japan's capital city of Tokyo (Barclay and Tavares 2002: 4). Since 1975, the number of reported penal code offenses has continually risen, reaching 2,690,267 in 1998 (UNAFEI 2004: 13). Nearly 66 percent of reported penal code offenses in 1998 were larceny. Approximately 90 percent of the penal code offenses over a decade were for larceny, traffic, and professional negligence (UNAFEI 2004: 14).

The Correction Bureau administers prisons, juvenile facilities, houses of detention, juvenile training schools, women's guidance homes, and juvenile classification homes. In 2004, Japan's 189 prisons, juvenile prisons, and detention houses held 73,734 inmates (including prerial and remand inmates), of whom 5.8 percent were female (ICPS 2005). There are eight juvenile prisons, which hold offenders up to twenty-six years old, six women's prisons, and five medical prisons (UNAFEI 2004: 9). Based on the 2004 national population, the prison population rate was 58 per 100,000 of national population (ICPS 2005). Between 1990 and 2000 the prison population increased in Japan by 24 percent, and between 1999 and 2000 it increased by 9 percent (Barclay and Tavares 2002: 7).

The main sentences handed down to convicted offenders are: "death; imprisonment with or without labor for life or for a predetermined term; fine; penal detention; and minor fine (Penal Code Article 9)" (UNAFEI 2004: 27). In 1998, 70.1 percent of those sentenced to incarceration were given terms of one year to less than three years (UNAFEI 2004: 28). Only 0.3 percent were given prison terms of more than ten years to twenty years. Forty-seven life sentences and seven capital punishment sentences were handed down in the same year. Most offenders are given community-based sentences, thus preventing the crowding of Japan's penal system. By the end of 1998, there were 52,715 inmates in all of Japan's penal institutions, which amounts to only 82.9 percent of the system's total capacity (UNAFEI 2004: 34). Incarceration in Japan falls under public safety, retributive, and rehabilitation philosophies of punishment.

Legal Criteria

"Penal law only attaches blame to an individual who can understand, feel in an intuitive sense, observe the socioethical norms on which penal law is based, and have the mental ability to distinguish between right and wrong concerning their concrete acts and to regulate their conduct according to the differentiation." (Nakastone 2000).

In addressing criminal responsibility, Article 39 (enacted 1907 and influenced by German code) states: "an incompetent person shall not be punished; a person with diminished competence shall be given a mitigation of punishment." However, there were no guidelines for people acquitted due to insanity (Nakatani 2000: 594). As stated by Nakatani (2000), "Japan is unique in having no specialized legal provision for mentally ill criminal offenders" (593).

Burden of Proof

The prosecutor bears the persuasive burden of proof for the existence of all requirements of the crime.

Form of Verdict

Offenders can be found to be criminally irresponsible or to have diminished responsibility (Nakatani 2000).

Who Decides?

A judge determines the verdict.

Role of Experts

Article 24 of the Law related to Mental Health and Welfare of the Person with Mental Disorder[1] requires the police to notify the prefectural governor if an individual is a danger to himself or others due to a mental disorder (Shiraishi et al.: 10). Under Articles 25-2 and 26, public prosecutors, the head of a probation office, the head of a correctional institution, and administrators of psychiatric hospitals are also required to notify the prefectural government of situations involving mentally disordered individuals (Shiraishi et al.: 10). The prefectural governor then appoints a Designated Physician to examine the individual (Article 27). The prefectural governor can order involuntary admission if two or more of the designated physicians agree that the person is likely to hurt himself (Nakatani 2000: 594; Satsumi, Inada, and Yamauchi 1998). Experts can be retained by the prosecution, defense, or by the court (Satsumi and Oda 1995).

What Happens to the Defendant?

The Mental Health Law states in Article 25:

> When a public prosecutor decides not to prosecute a suspect or a defendant who is mentally disordered or is suspected of mental disorder, if the judgment of a court is irrevocably established (excluding those of imprisonment with or without forced labor, or penal detention, without suspension of execution of the sentence), or if it is deemed particularly necessary, he/she shall immediately notify the same to the prefectural governor.

Offenders acquitted due to insanity are treated like any other involuntarily committed patient and handled in accordance with the Mental Health and Welfare Law (Nakatani 2000: 593). At this point, the criminal court is no longer involved. Those found guilty may receive treatment in prison. Generally, simple pretrial evaluations are conducted in order to identify mentally ill offenders before trials. More extensive evaluations are given in difficult cases or "to support or contest judges' decisions concerning the responsibility of the mentally ill offender" (Satsumi, Inada, and Yamauchi 1998: 198).

After the case has been filed, a judge will order the offender to undergo psychiatric evaluation at a hospital to determine whether the individual is criminally insane (JCLU 2002). The findings are examined by a judge and a mental health examiner. The court may then decide whether the defendant who has committed serious crimes or who has deficient mental capacities should be hospitalized or simply required to make regular hospital visits. Thus, mentally ill offenders may be ordered to undergo inpatient or outpatient treatment (JCLU 2002). If the individual is not deemed to be a danger to the public, then the court may not order treatment.

If hospitalized, defendants are sent to special units at public hospitals meeting standards established by the Ministry of Health, Labor and Welfare. The hospitals make status reports every six months and the panels (composed of judges and psychiatrists) decide whether to continue hospitalization or to discharge the defendant. If a panel orders discharge, the defendant is required to report to a similar hospital unit for regular checks by the doctor for a three year period. After that, the court is empowered to decide how to continue and may order the defendant to undergo treatment for another two years (JCLU 2002).

Under the Ministry of Health's draft guidelines, mentally ill offenders who were acquitted of murder or arson or who were never indicted or who received lighter sentences will be subject to compulsory treatment (*The Japan Times* 2004). These individuals would undergo a three-stage treatment process, the first of which is a three-month "acute" phase, followed by a nine-month period of "recovery," and finally, a six-month period to prepare for reintegration. Ultimately, patients are expected to be released within eighteen months of their admission.

Article 39 of Japan's Penal Code states that "an act if committed by an insane shall not be punished. Penalty may be reduced for an act of a quasi-insane person" (FIDH 2003). If a person is not believed to be harmful to self or others, he or she can no longer be involuntarily committed. This is usually determined by the leading doctor in each case (Nakatani 2000).

Frequency of Use

Involuntarily committed patients as a percentage of total patient population decreased from 15 percent in 1980 to 1 percent (3247) in 2000 (Semba 2003).

In 2003, approximately 1100 offenders were patients in psychiatric hospitals, 600 of whom were ordered there by the court (Semba 2003).

According to Inada et al. (1995), approximately 0.01 to 0.12 percent of criminal offenders handled by the Tokyo District Public Prosecutor's office are placed on "Pre-Prosecution Psychiatric Justice," or PPPJ (223). Inada et al. reviewed 1,245,352 criminal cases that were handled by the Tokyo District Public Prosecutor's Office from 1987 to 1991. Approximately 0.1 percent (1,361) of cases were put on PPPJ. Of the cases put on PPPJ, 91 percent were male. The average age was thirty-eight. A majority of the individuals were diagnosed with schizophrenic psychoses. The offenses with which they were charged were distributed as follows: larceny (26.2 percent), injury/violence (18.3 percent), homicide (6.6 percent), house intrusion (6.0 percent), burglar (5.1 percent), arson (5.0 percent), swindling (5.0 percent), property damage (3.9 percent), threat (1.5 percent), and other criminal offenses (5.4 percent). Charges of offenses of "specially enacted law" relating to stimulant control, weapons, prostitution, and others accounted for 13.8 percent (225). Of the 1,361 cases, 43.0 percent were prosecuted (586) and 56.9 percent (774) released. Of those released, 32.3 percent (440) were reported to the prefectural governor by the prosecutor.

Satsumi and Oda (1995) examined 185 individuals who were sent for evaluations to the University of Tsukuba's Department of Mental Health in the Institution of Social Medicine. Males made up 75 percent of the group. The individuals, all of whom were twenty to thirty-nine years old, were categorized as having mood disorders, schizophrenia, or schizophrenic-related disorders, such as schizotypal personality disorder. Murder accounted for 57 percent of the charges. Overall, 70 percent of the individuals had committed serious felonies. Other crimes with which they were charged included injury (8 percent), robbery (6 percent), and rape or indecent assault (4 percent). Ultimately, 33 percent were found to have diminished responsibility, 6 percent were deemed completely responsible, and 61 percent were found to have no responsibility.

Satsumi, Inada, and Yamauchi (1998) studied 359 offenders between 1987 and 1991 who were believed by the prosecutor to be mentally ill and who therefore were given pretrial evaluations. The offenders had committed 367 offenses, including larceny (28 percent), physical injury or violence (14 percent), homicide (11 percent), arson (7 percent), intrusion on habitation (6 percent), and others (18 percent) (Satsumi, Inada, and Yamauchi 1998: 198). Of the 359 offenders, half were prosecuted. Of those prosecuted, 41 percent were deemed irresponsible, 15 percent had diminished capacity, and 44.6 percent were held completely responsible (Satsumi, Inada, and Yamauchi 1998: 202).

From 1994 to 1998, slightly over 3,800 offenders were found to be criminally irresponsible or have diminished responsibility. The prefectural governor ordered the admission of 58 percent, whereas 21.1 percent were admitted by others (Nakatani 2000: 594).

Note

1. Chapter 5, section 3.

References

Barclay, Gordon, and Cynthia Tavares. 2002. "International Comparisons of Criminal Justice Statistics 2000." Issue 05/02. Retrieved June 15, 2004, <www.homeoffice.gov/uk/rds/pdfs2/hosb502.pdf>.

Central Intelligence Agency (CIA). 2005. "Japan." The World Factbook. <www.odci.gov/cia/publications/factbook/geos/it.html>.

Inada, Toshiya, Fumiko Minagawa, Satoru Iwashita, and Tatsuji Tokui. 1995. "Mentally Disordered Criminal Offenders: Five Years' Data from the Tokyo District Public Prosecutor's Office." *International Journal of Law and Psychiatry* 18, no. 2: 221–30. Retrieved online June 6, 2005, <www.sciencedirect.com>, Elsevier Sciences, Ltd.

International Centre for Prison Studies (ICPS). 2005. "World Prison Brief: Entire World—Prison Population Totals, Prison Brief for Japan." International Centre for Prison Studies, Kings College London. Retrieved May 10, 2005, <www.kcl.ac.uk/depsta/rel/icps/worldbrief/world_brief.html>.

International Federation for Human Rights (FIDH). 2003. "International Mission of Investigation, The Death Penalty in Japan: A Practice Unworthy of a Democracy." May 2003.

Japanese Civil Liberties Union. July 26, 2002. "The New Law Jeopardizes Rights of People with Mental Disabilities." General Assembly Memorial Symposium: *Crime and Human Rights of People with State of Insanity*, Jinken Shimbun, No. 337. Speakers: Yoichi Kitamura, Nobuko Kobayashi. Translation by Satoshi Ueno and Nobuko Kobayashi. Retrieved June 28, 2001, <www.jclu.org/katsudou/universal_principle/articles/337mental.html>.

The Japan Times. March 5, 2004. "Discharged after 18 Months, Mentally Ill Criminals to Get Rehab Boost." *The Japan Times Ltd.* Downloaded May 16, 2005, <http://search.japantimes.co.jp/print/news/nn03-2004/nn20040305a2.htm>.

Library of Congress. 1994. "Japan: The Criminal Justice System." *Library of Congress Country Studies*. Washington, D.C.: Library of Congress. Retrieved June 25, 2004, <http://memory.loc.gov/frd/cs/>.

Mental Health Law. 1988. The Mental Health Division of the Health Service Bureau of the Ministry of Health and Welfare of Japan.

Ministry of Justice. 1998. *Public Prosecutors Office*. Retrieved June 24, 2005, <www.moj.go.jp/ENGLISH/index.html>.

Nakastone, Yogi.   2000.   "Psychiatry and Law in Japan." *International Journal of Law and Psychiatry* 23, nos. 5–6: 589–604.

Nakatani, Yoji. 2000. "Psychiatry and the Law in Japan." *International Journal of Law and Psychiatry* 23, nos. 5–6: 589–604.

Prisoners Abroad. 2004. "Fact Sheet: Japan Criminal Justice System." London. Retrieved May 9, 2005, <www.prisonersabroad.org.uk>.

Satsumi, Yuki, and Susumu Oda. 1995. "Mentally Ill Offenders Referred for Psychiatric Examination in Japan: Descriptive Statistics of a University Unit of Forensic Assessment." *International Journal of Law and Psychiatry* 18, no. 3: 323–31. Retrieved online June 6, 2005, <www.sciencedirect.com>, Elsevier Sciences, Ltd.

Satsumi, Yuki, Toshiya Inada, and Tadamitsu Yamauchi. 1998. "Criminal Offenses among Discharged Mentally Ill Individuals. Determinants of the Duration from Discharge and Absence of Diagnostic Specificity." *International Journal of Law and Psychiatry* 21, no. 2: 197–207. Retrieved online June 6, 2005, <www.sciencedirect .com>, Elsevier Sciences, Ltd.

Semba, Tsuneo. 2003. "Establishment of the Act for Observation of Insane Persons Charged with Offenses: Its Significance and Future." Presidential Address, Japanese Association of Psychiatric Hospitals. August 2003. Retrieved May 16, 2005, <www .nisseikyo.or.jp/home/top_english/kanto_e/200308.html>.

Shiraishi, Hiromi, Yoshito Igarashi, Tazekazu Ikehara, Tomoko Kimura, Tadashi Takeshima, Teruyuki Yamamoto, and Sachiko Ohi. 2000. *"Law related to Mental Health and Welfare of the Person with Mental Disorder (Full Text as of Date of Enforcement in 2000)."* Health Science Research Grant (H12-Syogai-007), Research for Ethics and Social Psychiatry, Tokyo Institute of Psychiatry.

United Nations Asian and Far East Institute (UNAFEI) for the Prevention of Crime and the Treatment of Offenders. 2004. "Criminal Justice in Japan." Retrieved June 17, 2004, <www.unafei.or.jp/english/publications/criminal_justice.html>.

Part VIII

AFRICA

21

Nigeria

NIGERIA IS LOCATED IN WESTERN AFRICA, bounded by Cameroon to the east, Chad to the northeast, Niger to the north, Benin to the west, and the Atlantic Ocean to the south. Nigeria covers an area of 356,669 square miles. It is the most populated of Africa's countries, with 133 million inhabitants. The population is largely rural, and only about 15 percent live in cities. Nigeria is a secular state, but two main religions are widely practiced in the country: Christianity and Islam. Small proportions of the people have traditional religious beliefs indigenous to Africa, or are atheists.

Most Nigerians speak more than one language. English, the country's official language, is widely spoken, especially among educated individuals. In many Nigerian cities, standard English is spoken side by side with the "pidgin," or a mixture of English and local languages. About four hundred native Nigerian languages have been identified, and some are threatened with extinction. The most common of the native languages are Hausa, Yoruba, and Igbo.

Nigeria gained its independence on October 1, 1960 and became a federation with three largely self-governing regions—northern, western, and eastern (Winslow 2005). A fourth region—the midwest—was added when Nigeria declared itself to be a federal republic and drew up a new constitution. The 1999 Constitution, which was heavily influenced by the 1979 Constitution, was enacted on May 29, 1999 (U.S. Department of State 2004). The constitution sets forth an independent judiciary, although it has been influenced by the executive and legislative branches and has been subject to corruption (Winslow 2005).

Background

By the late 1800s, madness among Nigerians was a concern to the British (Keller 2001). A ward for the mentally ill at Lagos prison was overcrowded. The first asylum was in Calabar in 1904 (Ayonrinde et al. 2004). In 1906, a "lunacy ordinance" was passed that ordered the construction of mental institutions. Another facility, the Yaba Asylum, was built in Lagos in 1907. These early asylums in Nigeria functioned like prisons and did not provide mental health treatment (Keller 2001: 310); rather, they "provided essentially emergency and custodial interventions" (Ayonrinde et al. 2004: 1). They also only employed medical officers, not psychiatrists (Ayonrinde et al. 2004). According to Sadowsky, most patients in colonial Nigeria were "male, urban, insane criminals." Care at the asylums amounted to sedation rather than treatment (Keller 2001: 311). In 1916, the West Nigerian Criminal Code adopted an insanity test comparable to *M'Naghten* (Bienen 1976).

Amidst the presence of westernized medical practices and procedures, many Nigerians associated insanity with the supernatural rather than the physical. Thus, treatment for "madness" was often sought from traditional healers who turned to rituals and prayer as cures (Bienen 1976).

In 1960, an estimated 53 mental patients were deemed "criminal lunatics." In 1967, this figure rose to 124, and in 1969, 74 of the 1,853 "mental patients" were considered criminal (Bienen 1976: 222).

The Constitution recognizes the rights of the accused, including the right to a fair public hearing, the right to be presumed innocent until proven guilty, and the right to a legal defense (Constitution 1999).

All homicides are either classified as murder or manslaughter, of which the former receives a mandatory death sentence after conviction (Bienen 1976: 224). If an accused individual who is being questioned by the magistrate "openly offers an unsolicited guilty plea" (Winslow 2005), the court may order the individual to undergo a psychiatric examination to determine mental competency. At any point during a trial, issues surrounding insanity and fitness to stand trial may be brought up.

Nigerian law is largely derived from the English common law system, from native practices, or from Islam (Ayuba et al. 2004: 211). In northern Nigeria, laws are set forth through the Nigerian Penal Code of the North and the Northern Nigerian Criminal Procedure Code (Bienen 1976: 224 [see footnote 1]). The Criminal Code Act (chapter 77) contains the "Laws of the Federation of Nigeria 1990." The High Court tries offenses contained in the Nigerian Criminal Code.

Since 2000, twelve northern Nigerian states have implemented Shari'a into the courts and criminal legislation (Human Rights Watch [HRW] 2004: 1, 14).[1] This has caused much apprehension among the Christian populations in Nigeria and has stimulated a global dialogue regarding human rights violations under Shari'a law. Crimes that may be punished under Shari'a law include adultery, theft, and alcohol consumption (HRW 2004: 13). The punishments that offenders can receive include, but are not limited to, death, imprisonment, caning, amputation, and restitution (HRW 2004).

In 2004, there were 39,153 inmates (including remand and pretrial detainees), which amounted to a prison population rate of 31 per 100,000 of national population (ICPS 2004). In 2002, there were 147 penal facilities and 83 satellite institutions. Approximately 2 percent of Nigerian inmates are female.

Legal Criteria

The criteria for determining insanity are listed in the Criminal Code Act 1990.[2] Section 26 of the Criminal Code Act states:

> Subject to the express provisions of this code relating to acts done upon compulsion or provocation or in self-defence, a person is not criminally responsible for an act done or omission made under such circumstances of sudden or extraordinary emergency that an ordinary person possessing ordinary power of self-control could not reasonably be expected to act otherwise.[3]

Section 28 closely resembles *M'Naghten*:

> A person is not criminally responsible for an act or omission if at the time of doing the act or making the omission he is in such a state of mental disease or natural mental infirmity as to deprive him of capacity to understand what he is doing, or of capacity to control his actions, or of capacity to know that he ought not to do the act or make the omission.
>
> A person whose mind, at the time of his doing or omitting to do an act, is affected by delusions on some specific matter or matters, but who is not otherwise entitled to the benefit of the foregoing provisions of this section, is criminally responsible for the act or omission to the same extent as if the real state of things had been such as he was introduced by the delusions to believe to exist.[4]

Section 29 states:

> (1) Save as provided in this section, intoxication shall not constitute a defence to any criminal charge.

(2) Intoxication shall be a defence to any criminal charge if by reason thereof the person charged at the time of the act or omission complained of did not know that such act or omission was wrong or did not know what he was doing and—
   a. the state of intoxication was caused without this consent by the malicious or negligent act or another person; or
   b. the person charged was by reason of intoxication insane, temporarily or otherwise, at the time of such act or omission.

(3) Where the defence under the preceding subsection is established, then in a case falling under paragraph (a) thereof the accused person shall be discharged, and in a case failing under paragraph (b) sections 229 and 230 of the Criminal Procedure Act shall apply.

(4) Intoxication shall be taken into account for the purpose of determining whether the person charged had formed any intention, specific or otherwise, in the absence of which he would not be guilty of the offence.

(5) For the purposes of this section, "intoxication" shall be deemed to include a state produced by narcotics or drugs.[5]

The Zamfara State of Nigeria Shari'a Penal Code Law (Law No. 10, January 2000) states:

(i) There shall be no criminal responsibility except upon a mukallaf.
(ii) There shall be no criminal responsibility unless an unlawful act or omission is done intentionally or negligently.[6]

In addition, Zamfara's code reads:

No act is an offence which is done by a person involuntarily and without the ability of controlling his act by reason of "Act of God" or sudden illness which makes him incapable of avoiding that act.[7]

Maliki law, a system of religious law in Sunni Islam, is practiced in northern Nigeria. According to Ayuba et al. (2004: 211), the Penal Code Law states:

nothing is an offence which is done by a person who at the time of doing it, by reason of unsoundness of the mind is incapable of knowing the nature of the act or that he is doing what is wrong or either contrary to the law.[8]

Maliki law does not differentiate intentional from unintentional homicide, and according to Ayuba et al., an offender can receive the death penalty for culpable homicide. However, a mental disorder can be used as a mitigating element in sentencing (Ayuba et al. 2004: 212).

Burden of Proof

The accused bears the burden of demonstrating that he was insane at the time of the offense (Bienen 1976). Section 27 of the Criminal Code states:

> Every person is presumed to be of sound mind, and to have been of sound mind at any time which comes in question, until the contrary is proved.[9]

The burden is not "beyond a reasonable doubt," but "on the balance of the probabilities" (Bienen 1976: 228).

Form of Verdict

At the time of Bienen's study in 1974, the term "not Guilty by reason of insanity" replaced the older "guilty but insane" (62). The Nigerian Criminal Code does not allow for a "diminished responsibility" defense but does recognize an "irresistible impulse" defense (Bienen 1976: 228).

Who Decides?

There are no juries in western Nigeria as there are in Britain, whose laws provide the foundation for Nigerian criminal procedure (Bienen 1976). As such, procedures and instructions intended for jury trials remain in the Nigerian code. Thus, it is a judge within the Nigerian High Court who determines whether an accused is legally insane or not.

Role of Experts

Experts may provide testimony, although their evaluation is not necessary for an individual to be rendered insane (Bienen 1976). The judge has the right to deny the defense's use of expert testimony (Bienen 1976: 231). Often, a medical expert will examine a defendant for the first time a year after the commission of the offense. Thus, the expert testimony will reflect the defendant's mental state at the time of the evaluation rather than at the time of the crime.

Among those who were accused of homicide between 1966 and 1972, forty-four defendants exhibited signs of mental illness. Of those forty-four, only twenty were evaluated by a psychiatrist (Bienen 1976: 232). There were eight psychiatrists practicing in Nigeria at the time of this study, although

Bienen (1974) reports that only three were used in the determination of insanity (62).

Many individuals who experienced what would be dubbed as "mental illness" in westernized nations would visit traditional healers rather than medical experts. However, the testimonies of these healers is not or was not allowed in court (at least as of 1976). Thus, many defendants with histories of mental illness had no means of introducing past behavior in the courtroom (Bienen 1976).

Court Cases

The following excerpt is from a court opinion in a nonsuccessful insanity defense plea:

> The accused claimed in court that he was under the delusion he was slaughtering a ram when he killed his wife. He also testified that he had a previous history of such delusions. Some time earlier he had beaten one of his sons almost to the point of death under the delusion that he was a goat. At another time the accused claimed to have unwittingly stabbed himself in the stomach. On the occasion of the homicide for which he was on trial, he testified that an elderly man came and ordered him to slaughter the ram, when in fact he killed his wife. A herbalist who once treated the accused for symptoms of mental illness had died, and was unable to verify that he had been consulted. No member of the family of the accused testified as to his state of mind at the time of the crime or previous symptoms. The record states that if the accused had indeed suffered from delusions someone would have known about it. There was no cross examination of the accused as to his delusions. There was testimony that the victim had stated that she was afraid of her husband after the attack on her son, and that she had planned to seek a divorce.
>
> The court found that the threat to seek divorce was sufficient motive for the homicide. The insanity defence failed. Guilty of Murder. Appeal failed at the Court of Appeal. (Bienen 1976: 242; see *Arasiyu Aransi v. The State* [Abeokuta, 2C/71])

The following is a court opinion in a successful insanity defense plea:

> The accused was the barren wife of the deceased. She claimed her husband had wanted to use her [body parts] for ritual sacrifice to obtain wealth. The accused behaved abnormally during the trial, and she had been treated for symptoms of mental illness by a native doctor, whom, she claimed, had raped and imprisoned her. The court said there was some evidence that the accused was insane before the commission of the crime. The couple had gone to the place where the murder took place in order to have the accused treated by a traditional healer. The

court also saw the refusal of the wife to take food to her husband as a sign of mental illness.

The accused was found to have committed the homicide, but she was acquitted on grounds on insanity. The accused was remanded to Aro and remained there for eight months. (Bienen 1976: 245; see *Ajayi Anikara v. The State* [Akure, 36c/66])

What Happens to the Defendant?

Defendants who are found to be "insane" may be sent to Aro Hospital (Bienen 1974: 64). In Maliki law, mental disorders can be used as mitigating factors in cases of culpable homicide (Ayuba et al. 2004).

Frequency of Use

If a person is convicted of murder, the automatic sentence is death. Yet, Bienen (1976) suggests that the insanity defense is not used to a gratuitous extent. In a study of homicide cases tried in western Nigerian courts between 1966 and 1972, Bienen (1976) found that of the accused, 19 percent raised the issue of insanity (231). All forty-four of the cases where the issue of insanity was raised appeared to have some validity to their claim. Of the forty-four defendants who exhibited signs of mental illness, twenty were found guilty and given the death penalty (see table 21.1). Of those twenty, seventeen defendants had never seen a psychiatrist. Of the sixteen who were acquitted because of insanity (36 percent of the mentally ill), thirteen had been seen by a psychiatrist who testified at their trials. Overall, of the 205 accused, only 8 percent were eventually acquitted due to insanity. Thus, Bienen concludes that the availability of expert testimony appeared to be crucial to the successful use of the insanity defense.

Ayuba et al. (2004) studied 12,500 patients who, by order of court, were evaluated at the Jos University Teaching Hospital from 1980 to 1998 (211). The percent of the sample that had committed homicide was 1.3 (N=160), among whom 51 received a psychiatric diagnosis. Of the 45 males and 6 females with psychiatric disorders, 49 percent were diagnosed with schizophrenia, 29.4 percent with depression, 7.8 percent with mania, 9.8 percent with epilepsy or some other organic disorder, and 4 percent received other diagnoses (Ayuba et al. 2001: 213). About 47 percent (N=21) of the males were between the ages of thirty and thirty-nine and 67 percent (N=30) were farmers. Among the female homicide offenders, 33.3 percent (N=2) were between the ages of thirty and thirty-nine, and another 33.3 percent were between fifty and fifty-nine years of age. All but one of the female offenders were homemakers.

TABLE 21.1
Characteristics and Outcomes of Homicide Defendants: 1966–1972

	Mentally Ill Accused (%) N = 44	All Other Accused (%) N = 161
Sex of Accused		
Men	86	96
Women	14	4
	100%	*100%*
Relationship of Accused and Victim		
Marital and kinship	59	9
Lovers, former lovers	5	1
Business and economic relationships	9	10
Acquaintances	9	48
No prior relationship	16	31
No answer	2	1
	100%	*100%*
Alleged Motive		
Quarrel over personal relationships	30	8
Allegation of witchcraft	22	1
Associated with other crimes		
(robbery, rape, abortion)	2	9
Quarrel over property	5	22
Political and civil motives	5	41
Other motives, including accident	6	18
No motive	30	1
	100%	*100%*
High Court Verdict		
Guilty of murder	46	29
Guilty of manslaughter	2	11
Insanity acquittal	36	0
Acquitted and discharged	16	60
	100%	*100%*

Source: Bienen 1976, page 239, table 1.

Notes

1. These states are Bauchi, Borno, Gombe, Jigawa, Kaduna, Kano, Katsina, Kebbi, Niger, Sokoto, Yobe, and Zamfara.
2. Criminal Code Act, chapter 77, Laws of the Federation of Nigeria 1990.
3. Criminal Code Act, part I, chapter 5, section 26.
4. Criminal Code Act, part I, chapter 5, section 28.
5. Criminal Code Act, part I, chapter 5, section 29.
6. Zamfara State of Nigeria Shari'a Penal Code Law, chapter 2, section 63.
7. Zamfara State of Nigeria Shari'a Penal Code Law, chapter 2, section 79.

8. Penal Code Law, section 51.

9. Criminal Code Act, part I, chapter 5, section 27.

References

Ayonrinde, Oyedeji, Oye Gureje, and Rahmaan Lawal. 2004. "Psychiatric Research in Nigeria: Bridging Tradition and Modernisation." *British Journal of Psychiatry* 184 (June): 536–38.

Ayuba, Larry Nanjul, Moses David Audu, Ali Ruth Choji, and Mansfield Mela. 2004. "A Developing World Perspective on Homicide and Mental Disorder: An Eighteen-Year Retrospective Study (1980–1998) at Jos, Nigeria." *International Journal of Forensic Mental Health* 3, no. 2: 211–16. Retrieved July 21, 2005, <www.iafmhs.org/files/Nanjulfall04.pdf>.

Bienen, Leigh. 1974. "Criminal Homicide in Western Nigeria, 1966–1972." *Journal of African Law* 18, no. 1, Criminal Law and Criminology (Spring 1974): 57–78. Retrieved from JSTOR on May 18, 2005, <www.jstor.org>.

———. 1976. "The Determination of Criminal Insanity in Western Nigeria." *The Journal of Modern African Studies* 14, no. 2: 219–45. Retrieved online July 14, 2004, <www.jstor.org" www.jstor.org>.

Constitution of the Federal Republic of Nigeria (Constitution). 1999. Retrieved May 10, 2005, <www.nigeria-law.org/ConstitutionOfTheFederalRepublicOfNigeria.htm>.

Criminal Code Act, Chapter 77. *Laws of the Federation of Nigeria 1990.* Retrieved online May 20, 2004, <www.nigeria-law.org>.

Human Rights Watch (HRW). 2004. "'Political Shari'a'? Human Rights and Islamic Law in Northern Nigeria." *Human Rights Watch* 14, no. 9A (September). Retrieved April 24, 2006, <www.hrw.org/reports/2004/nigeria0904/nigeria0904.pdf>.

International Centre for Prison Studies (ICPS). 2005. "World Prison Brief: Entire World—Prison Population Totals, Prison Brief for Nigeria." International Centre for Prison Studies, Kings College London. Retrieved May 10, 2005, <www.kcl.ac.uk/depsta/rel/icps/worldbrief/world_brief.html>.

Keller, Richard. 2001. "Madness and Colonization: Psychiatry in the British and French Empires, 1800–1962." *Journal of Social History* 35, no. 2: 295–326. Retrieved from Project Muse website July 14, 2004, <http://must.jhu.edu.proxyau.wrlc.org>.

Sadowsky, Jonathan. *Imperial Bedlam: Institutions of Madness in Colonial Southwest Nigeria.* Medicine and Society 10. Berkeley: University of California Press, 1999.

United States Department of State. 2004. "Background Note: Nigeria." Washington, D.C.: U.S. Department of State. Retrieved online June 14, 2004, <www.state.gov/r/pa/ei/bgn/2836.htm>.

Winslow, Robert. 2005. "Nigeria" from *Crime and Society: A Comparative Criminology Tour of the World.* Retrieved May 24, 2005, <www.rohan.sdsu.edu/faculty/rwinslow/index.html>.

Zamfara State of Nigeria Shari'a Penal Code Law. 2002. <www.zamfaraonline.com/sharia/introduction.html>.

22

South Africa

SOUTH AFRICA OCCUPIES THE SOUTHERNMOST portion of the African continent, bordered on the north by Namibia, Botswana, Zimbabwe, Mozam-
bique, and Swaziland; on the east and south by the Indian Ocean; and on the
west by the Atlantic Ocean. Black Africans comprise three-fourths of South
Africa's population, and whites, coloreds (people of mixed race), and Asians
(mainly Indians) make up the remainder of the 42.7 million people.

Until recently, whites dominated the majority of the population under
the political genre of racial segregation known as apartheid. Apartheid
ended in the early 1990s, but South Africa is still recovering from the racial
inequalities of political power, opportunity, and lifestyle. The end of
apartheid led to the lifting of trade sanctions against South Africa imposed
by the international community. It also led to a total reorganization of the
government, which since 1994, has been a nonracial democracy based on
majority rule.

South Africa is divided into nine provinces: Gauteng, Limpopo,
Mpumalanga, Northwest Province, Free State, Eastern Cape, Northern Cape,
Western Cape, and KwaZulu-Natal.

Until apartheid ended in 1994, Afrikaans and English were official languages, although they represent the native languages of only 15 percent and 9
percent of the total population, respectively. Afrikaans is spoken not only by
Afrikaners but also by 83 percent of colored people. English is the primary
language of many whites, and is spoken by 95 percent of Asians. The 1994
Constitution added nine African languages to the list of recognized, official
languages: Zulu, Xhosa, Sesotho sa Leboa (Northern Sotho or Pedi), Tswana,

Sesotho (Southern Sotho), Tsonga, Venda, Ndebele, and siSwati. Most blacks can speak two or more of these languages, in addition to English and Afrikaans. Together, these eleven languages are the primary languages of 98 percent of South Africans. In practice, English retains a dominant position as the main medium of instruction in schools and most universities. Afrikaners pride themselves on their language and have struggled to keep it as a medium of instruction and resist any threat to exterminate it.

Of the four-fifths of South Africans who profess religious faith, 77 percent are Christians. The remaining 3 percent are Hindus (1.74 percent), Muslims (1.09 percent), and Jews (0.41 percent). There are also many independent African religions. Most people who claim no religious affiliation are African traditionalists. Their religion has a strong cultural base and rituals vary according to ethnic group.

Background

South African trials are derivatives of the English trial system, but juries are not used (Prisoners Abroad 2005). Arrestees plead guilty or not guilty before a magistrate, "with or without accessors" (Prisoners Abroad 2005: 2). The State must prove its case beyond a reasonable doubt.

Capital punishment was practiced until 1995, but whipping continues to be used for juvenile and young male offenders (Library of Congress [LOC] 1996). Throughout the early 1990s, over 30,000 young offenders were whipped annually (LOC 1996). In addition to incarceration, an offender may be sentenced to periodic imprisonment, fined, or sent to nonpenal institutions (LOC 1996).

During the colonial period, psychiatry was the government's weapon against African dissidents. According to Jessica Powers (2002), resistance to colonialism was deemed a psychiatric disorder.

Tara Hospital, located right outside of Johannesburg, was the first "therapeutic neuropsychiatric hospital" (Jones 2003) in South Africa that offered therapy to "previously neglected mental patients" (Jones 2003). It opened in 1946 and offered a different approach to handling mental illness. Instead of focusing on detention and eugenics, Tara Hospital offered a therapeutic environment.

When South Africa was unionized, there were eight mental institutions with 1,692 "European" patients, and 1,932 "non-European patients" (Jones 2003). These hospitals were built during a time of industrialization in the late 1800s, when the need for "formalized mental hospital beds" was on the rise (Jones 2003). However, black and white patients were segregated.

In 1916, the Commissioner of Mental Hygiene in the Department of the Interior, under which the penal system was operated, was given jurisdiction of mental hospitals (Jones 2003). According to Jones:

> Mental hospitals were very like prisons. They were closed detention centres that mostly housed the underprivileged, disorderly and miscreant.... Jail cells had always housed those deemed mad. Even when permanent mental institutions had been erected, they were quickly filled and prisons continued to serve as temporary holding areas for the mentally disordered.

Between 1995 and 1997, there were 1,512 homicides in the city of Pretoria, which is the capital of South Africa (Barclay and Tavares 2002: 4).

There are 186,739 persons (including pretrial and remand prisoners) incarcerated in South Africa where the incarceration rate is 413 per 100,000 of national population. Females make up 2.2 percent of the prison population. In 1993, there were eleven maximum-security prisons, one minimum-security prison, sixteen prison farms, two juvenile prisons, and eight female prisons. By 2003, there were 229 penal institutions and two private prisons. In 2004, there were a reported 224 penal institutions. The prison population in South Africa increased by 51 percent between 1990 and 2000 and by 8 percent between 1999 and 2000 (Barclay and Tavares 2002: 7).

Legal Criteria

> A person who commits an act which constitutes an offense and who at the time of such commission suffers from a mental defect or mental illness which makes him incapable of
>
> 1) appreciating the wrongfulness of his act or
> 2) acting in accordance with an appreciation of the wrongfulness of his act shall not be criminally responsible for such act. (Section 78 of CP Act of 1977)

There is no formal definition of mental illness for purpose of the insanity defense. For a mental disorder to constitute a mental illness or defect for these purposes, it must at least consist of "a pathological disturbance of the accused's mental capacity and not a mere temporary mental confusion which is not attributable to a mental abnormality but rather to external stimuli such as alcohol, drugs, or provocation" (*S. v. Stellmacher* 1982). "A malfunctioning of the mind which is caused by a blow to the head resulting in a concussion, consumption of drugs/alcohol, or administration of an anaesthetic is not an 'illness' or a 'disease' of mind because it is exogenous in its origin" (Burchell and Milton 1991).

A defendant may be found not fit to stand trial, yet this does not release him/her of responsibility. According to the Criminal Procedures Act of 1977: [CP]

> An accused who suffers from mental illness or defect may not be fit to stand trial. An accused is not triable if the mental illness or defect renders him not capable of understanding the proceedings so as to make a proper defense. (s. 77[1])

Burden of Proof

The burden is on the accused to establish insanity on a balance of probabilities (Milton et al. 1994: 82; see *S. v. Mahlinza* 1967). The burden is on the prosecutor to prove triability BRD if an accused alleges non-triability on account of mental illness (Milton et al. 1994: 82; see *S. v. Ebrahim* 1973).

Form of Verdict

A defendant may be found not guilty by reason of mental illness or mental defect.

Who Decides?

A judge decides. The judge may have two assessors in more serious cases.

Role of Experts

Psychiatric opinions are used frequently in court. In Supreme Court cases that could result in the administration of the death penalty, expert evaluations are mandatory (Scharf and Cochrane 1993). Experts are called upon to provide factual information.

What Happens to the Defendant?

If the court determines at any time that the defendant is mentally ill or has mental defects to the extent that he or she cannot understand the proceedings, the court may commit the defendant to a mental hospital or prison (Scharf and Cochrane 1993). An individual may be referred to observation for major and minor crimes (Kaliski 2001). To determine whether the defendant can mentally understand the proceedings, the court may order a thirty-day observation period (Section 79[2] of the CP). The Mental Health Act of 1973 defined *mental illness* as "disability or disease of the mind" (Kaliski 2001). Under Section 77, the defendant must be tested for competence to stand trial, and Section 78 specifies that the evaluation must examine whether the mental state of the offender disrupts his ability to appreciate wrongful actions (Kaliski 2001). According to Kaliski:

> . . . pathological and nonpathological incapacity can abrogate mens rea. Pathological incapacity derives from an inherent condition, such as mental illness, epileptic seizures etc. Nonpathological incapacity is loosely conceptualized as a circumstance which is not due to an internal disorder. . . . Over recent years (in some persuasive precedents) it has expanded to include alcohol intoxication and provocation. . . . Section 79(2) defines psychiatric observations which determine whether pathological incapacity due to mental illness or defect operations.

Under Section 28 of the Mental Health Act, a defendant becomes a "state patient" if found not competent to stand trial or found not to be criminally responsible. Though the charges are dropped, the defendant is institutionalized in a state psychiatric hospital for an indefinite term (Kaliski 2001). For the defendant's release, the attorney general must consent after examining the original offense. In determining the release of a "state patient" charged with a violent offense, the attorney general will collect patient records from psychiatrists, medical officers, and hospital administrators. If the defendant is found to have nonpathological incapacity, he will be acquitted.

If the defendant was charged for a capital crime, the following inquiry shall be conducted and reported on:

a. by the medical superintendent of a mental hospital designated by the court, or by a psychiatrist appointed by the medical superintendent at the request of the court;
b. by a psychiatrist appointed by the court and who is not in the full-time service of the state; and
c. by a psychiatrist appointed by the accused if he so wishes (Milton et al. 1994: 212; see CP Act 52 of 1977 s. 79[1][b]).

For noncapital offenses, the inquiry and report can be conducted by the medical superintendent of the mental hospital or by a psychiatrist appointed by the medical superintendent as required by the court. The reports must be available to the court, the prosecutor, and the accused. The report contains a description of the inquiry, a diagnosis, and psychiatric findings on triability and criminal capacity (CP Act 51 of 1997, s. 79[4]).

Frequency of Use

In 1991 and 1992, there were 485,099 prosecutions, of which 127 defendants were determined to be mentally disordered (Scharf and Cochrane 1993).

References

Barclay, Gordon, and Cynthia Tavares. 2002. "International Comparisons of Criminal Justice Statistics 2000." Issue 05/02. Retrieved June 15, 2004, <www.homeoffice.gov/uk/rds/pdfs2/hosb502.pdf>.

Burchell, J., and J. Milton. 1991. *Principles of Criminal Law*. Cape Town: Juta. Pages 208ff.

Hooper, J. F. 2004. "Forensic Psychiatry in South Africa." Psychiatry and the Law, Forensic Psychiatry Resource Page. University of Alabama. Retrieved May 16, 2005, <http://bama.ua.edu/~jhooper/southaf.html>.

International Centre for Prison Studies (ICPS). 2005. "World Prison Brief: Entire World—Prison Population Totals, Prison Brief for South Africa." International Centre for Prison Studies, Kings College London. Retrieved May 10, 2005, <www.kcl.ac.uk/depsta/rel/icps/worldbrief/world_brief.html>.

International Constitutional Law (ICL). 1997. "South Africa—Constitution." A. Tschentscher, ed. Retrieved May 11, 2005, <www.oefre.unibe.ch/law/icl/info.html>.

Jones, Tiffany F. 2003. "Prospects of a Progressive Mental Health System in 1940s South Africa: Hereditarianism, Behaviourism and Radical Therapies." Workshop on South Africa in the 1940s, Southern African Research Centre, Kingson, September 2003. Retrieved online June 28, 2004, <www.queensu.ca/sarc/Conferences/1940s/Jones.htm>.

Kaliski, Sean Z. 2001. *Forensic Psychiatry in South Africa*. Retrieved online June 14, 2004, <http://bama.ua.edu/~jhooper/southaf.html>.

Library of Congress. 1996. "South Africa: Penal Code." *Library of Congress Country Studies*. Washington, D.C.: Library of Congress. Retrieved June 25, 2004, <http://memory.loc.gov/frd/cs/>.

Milton, John, Stephan E. van der Merwe, and Dirk van Zyl Smit. 1994. "South Africa" in L. Dupont and C. Fijnaut, eds., *International Encyclopaedia of Laws—Criminal Law*. The Netherlands: Kluwer Law International.

Powers, Jessica. 2002. "African History, Insanity and Resistance to Colonialism." Creative Marketeam Canada Ltd., doing business as Suite101.com. Retrieved online June 28, 2004, <www.suite101.com/article.cfm/african_history/96489>.

Prisoners Abroad. 2005. "Fact Sheet: Criminal Justice System South Africa." London. Retrieved May 9, 2005, <www.prisonersabroad.org.uk>.

Report of the Commission of Enquiry into the Responsibility of Mentally Deranged Persons and Related Matters (RP 60/1967). Paras. 9.30. et seq. CP Act of 1977, section 78.

Republic of South Africa Government Gazette 30, no. 18492. 1997. "Criminal Procedure Amendment Act." Cape Town, Republic of South Africa. Retrieved June 14, 2004 <www.gov/za/gazette/acts/1997/a76-97.pdf>.

R. v. Booth 1978 Kotze 50 at 52.

R. v. Von Zell 1953 (3) SA (A) at 308.

R. v. Zulch 1967 TPD 400 at 403.

Scharf, Wilfried, and Rona Cochrane. 1993. "South Africa." World Factbook of Criminal Justice Statistics. NCJ 199270. United States Department of Justice, Office of Justice Programs, Bureau of Justice Statistics. Retrieved online June 10, 2004, <www.ojp.usdoj.gov/bjs/pub/ascii/wfcjsaf.txt>.

S. v. Ebrahim 1973 (1) SA 868 A 871.

S. v. Mahlinza 1967 (1) SA 408 (A) 419.

S. v. Mnyanda 1976 (2) SA 751 (A).

S. v. Stellmacher 1982 (2) SA 181 (SWA) at 187H (translation).

S. v. Webb (2) 1971 (2) SA 343 (T) at 344-345).

Winslow, Robert. 2005. "South Africa" from *Crime and Society: A Comparative Criminology Tour of the World.* Retrieved May 24, 2005, <www-rohan.sdsu.edu/faculty/rwinslow/index.html>.

Part IX
THE PACIFIC

23

Australia

A USTRALIA IS LOCATED IN THE southern hemisphere between the Indian and Pacific Oceans. It is a federation of six states—New South Wales, Queensland, South Australia, Tasmania, Victoria, and Western Australia—and two territories: Northern Territory and Australian Capital Territory (ACT), the site of the nation's capital. It extends for about 4,000 kilometers from east to west and for about 3,700 kilometers from north to south. Its coastline measures some 25,760 kilometers. Australia is 7,682,300 square kilometers, making it the smallest continent in the world but the sixth largest country.

Australia is one of the most urbanized countries in the world. Its population is estimated at just over 19 million. Approximately 85 percent live in urban centers, with about a third residing in the two largest cities, Sydney and Melbourne.

Australia is a federal parliamentary democracy and a member of the Commonwealth of Nations. The Constitution of Australia, which became effective in 1901, is based on British parliamentary traditions, and includes elements of the United States system. The head of the state is the British sovereign, and the head of the government is the Australian prime minister, who is responsible to the Australian Parliament. All powers not delegated to the federal government are reserved to the states.

The official language of Australia is English.

Australia has no single established church, and its Constitution guarantees freedom of worship. The population is predominantly Christian. The largest single denominations are Roman Catholic (16 percent of the population) and the Anglican Church [of] Australia (26 percent). Jewish, Buddhist, and Muslim worshippers make up a small portion of the population.

Background

Each Australian territory or state, in essence, has its own prison and mental health system (Mullen et al. 2000). Relevant criminal and mental health legislation throughout Australia is as follows (Law Reform Commission (LRC) 1997a):

New South Wales: Crimes Act 1900; Criminal Procedure Act 1986; Sentencing Act 1989; Mental Health Act 1990; Mental Health (Criminal Procedure) Act 1990; Evidence Act 1995; Crimes Amendment (Mandatory Life Sentences) Act 1996; Crimes Amendment (Diminished Responsibility) Act 1997 (No. 106); Mental Health Legislation Amendment Bill 1997

Queensland: Criminal Code; Mental Health Act 1974

South Australia: Criminal Law Consolidation Act 1935; Criminal Law (Sentencing Act) 1988

Tasmania: Criminal Code Act of 1924; Corrections Act 1992; Mental Health Act 1996; Criminal Justice (Mental Impairment) Act 1999

Victoria: Crimes Act 1958; Sentencing Act 1991; Crimes (Criminal Trials) Act 1993

Western Australia: Criminal Code

Australia Capital Territory: Crimes Act 1900

Northern Territory: Criminal Code

New South Wales first introduced the notion of diminished responsibility in 1974. The new legislation was based on that used by the United Kingdom. Convicted murderers received mandatory life sentences at the time. Under the diminished responsibility defense in New South Wales, mentally impaired individuals convicted of murder who did not meet the mental illness criteria could avoid a life sentence (LRC 1997a: 3.2).

Forensic psychiatric services are found throughout all territories and states. For example, there are district mental health inpatient units in Queensland for individuals charged with crimes but who are unfit to stand trial (Jager 2001: 388). The Victorian Institute of Mental Health provides services in hospitals, communities, prisons, and courts, while in Western Australia teams of mental health and social workers provide services in most prisons (Jager 2001: 389–90). Other forensic psychiatric facilities include the Long Bay Prison Hospital in Sydney, Glendale Hospital in South Australia, the Community Forensic Mental Health Clinic in Melbourne, Canberra Hospital in the Australian Capital Territory, and Risdon Prison in Tasmania (Jager 2001).

Between 1998 and 2000, there were five homicides in Canberra and 180 in Sydney (Barclay and Tavares 2002: 4). In 2003, there were 123 penal facilities in Australia. By mid-2004, there were 23,363 inmates (including pretrial and remand prisoners), equivalent to a prison population rate of 117 per 100,000 of national population (ICPS 2005). An estimated 6.9 percent of the prison population was female. The prison population rose by 52 percent between 1990 and 2000, yet there was only a 1 percent increase between 1999 and 2000 (Barclay and Tavares 2002: 7).

Legal Criteria

The Standing Committee of Attorneys General of the States and the Commonwealth created a Model Criminal Code in 1995 (Mullen et al. 2000). It included a defense of mental impairment similar to the *M'Naghten* criteria, but it also required that the defendants not only be unable to understand the nature of their acts and not know it was wrong, but they must not have been able to control their own behavior (Mullen et al. 2000: 435).[1] Mental impairment, which is an "underlying pathological infirmity of the mind, whether of long or short duration and whether permanent or temporary, but does not include a condition that results from the reaction of a healthy mind to extraordinary external stimuli,"[2] includes "senility, intellectual disability, mental illness, brain damage, and severe personality disorder"[3] (see McSherry 1997: 184).

The defense of mental illness may be used in situations where the defendant's mental conditions "affect the accused's cognitive process to such an extent as to render that person incapable of knowing the nature or quality of his or her act, or incapable of knowing that that act was wrong" (LRC 1997a: 3.7).

Diminished responsibility in New South Wales was defined in the Crimes Act 1900 (NSW) (s 23A) as (LRC 1997a: 3.5):

1. Where, on the trial of a person for murder, it appears that at the time of the acts or omissions causing the death charged the person was suffering from such abnormality of mind (whether arising from a condition or arrested or retarded development of mind or any inherent causes or induced by diseases or injury) as substantially impaired his mental responsibility for the acts or omissions, he shall not be convicted of murder.
3. A person who, but for subsection (1) would be liable, whether as principal or as accessory, to be convicted of murder shall be liable instead to be convicted of manslaughter.
4. The fact that a person is by virtue of subsection (1) not liable to be convicted or murder in respect of a death charged shall not affect the question whether any other person is liable to be convicted of murder in respect of that death.

5. Where, on the trial of a person for murder, the person contends:
   a. That he is entitled to be acquitted on the ground that he was mentally ill at the time of the acts or omissions causing the death charged; or
   b. That he is by virtue of subsection (1) not liable of murder,
   evidence may be offered by the Crown tending to prove the other of those contentions, and the Court may give directions as to the stage of the proceedings at which that evidence may be offered.

Schedule 1 Amendments, Section 23A of the Crimes Amendment (Diminished Responsibility) Act 1997 of New South Wales revised the Crimes Act 1900 and defines diminished responsibility as (LRC 1997c: 3–4):

1. A person who would otherwise be guilty of murder is not to be convicted of murder if:
   a. At the time of the acts or omissions causing the death concerned, the person's capacity to understand events, or to judge whether the person's actions were right or wrong, or to control himself or herself, was substantially impaired by an abnormality of mind arising from an underlying condition, and
   b. the impairment was so substantial as to warrant liability for murder being reduced to manslaughter.
2. For the purposes of subsection (1)(b), evidence of an opinion that an impairment was so substantial as to warrant liability for murder being reduced to manslaughter is not admissible.
3. If a person was intoxicated at the time of the acts or omissions causing the death concerned, and the intoxication was self-induced intoxication (within the meaning of section 428A), the effects of that self-induced intoxication are to be disregarded for the purpose of determining whether the person is not liable to be convicted of murder by virtue of this section.
4. The onus is on the person accused to prove that he or she is not liable to be convicted of murder by virtue of this section.
5. A person who but for this section would be liable, whether as principal or accessory, to be convicted of murder is to be convicted of manslaughter instead.
6. The fact that a person is not liable to be convicted of murder in respect of a death by virtue of this section does not affect the question of whether any other person is liable to be convicted of murder in respect of that death.
7. If, on the trial of a person for murder, the person contends:
   a. that the person is entitled to be acquitted on the ground that the person was mentally ill at the time of the acts or omissions causing the death concerned, or
   b. that the person is not liable to be convicted of murder by virtue of this section,
   evidence may be offered by the prosecution tending to prove the other of those contentions, and the Court may give directions as to the stage of the proceedings at which that evidence may be offered.

8. In this section:
   underlying condition means a pre-existing mental or physiological condition, other than a condition of a transitory kind.

The 1997 Act also amended section 405AB to read (LRC 1997c: 4–5):

Notice of intention to adduce evidence of substantial impairment

1. On trial for murder, the defendant must not, without the leave of the Court, adduce evidence tending to prove a contention by the defendant that the defendant is not liable to be convicted of murder by virtue of section 23A, unless the defendant gives notice, as prescribed by the regulations, of his or her intention to raise that contention.
2. Without limiting subsection (1), the defendant must not, without the leave of the Court, call any other person to give evidence tending to prove a contention by the defendant that the defendant is not liable to be convicted of murder by virtue of section 23A unless the notice under this section includes:
   a. the name and address of the other person, and
   b. particulars of the evidence to be given by the other person.
3. Any evidence tendered to disprove a contention that the defendant is not liable to be convicted of murder by virtue of section 12A may, subject to any direction of the Court, be given before or after evidence is given to prove that contention.
4. Any notice purporting to be given under this section on behalf of the defendant by his or her legal practitioner is taken, unless the contrary is proved, to have been given with the authority of the defendant.

The amendment also reads (LRC 1997c: 5–6):

Replacement of defence of diminished responsibility—application of new defence

Section 23A, as substituted by the *Crimes Amendment (Diminished Responsibility) Act 1997*, does not apply to or in respect of a murder that is alleged to have been committed before that substitution. This Act continues to apply to and in respect of such an alleged murder as if the *Crimes Amendment (Diminished Responsibility) Act* had not been enacted.

Application of requirement to give notice of defence

Section 405AB, as inserted by the *Crimes Amendment (Diminished Responsibility) Act 1997*, does not apply to or in respect of a trial for murder if the murder is alleged to have been committed before the commencement of this section.

In New South Wales, a diminished responsibility defense may only be used in murder cases (LRC 1997a: 3.7). It refers to a "substantial impairment caused by an abnormality of mind. This may cover, for example, uncontrollable urges and extreme emotional states, as well as cognitive disorders falling outside the defence of mental illness" (LRC 1997a: 3.7). "Abnormality of the mind" was described by Lord Parker CJ in *R v. Byrne* [1960] as:

> A state of mind so different from that of ordinary human beings that a reasonable man would term it abnormal. It appears . . . to be wide enough to cover the mind's activities in all aspects, not only the perception of physical acts and matters, and the ability to form a rational judgment as to whether an act is right or wrong, but also the ability to exercise will-power to control physical acts in accordance with that rational judgment. (LRC 1997a: 3.33)

It should be noted that the term "abnormality of the mind" used in the diminished responsibility defense has also been described as ambiguous and ill-defined. In *R v. Chayna* [1993], the Chief Justice stated:

> The variety of psychiatric opinion with which the jury were confronted strongly suggests that the operation of s 23A of the *Crimes Act* depends upon concepts which medical experts find at least ambiguous and, perhaps, unscientific. . . . It appears to me that the place in the criminal law of s 23A is a subject ripe for reconsideration. (LRC 1997a: 3.33; see *R v. Chayna* at 189 and 191)

In Queensland, the courts or the Mental Health Tribunal, which is made up by a Supreme Court judge and two psychiatric assessors, determines whether the defense of diminished responsibility may be used (LRC 1997a: 3.81; see Mental Health Act 1974 (Qld).

The courts in New South Wales have repeatedly rejected the claim of self-induced intoxication as a defense of diminished responsibility because it "does not cause damage or destruction of brain cells" that is permanent, and thus is not an "injury" under s 23A of the Crimes Act of 1900 (NSW) (LRC 1997a: 3.68). Amendments to the Crimes Act of 1900 (NSW) in 1996[4] set forth that in cases where a defendant is acquitted of murder due to intoxication, evidence of self-induced intoxication cannot be used to determine whether the person meets the criteria for mens rea for manslaughter (LRC 1997a: 3.71). If the intoxicated state was not self-induced, then evidence of the defendant's state may be used to determine mens rea for manslaughter.

Mental impairments do not include personality disorders in South Australia, New South Wales, and Tasmania (Mullen et al. 2000: 451). Legislation where personality disorders may be relevant to an insanity defense is found in the Australian Capital Territory and Northern Territory. In Victoria, personality disorders may be recognized as a component of mental impairment on a limited basis. There is a volitional factor in South Australia, but not in Victoria or the Australian Capital Territory (Mullen et al. 2000: 436).

In South Australia, the insanity defense was used almost exclusively in se-vere cases under criteria similar to those of *M'Naghten* (Burvill et al. 2003: 14–15). Defendants could be found NGRI and subject to indefinite detention. After the Criminal Law Consolidation (Mental Impairment) Amendment Act in 1995, with the addition of a volitional prong and the widening of the crite-ria for mental impairment, defendants could be treated either in a custodial setting or within the community. Thus, frequency of the mental impairment defense increased among cases involving minor crimes.

Today, automatism from dissociation as a defense can lead to a full ac-quittal (McSherry 2004). McSherry describes dissociation as a "fleeting mental state" due to an inability to control one's conduct and lack of self-control (447).

Burden of Proof

The Criminal Code Act of 1995 states that the defendant or the prosecutor can raise the issue of mental illness (Ridgway 1996: section 41).[5] It also states that a defendant is presumed not to have a mental impairment unless "proved on the balance of probabilities (by the prosecution or the defence) that the person was suffering from such a mental impairment"[6] (see McSherry 1997: 194).

Section 23A Crimes Amendment (Diminished Responsibility) Act 1997 of New South Wales revised the Crimes Act 1900 and states, "The onus is on the person accused to prove that he or she is not liable to be convicted of murder by virtue of this section." Thus, under the New South Wales Crimes Act 1900, the burden of proof lies with the accused in murder cases (LRC 1997a).[7]

In New South Wales, the prosecutor must show beyond a reasonable doubt that the offender did commit homicide. The prosecutor must also demon-strate that the defendant "had the requisite mental state for murder at the time of the killing" (LRC 1997a: 3.6). Once this is demonstrated, the defendant is responsible for showing the following in order to use the defense of dimin-ished responsibility (LRC 1997a: 3.6):

1. that at the time of the killing, the accused was suffering from an abnormality of the mind;
2. that the abnormality of mind arose from one of the causes listed within the parentheses in s 23A(1), that is from a condition or arrested or retarded de-velopment of mind, or from any inherent cause, or induced by disease or in-jury, and
3. that the abnormality of mind substantially impaired the accused's mental re-sponsibility for the killing.

In Queensland, individuals charged with an offense may be referred to the Tribunal if a close relative, legal advisor, or Crown Law Officer believes that the defendant was mentally ill when the crime was committed (LRC 1997a: 3.81). The defendant may refer him- or herself as well. Further, if a defendant submits a plea of "guilty" during a trial and the court has reason to believe that he or she was mentally ill during the commission of the crime, the court may submit a plea of "not guilty" and order the defendant to undergo psychiatric evaluation (LRC 1997a: 3.81). A defendant may still use the defense of diminished responsibility if the case is not sent to the Tribunal (LRC 1997a: 3.81).

In cases of automatism, where a defendant engages in "involuntary conduct resulting from some form of impaired consciousness" (McSherry 2004: 449), the defense will argue that extreme provocation or an "extraordinary external stress" (447) resulted in a dissociative state. Automatism can result from "a blow to the head, sleep disorders, the consumption of alcohol or other drugs, neurological disorders, hypoglycemia, epilepsy, and dissociation arising from extraordinary external stress" (McSherry 2004: 450). If the issue is raised, the prosecutor bears the burden of disproving the claim (McSherry 2004).

Form of Verdict

Despite the Model Criminal Code's criteria for mental impairment (insanity), Australian regions retain their own practices and legislation (Mullen et al. 2000). For example, "mental dysfunction" is used in the Australian Capital Territory while New South Wales has a diminished responsibility defense and an insanity defense (Mullen et al. 2000).

Queensland, Western Australia, the Northern Territory and Tasmania have an insanity defense (McSherry 1997: 183). The diminished responsibility defense is also used in Queensland, the Australian Capital Territory, and the Northern Territory (LRC 1997a: 3.2; McSherry 2001).[8] The Northern Territory refers to insanity as an "abnormality of the mind" (McSherry 1997: 183). A defendant can raise a defense of "non-mental disorder automatism due to association," "provocation leading to partial loss of self-control," or "mental disorder automatism" (McSherry 2004: 448).

Who Decides?

In every region but Queensland, the court decides whether a defendant has a mental impairment or is insane (Mullen et al. 2000: 436). Mentally ill offenders in the Australian Capital Territory, New South Wales, the Northern Territory, Queensland, Tasmania, and Victoria can be directed into the mental health system rather than prison (Mullen et al. 2000: 451).

A defendant in New South Wales can choose to be tried by a judge rather than by a jury (LRC 1997a: 3.26). In Queensland, "the Tribunal has the power to determine whether the accused suffered from diminished responsibility as defined in s 304A of the Criminal Code (Qld)" (LRC 1997a: 3.81). The Tribunal is made up of a judge of the Supreme Court and two psychiatrists (Mullen et al. 2000).

Role of Experts

In New South Wales, expert opinion is necessary to validate the defendant's three-pronged criteria for meeting the defense of diminished responsibility (LRC 1997a: 3.38). Psychiatrists sit in tribunals in Queensland.

Under the Crimes Amendment (Diminished Responsibility) Act 1997 in New South Wales, "evidence of an opinion" on whether the defendant's impairment is "substantial" enough to reduce a murder charge to manslaughter is not permitted, so the jury is responsible for the determination (McSherry 2001: 19–20).[9]

What Happens to the Defendant?

Defendants can be found unfit to plead, in which case they are hospitalized (Mullen et al. 2000).

A person who successfully uses the defense of mental illness is acquitted yet held in "strict custody" in a penal or mental facility. In order to be released, the Mental Health Review Tribunal must ensure that the offender is not a danger to himself or others (LRC 1997a, see footnote 9).

In New South Wales, "there is no specific provision to allow diminished responsibility offenders to receive medical or psychiatric treatment" (LRC 1997a: 3.3). A defendant who successfully uses the diminished responsibility defense will receive a manslaughter conviction, which results in a twenty-five-year penal sentence. If the defense is not successful, the defendant may be convicted of murder and may be sentenced to life in prison (LRC 1997a: 3.6). However, murder convictions are no longer required to result in mandatory life sentences (LRC 1997a: 3.14). Automatism defenses, used successfully, can result in an acquittal (McSherry 1997).

In Queensland, if a defendant enters a successful diminished responsibility defense, the tribunal ceases the murder prosecution (LRC 1997a: 3.81). This does not preclude the court from prosecuting the defendant for other relevant offenses. If the tribunal does not find diminished responsibility, the defendant can still use the defense and "evidence of the Tribunal's determination is not admissible" (LRC 1997a: 3.81), although medical reports received or produced by the tribunal may be admitted into future proceedings against the defendant (3.81).

In Victoria, the Commonwealth Crimes Act of 1914 provides for alternatives to incarceration through the use of hospitals (LRC 1997a: 3.112).

Regarding cases involving automatism, a successful use of the defense "non-mental disorder automatism due to dissocation" can result in an acquittal (McSherry 2004: 448). If the defendant was provoked and therefore partially lacked self-control, murder charges can be changed to manslaughter. If the dissociation was a result of a mental disorder, the defendant can be held not criminally responsible but detained in a psychiatric hospital.

Frequency of Use

Between 1990 and 1993 in New South Wales, the Judicial Commission found that the most frequent uses of the diminished responsibility defense applied to individuals with depression and schizophrenia, brain damage, personality disorders, and post-traumatic stress syndrome (LRC 1997, see footnote 10). This study included sentenced homicide offenders in New South Wales and showed that the defense of diminished responsibility was raised in 14 percent of the cases (LRC 1997: 3.9). Of those, 61 percent resulted in manslaughter conviction.

Mullen et al. (2000) suggest that recent legislation has led to an increased use of mental impairment defenses (440). One study of 143 homicide cases in Victoria from 1997 to 2001 found that a provocation as defense is used quite often at trial (McSherry 2004: 454).

Types of Offenses

The diminished responsibility defense applies only to murder cases. However, the mental impairment defense is being used more often for less serious crimes, as seen in South Australia and Victoria (Mullen et al. 2000: 440).

In NSW, under section 22A of the Crimes Act of 1900 (NSW), "a woman will be convicted of infanticide if she kills her child aged less than twelve months, where the balance of her mind is disturbed as a result of giving birth or by reason of the effect of lactation" (LRC 1997a: 3.22).

Notes

1. Section 7.3(1).
2. Section 7.3(9).
3. Section 7.3(8).
4. Section 428e.
5. Section 52(3)(b).
6. Section 7.3(3).
7. Section 23a.
8. See Criminal Code (WLD) s 304A; Crimes Act 1900 (ACT) s 14; Criminal Code (NT) s 37.
9. See Section 23A(2).

References

Barclay, Gordon, and Cynthia Tavares. 2002. "International Comparisons of Criminal Justice Statistics 2000." Issue 05/02. Retrieved June 15, 2004, <www.homeoffice.gov/uk/rds/pdfs2/hosb502.pdf>.

Burvill, Michael, Sue Dusmohamed, Nichole Hunter, and Helen McRostie. 2003. "The Management of Mentally Impaired Offenders within the South Australian Criminal Justice System." *International Journal of Law and Psychiatry* 26: 13–31. Retrieved online June 6, 2005, <www.sciencedirect.com>, Elsevier Sciences, Ltd.

Forensic Glossary. <www.forensiceducation.com/sourcebooks/glossary/n.htm>.

International Centre for Prison Studies (ICPS). 2005. "World Prison Brief: Entire World—Prison Population Totals, Prison Brief for Australia." International Centre for Prison Studies, Kings College London. Retrieved May 9, 2005, <www.kcl.ac.uk/depsta/rel/icps/worldbrief/world_brief.html>.

Jager, Alan D. 2001. "Forensic Psychiatric Services in Australia." *International Journal of Law and Psychiatry* 24: 387–98. Retrieved online June 6, 2005, <www.sciencedirect.com>, Elsevier Sciences, Ltd.

Law Reform Commission. 1993. "Report 31 (1993)—Provocation, Diminished Responsibility and Infanticide," Chapters 4–5. Law Reform Commission Publications, Digest of Law Reform Commission References. Retrieved June 11, 2004, <www.lawlink.nsw.gov.au/lrc.nsf/pages/digest.085>.

———. 1997a. "Report 82 (1997)—Partial Defences to Murder: Diminished Responsibility." Law Reform Commission Publications, Digest of Law Reform Commission References. Retrieved June 11, 2004, <www.lawlink.nsw.gov.au/lrc.nsf/pages/digest.085>.

———. 1997b. "Report 83 (1997)—Partial Defences to Murder: Provocation and Infanticide," Chapters 1–3. Law Reform Commission Publications, Digest of Law Reform Commission References. Retrieved June 11, 2004, <www.lawlink.nsw.gov.au/lrc.nsf/pages/digest.085>.

————. 1997c. "Crimes Amendment (Diminished Responsibility) Act 1997 No 106." New South Wales. Retrieved June 10, 2004, <www.lawlink.nsw.gov.au/lrc.nsf/pages/digest.085>.

McSherry, Bernadette. 1997. "The Reformulated Defence of Insanity in the Australian Criminal Code Act 1995 (Cth)." *International Journal of Law and Psychiatry* 20, no. 2: 183–97. Retrieved online June 6, 2005, <www.sciencedirect.com>, Elsevier Sciences, Ltd.

————. 2001. "Expert Testimony and the Effects of Mental Impairment: Reviving the Ultimate Issue Rule." *International Journal of Law and Psychiatry* 24: 13–21. Retrieved online June 6, 2005, <www.sciencedirect.com>, Elsevier Sciences, Ltd.

————. 2004. "Criminal Responsibility, 'Fleeting' States of Mental Impairment, and the Power of Self-control." *International Journal of Law and Psychiatry* 27: 445–57. Retrieved online June 6, 2005, <www.sciencedirect.com>, Elsevier Sciences, Ltd.

Mullen, Paul E., Sue Briggs, Tom Dalton, and Michael Burt. 2000. "Forensic Mental Health Services in Australia." *International Journal of Law and Psychiatry* 23, nos. 5–6: 433–52. Retrieved online June 6, 2005, <www.sciencedirect.com>, Elsevier Sciences, Ltd.

Ridgway, Peter. 1996. "Sleepwalking—Insanity or Automatism." *Murdoch University Electronic Journal of Law* 3, no. 1. Queensland: Murdoch University. Retrieved online April 15, 2004, <www.murdoch.edu/au/elaw/issues/v3n1/ridgway.html>.

R v. Burgess [1991] 2 QB 92 at 99.

R v. Byrne [1960] 2 QB 396.

R v. Chayna [1993] 66 A Crim R 178.

R v. Falconer (1990) 171 CLR 30 at 42.

R v. Falconer (1990) 171 CLR 30 at 61 per Deane and Dawson JJ.

R v. Falconer (1990) 171 CLR 30 at 72 per Toohey J.

R v. Holmes [1960] WAR 122 at 125.

R v. Tolsen [1889] QBD 168 at 187 per Stephen J.

U.S. Department of State. 2003. "Background Note: Australia." Washington, D.C.: U.S. Department of State. Retrieved online June 14, 2004, <www.state.gov/r/pa/ei/bgn/2698.htm>.

Part X

24

Concluding Remarks

O F THE TWENTY-TWO COUNTRIES included in this study, only one—Sweden—does not allow for a defense of insanity. After abolishing the defense in 1965, it passed legislation applicable to all mentally ill persons, including those charged with having committed criminal offenses.

Of the remaining twenty-one countries, the most commonly used criteria for determining whether defendants should be held responsible for their criminal behavior is the *M'Naghten* rules or a modified version of those rules. Different societies expanded on the phrases "not to know the values and quality of the act" and "or if he did not know that what he was doing was wrong." Traditionally "to know" was interpreted in a narrowly cognitive manner. Over time it has come to include a more expanded interpretation that includes terms such as "unable to appreciate." In addition to *M'Naghten*, many of the countries also include a version of the Irresistible Impulse Test. Nine of the twenty-one countries employ a combination of the *M'Naghten* and "irresistible impulse" criteria. Seven societies use the traditional *M'Naghten* rules or the more expanded version.

The burden of proof varies considerably. In four countries, the burden is on the prosecutor to prove sanity or responsibility beyond a reasonable doubt or on the balance of probabilities. In the remaining countries, the burden is on the defense to prove insanity, mostly by a preponderance of the evidence or on the balance of probability.

In almost all of the societies, the United States being the rare exception, and to a lesser extent Australia, Canada, and Great Britain, a judge determines the defendant's fate. The United States involves a jury more than any of the twenty-two countries included in the study.

The most frequently used verdict in eleven countries is "not guilty by reason of insanity." "Guilty but mentally ill" is used in a couple of countries, and terms such as "state of irresponsibility," "state of insanity," and "acquittal due to unsound mind" are used in most of the other societies.

All of the countries call upon experts in psychology, psychiatry and/or social work to examine the defendant before the trial, often to determine if he or she is fit to stand trial, during the trial to provide insight into the defendant's responsibility or lack of it for his or her criminal behavior, and after the trial if a judge or jury has found the defendant not guilty by reason of insanity to advise the court about what should be done with the defendant. Psychiatric experts are also called upon by the court to determine if and when the defendant should be released from the mental hospital to which he or she has been committed.

In all of the countries, a defendant who is found not guilty by reason of insanity does not walk out of the court a free person; he or she is committed for an undetermined period of time to a mental hospital. The defendant's release is usually determined by a judge on the advice of medical experts.

While often given a great deal of media attention because of the nature of the criminal act the defendant committed, most often homicide, the percentage of cases in which defendants opt to plead insanity is very small, usually less than three percent.

With the downfall of the Soviet Union, only China, of all the countries included in this study, uses psychiatry followed by involuntary commitment to a mental institution against political dissidents. Thousands of members of the Falun Gong, for example, have been committed to mental institutions.

The insanity defense has attracted a great deal of attention for hundreds of years by the media, and by legal scholars and medical experts because it involves such basic issues as responsibility, and the commission of heinous offenses, sometimes against heads of state or other prominent members of society.

Index

Index

About the Authors

Rita J. Simon is University Professor in the School of Public Affairs and the Washington College of Law at American University. She is author or editor of numerous books, including *Women's Roles and Statuses the World Over* (with Stephanie Hepburn, Lexington Books, 2006), and *Adoption Across Borders* (with Howard Altstein, Rowman & Littlefield, 2000).

Heather Ahn-Redding is Assistant Professor of Criminal Justice at High Point University. She received her doctorate in Justice, Law and Society from American University's School of Public Affairs. She is coauthor of *Illicit Drug Policies, Trafficking, and Use the World Over* (with Caterina Gouvis Roman and Rita J. Simon, Lexington Books, 2005) and *The Crimes Women Commit: The Punishments They Receive* (with Rita J. Simon, Lexington Books, 2005).